# Ansible for DevOps

## Server and configuration management for humans

## Jeff Geerling

# Ansible for DevOps

## Server and configuration management for humans

Jeff Geerling

ISBN 978-0-9863934-1-9

Leanpub

This is a Leanpub book. Leanpub empowers authors and publishers with the Lean Publishing process. Lean Publishing is the act of publishing an in-progress ebook using lightweight tools and many iterations to get reader feedback, pivot until you have the right book and build traction once you do.

This book is dedicated to my wife, Natalie, and my children.

Editing by Margie Newman and Katherine Geerling.

Cover photograph and illustration © 2011 Jeff Geerling.

Ansible is a software product distributed under the GNU GPLv3 open source license.

# Contents

# Foreword

Over the last few years, Ansible has rapidly become one of the most popular IT automation tools in the world. We've seen the open source community expand from the beginning of the project in early 2012 to over 1200 individual contributors today. Ansible's modular architecture and broad applicability to a variety of automation and orchestration problems created a perfect storm for hundreds of thousands of users worldwide.

Ansible is a general purpose IT automation platform, and it can be used for a variety of purposes. From configuration management: enforcing declared state across your infrastructure, to procedural application deployment, to broad multi-component and multi-system orchestration of complicated interconnected systems. It is agentless, so it can coexist with legacy tools, and it's easy to install, configure, and maintain.

Ansible had its beginnings in 2012, when Michael DeHaan, the project's founder, took inspiration from several tools he had written prior, along with some hands-on experience with the state of configuration management at the time, and launched the project in February of 2012. Some of Ansible's unique attributes like its module-based architecture and agentless approach quickly attracted attention in the open source world.

In 2013, Said Ziouani, Michael DeHaan, and I launched Ansible, Inc. We wanted to harness the growing adoption of Ansible in the open source world, and create products to fill the gaps in the IT automation space as we saw them. The existing tools were complicated, error-prone, and hard to learn. Ansible gave users across an IT organization a low barrier of entry into automation, and it could be deployed incrementally, solving as few or as many problems as the team needed without a big shift in methodology.

This book is about using Ansible in a DevOps environment. I'm not going to try to define what DevOps is or isn't, or who's doing it or not. My personal interpretation of the idea is that DevOps is meant to shorten the distance between the developers writing the code, and the operators running the application. Now, I don't believe adding a new "DevOps" team in between existing development and operations teams achieves that objective! (Oops, now I'm trying for a definition, aren't I?)

Well, definitions aside, one of the first steps towards a DevOps environment is choosing tools that can be consumed by both developers and operations engineers. Ansible is one of those tools: you don't have to be a software developer to use it, and the playbooks that you write can easily be self-documenting. There have been a lot of attempts at "write once, run anywhere" models of application development and deployment, but I think Ansible comes the closest to providing a common language that's useful across teams and across clouds and different datacenters.

The author of this book, Jeff, has been a long-time supporter, contributor, and advocate of Ansible, and he's maintained a massive collection of impressive Ansible roles in Galaxy, the public role-sharing service maintained by Ansible, Inc. Jeff has used Ansible extensively in his professional career, and is eminently qualified to write to the end-to-end book on Ansible in a DevOps environment.

As you read this book, I hope you enjoy your journey into IT automation as much as we have. Be well, do good work, and automate everything.

Tim Gerla
Ansible, Inc. Co-Founder & CTO

# Preface

Growing up, I had access to a world that not many kids ever get to enter. At the local radio stations where my dad was chief engineer, I was fortunate to get to see networks and IT infrastructure up close: Novell servers and old Mac and Windows workstations in the '90s; Microsoft and Linux-based servers; and everything in between. Best of all, he brought home decommissioned servers and copies of Linux burned to CD.

I began working with Linux and small-scale infrastructures before I started high school, and my passion for infrastructure grew as I built a Cat5 wired network and a small rack of networking equipment for a local grade school. When I started developing full-time, what was once a hobby became a necessary part of my job, so I invested more time in managing infrastructure efficiently. Over the past ten years, I've gone from manually booting and configuring physical and virtual servers; to using relatively complex shell scripts to provision and configure servers; to using configuration management tools to manage many cloud-based servers.

When I began converting my infrastructure to code, some of the best tools for testing, provisioning, and managing my servers were still in their infancy, but they have since matured into fully-featured, robust tools that I use every day. Vagrant is an excellent tool for managing local virtual machines to mimic real-world infrastructure locally (or in the cloud), and Ansible — the subject of this book — is an excellent tool for provisioning servers, managing their configuration, and deploying applications, even on my local workstation!

These tools are still improving rapidly, and I'm excited for what the future holds. The time I invest in learning new infrastructure tools well will be helpful for years to come. (Ansible, Docker, and Vagrant seem a potent combination for both local and production infrastructure, but that's a little outside of *this* book's scope.)

In these pages, I'll share with you all I've learned about Ansible: my favorite tool for server provisioning, configuration management, and application deployment. I hope you enjoy reading this book as much as I did writing it!

— Jeff Geerling, 2015

# Who is this book for?

Many of the developers and sysadmins I work with are at least moderately comfortable administering a Linux server via SSH, and manage between 1-100 servers.

Some of these people have a little experience with configuration management tools (usually with Puppet or Chef), and maybe a little experience with deployments and continuous integration using tools like Jenkins, Capistrano, or Fabric. I am writing this book for these friends who, I think, are representative of most people who have heard of and/or are beginning to use Ansible.

If you are interested in both development and operations, and have at least a passing familiarity with managing a server via the command line, this book should provide you with an intermediate- to expert-level understanding of Ansible and how you can use it to manage your infrastructure.

# Typographic conventions

Ansible uses a simple syntax (YAML) and simple command-line tools (using common POSIX conventions) for all its powerful abilities. Code samples and commands will be highlighted throughout the book either inline (for example: `ansible [command]`), or in a code block (with or without line numbers) like:

```
1   ---
2   # This is the beginning of a YAML file.
```

Some lines of YAML and other code examples require more than 70 characters per line, resulting in the code wrapping to a new line. Wrapping code is indicated by a \ at the end of the line of code. For example:

```
1   # The line of code wraps due to the extremely long URL.
2   wget http://www.example.com/really/really/really/long/path/in/the/ur\
3   l/causes/the/line/to/wrap
```

When using the code, don't copy the \ character, and make sure you don't use a newline between the first line with the trailing \ and the next line.

Links to pertinent resources and websites are added inline, like the following link to Ansible[1], and can be viewed directly by clicking on them in eBook formats, or by following the URL in the footnotes.

Sometimes, asides are added to highlight further information about a specific topic:

 Informational asides will provide extra information.

 Warning asides will warn about common pitfalls and how to avoid them.

 Tip asides will give tips for deepening your understanding or optimizing your use of Ansible.

When displaying commands run in a terminal session, if the commands are run under your normal/non-root user account, the commands will be prefixed by the dollar sign ($). If the commands are run as the root user, they will be prefixed with the pound sign (#).

## Please help improve this book!

New revisions of this book are published on a regular basis (you're reading version 1.13). If you think a particular section needs improvement or find something missing, please contact me via Twitter (@geerlingguy[2]), a comment on this book's Feedback page on LeanPub[3], or whatever method is convenient for you.

---

[1] http://www.ansible.com/

[2] https://twitter.com/geerlingguy

[3] https://leanpub.com/ansible-for-devops/feedback

All known issues with Ansible for DevOps will be aggregated on the book's online
Errata[4] page.

## About the Author

Jeff Geerling is a developer who has worked in programming and reliability engineering for companies with anywhere between one to thousands of servers. He also
manages many virtual servers for services offered by Midwestern Mac, LLC and has
been using Ansible to manage infrastructure since early 2013.

---

[4]https://www.ansiblefordevops.com/errata

# Introduction

## In the beginning, there were sysadmins

Since the beginning of networked computing, deploying and managing servers reliably and efficiently has been a challenge. Historically, system administrators were walled off from the developers and users who interact with the systems they administer, and they managed servers by hand, installing software, changing configurations, and administering services on individual servers.

As data centers grew, and hosted applications became more complex, administrators realized they couldn't scale their manual systems management as fast as the applications they were enabling. That's why server provisioning and configuration management tools came to flourish.

Server virtualization brought large-scale infrastructure management to the fore, and the number of servers managed by one admin (or by a small team of admins), has grown by an order of magnitude. Instead of deploying, patching, and destroying every server by hand, admins now are expected to bring up new servers, either automatically or with minimal intervention. Large-scale IT deployments now may involve hundreds or thousands of servers; in many of the largest environments, server provisioning, configuration, and decommissioning are fully automated.

## Modern infrastructure management

As the systems that run applications become an ever more complex and integral part of the software they run, application developers themselves have begun to integrate their work more fully with operations personnel. In many companies, development and operations work is integrated. Indeed, this integration is a requirement for modern test-driven application design.

As a software developer by trade, and a sysadmin by necessity, I have seen the power in uniting development and operations—more commonly referred to now as DevOps or Reliability Engineering. When developers begin to think of infrastructure as *part of their application,* stability and performance become normative. When sysadmins (most of whom have intermediate to advanced knowledge of the applications and languages being used on servers they manage) work tightly with developers, development velocity is improved, and more time is spent doing 'fun' activities like performance tuning, experimentation, and getting things done, and less time putting out fires.

 *DevOps* is a loaded word; some people argue using the word to identify both the *movement* of development and operations working more closely to automate infrastructure-related processes, and the *personnel* who skew slightly more towards the system administration side of the equation, dilutes the word's meaning. I think the word has come to be a rallying cry for the employees who are dragging their startups, small businesses, and enterprises into a new era of infrastructure growth and stability. I'm not too concerned that the term has become more of a catch-all for modern infrastructure management. My advice: spend less time arguing over the definition of the word, and more time making it mean something *to you.*

## Ansible and Ansible, Inc.

Ansible was released in 2012 by Michael DeHaan (@laserllama[5] on Twitter), a developer who has been working with configuration management and infrastructure orchestration in one form or another for many years. Through his work with Puppet Labs and Red Hat (where he worked on Cobbler[6], a configuration management tool and Func[7], a tool for communicating commands to remote servers), and some other projects[8], he experienced the trials and tribulations of many different organizations and individual sysadmins on their quest to simplify and automate their infrastructure management operations.

---

[5]https://twitter.com/laserllama
[6]http://www.cobblerd.org/
[7]https://fedorahosted.org/func/
[8]https://www.ansible.com/blog/2013/12/08/the-origins-of-ansible

Additionally, Michael found many shops were using separate tools[9] for configuration management (Puppet, Chef, cfengine), server deployment (Capistrano, Fabric), and ad-hoc task execution (Func, plain SSH), and wanted to see if there was a better way. Ansible wraps up all three of these features into one tool, and does it in a way that's actually *simpler* and more consistent than any of the other task-specific tools!

Ansible aims to be:

1. **Clear** - Ansible uses a simple syntax (YAML) and is easy for anyone (developers, sysadmins, managers) to understand. APIs are simple and sensible.
2. **Fast** - Fast to learn, fast to set up—especially considering you don't need to install extra agents or daemons on all your servers!
3. **Complete** - Ansible does three things in one, and does them very well. Ansible's 'batteries included' approach means you have everything you need in one complete package.
4. **Efficient** - No extra software on your servers means more resources for your applications. Also, since Ansible modules work via JSON, Ansible is extensible with modules written in a programming language you already know.
5. **Secure** - Ansible uses SSH, and requires no extra open ports or potentially-vulnerable daemons on your servers.

Ansible also has a lighter side that gives the project a little personality. As an example, Ansible's major releases are named after Led Zeppelin songs (e.g. 2.0 was named after 1973's "Over the Hills and Far Away", 1.x releases were named after Van Halen songs). Additionally, Ansible will use cowsay, if installed, to wrap output in an ASCII cow's speech bubble (this behavior can be disabled in Ansible's configuration).

Ansible, Inc.[10] was founded by Saïd Ziouani (@SaidZiouani[11] on Twitter) and Michael DeHaan, and oversees core Ansible development and provides services (such as Automation Jump Start[12]) and extra tooling (such as Ansible Tower[13]) to organizations using Ansible. Hundreds of individual developers have contributed

---

[9]http://highscalability.com/blog/2012/4/18/ansible-a-simple-model-driven-configuration-management-and-c.html

[10]http://www.ansible.com/

[11]https://twitter.com/SaidZiouani

[12]http://www.ansible.com/services

[13]https://www.ansible.com/tower

patches to Ansible, and Ansible is the most starred infrastructure management tool on GitHub (with over 10,000 stars as of this writing).

In October 2015, Red Hat acquired Ansible, Inc., and has proven itself to be a good steward and promoter of Ansible. I see no indication of this changing in the future.

## Ansible Examples

There are many Ansible examples (playbooks, roles, infrastructure, configuration, etc.) throughout this book. Most of the examples are in the Ansible for DevOps GitHub repository[14], so you can browse the code in its final state while you're reading the book. Some of the line numbering may not match the book *exactly* (especially if you're reading an older version of the book!), but I will try my best to keep everything synchronized over time.

## Other resources

We'll explore all aspects of using Ansible to provision and manage your infrastructure in this book, but there's no substitute for the wealth of documentation and community interaction that make Ansible great. Check out the links below to find out more about Ansible and discover the community:

- Ansible Documentation[15] - Covers all Ansible options in depth. There are few open source projects with documentation as clear and thorough.
- Ansible Glossary[16] - If there's ever a term in this book you don't seem to fully understand, check the glossary.
- Ansible Mailing List[17] - Discuss Ansible and submit questions with Ansible's community via this Google group.
- Ansible on GitHub[18] - The official Ansible code repository, where the magic happens.

---

[14]https://github.com/geerlingguy/ansible-for-devops

[15]https://docs.ansible.com/ansible/

[16]https://docs.ansible.com/ansible/glossary.html

[17]https://groups.google.com/forum/#!forum/ansible-project

[18]https://github.com/ansible/ansible

- Ansible Example Playbooks on GitHub[19] - Many examples for common server configurations.
- Getting Started with Ansible[20] - A simple guide to Ansible's community and resources.
- Ansible Blog[21]

I'd like to especially highlight Ansible's documentation (the first resource listed above); one of Ansible's greatest strengths is its well-written and extremely relevant documentation, containing a large number of relevant examples and continously-updated guides. Very few projects—open source or not—have documentation as thorough, yet easy-to-read. This book is meant as a supplement to, not a replacement for, Ansible's documentation!

---

[19]https://github.com/ansible/ansible-examples
[20]https://www.ansible.com/get-started
[21]https://www.ansible.com/blog

# Chapter 1 - Getting Started with Ansible

## Ansible and Infrastructure Management

### On snowflakes and shell scripts

Many developers and system administrators manage servers by logging into them via SSH, making changes, and logging off. Some of these changes would be documented, some would not. If an admin needed to make the same change to many servers (for example, changing one value in a config file), the admin would manually log into *each* server and repeatedly make this change.

If there were only one or two changes in the course of a server's lifetime, and if the server were extremely simple (running only one process, with one configuration, and a very simple firewall), *and* if every change were thoroughly documented, this process wouldn't be a problem.

But for almost every company in existence, servers are more complex—most run tens, sometimes hundreds of different applications or application containers. Most servers have complicated firewalls and dozens of tweaked configuration files. And even with change documentation, the manual process usually results in some servers or some steps being forgotten.

If the admins at these companies wanted to set up a new server *exactly* like one that is currently running, they would need to spend a good deal of time going through all of the installed packages, documenting configurations, versions, and settings; and they would spend a lot of unnecessary time manually reinstalling, updating, and tweaking everything to get the new server to run close to how the old server did.

Some admins may use shell scripts to try to reach some level of sanity, but I've yet to see a complex shell script that handles all edge cases correctly while synchronizing multiple servers' configuration and deploying new code.

1

## Configuration management

Lucky for you, there are tools to help you avoid having these *snowflake servers*—servers that are uniquely configured and impossible to recreate from scratch because they were hand-configured without documentation. Tools like CFEngine[22], Puppet[23] and Chef[24] became very popular in the mid-to-late 2000s.

But there's a reason why many developers and sysadmins stick to shell scripting and command-line configuration: it's simple and easy-to-use, and they've had years of experience using bash and command-line tools. Why throw all that out the window and learn a new configuration language and methodology?

Enter Ansible. Ansible was built (and continues to be improved) by developers and sysadmins who know the command line—and want to make a tool that helps them manage their servers exactly the same as they have in the past, but in a repeatable and centrally managed way. Ansible also has other tricks up its sleeve, making it a true Swiss Army knife for people involved in DevOps (not just the operations side).

One of Ansible's greatest strengths is its ability to run regular shell commands verbatim, so you can take existing scripts and commands and work on converting them into idempotent playbooks as time allows. For someone (like me) who was comfortable with the command line, but never became proficient in more complicated tools like Puppet or Chef (which both required at least a *slight* understanding of Ruby and/or a custom language just to get started), Ansible was a breath of fresh air.

Ansible works by pushing changes out to all your servers (by default), and requires no extra software to be installed on your servers (thus no extra memory footprint, and no extra daemon to manage), unlike most other configuration management tools.

---

[22]http://cfengine.com/
[23]http://puppetlabs.com/
[24]http://www.getchef.com/chef/

**Idempotence** is the ability to run an operation which produces the same result whether run once or multiple times (source[25]).

An important feature of a configuration management tool is its ability to ensure the same configuration is maintained whether you run it once or a thousand times. Many shell scripts have unintended consequences if run more than once, but Ansible deploys the same configuration to a server over and over again without making any changes after the first deployment.

In fact, almost every aspect of Ansible modules and commands is idempotent, and for those that aren't, Ansible allows you to define when the given command should be run, and what constitutes a changed or failed command, so you can easily maintain an idempotent configuration on all your servers.

# Installing Ansible

Ansible's only real dependency is Python. Once Python is installed, the simplest way to get Ansible running is to use `pip`, a simple package manager for Python.

**If you're on a Mac**, installing Ansible is a piece of cake:

1. Install Homebrew[26] (get the installation command from the Homebrew website).
2. Install Python 2.7.x (`brew install python`).
3. Install Ansible (`sudo pip install ansible`).

You could also install Ansible via Homebrew with `brew install ansible`. Either way (`pip` or `brew`) is fine, but make sure you update Ansible using the same system with which it was installed!

**If you're running Windows** (i.e. you work for a large company that forces you to use Windows), it will take a little extra work to everything set up. There are two ways you can go about using Ansible if you use Windows:

---

[25]http://en.wikipedia.org/wiki/Idempotence#Computer_science_meaning

[26]http://brew.sh/

1. The easiest solution would be to use a Linux virtual machine (with something like VirtualBox) to do your work. For detailed instructions, see Appendix A - Using Ansible on Windows workstations.
2. Ansible runs (somewhat) within an appropriately-configured Cygwin[27] environment. For setup instructions, please see my blog post Running Ansible within Windows[28]), and note that *running Ansible directly within Windows is unsupported and prone to breaking.*

**If you're running Linux**, chances are you already have Ansible's dependencies installed, but we'll cover the most common installation methods.

If you have `python-pip` and `python-devel` (`python-dev` on Debian/Ubuntu) installed, use `pip` to install Ansible (this assumes you also have the 'Development Tools' package installed, so you have `gcc`, `make`, etc. available):

```
$ sudo pip install ansible
```

Using pip allows you to upgrade Ansible with `pip install --upgrade ansible`.

*Fedora/Red Hat Enterprise Linux/CentOS:*

The easiest way to install Ansible on a Fedora-like system is to use the official yum package. If you're running Red Hat Enterprise Linux (RHEL) or CentOS, you need to install EPEL's RPM before you install Ansible (see the info section below for instructions):

```
$ yum -y install ansible
```

---

[27]http://cygwin.com/
[28]https://servercheck.in/blog/running-ansible-within-windows

On RHEL/CentOS systems, `python-pip` and `ansible` are available via the EPEL repository[29]. If you run the command `yum repolist | grep epel` (to see if the EPEL repo is already available) and there are no results, you need to install it with the following commands:

```
# If you're on RHEL/CentOS 6:
$ rpm -ivh http://dl.fedoraproject.org/pub/epel/6/x86_64/\
epel-release-6-8.noarch.rpm
# If you're on RHEL/CentOS 7:
$ yum install epel-release
```

*Debian/Ubuntu:*

The easiest way to install Ansible on a Debian or Ubuntu system is to use the official apt package.

```
$ sudo apt-add-repository -y ppa:ansible/ansible
$ sudo apt-get update
$ sudo apt-get install -y ansible
```

 If you get an error like "sudo: add-apt-repository: command not found", you're probably missing the `python-software-properties` package. Install it with the command:

```
$ sudo apt-get install python-software-properties
```

**Once Ansible is installed,** make sure it's working properly by entering `ansible --version` on the command line. You should see the currently-installed version:

---

[29]https://fedoraproject.org/wiki/EPEL

```
$ ansible --version
ansible 2.1.0.0
```

# Creating a basic inventory file

Ansible uses an inventory file (basically, a list of servers) to communicate with your servers. Like a hosts file (at /etc/hosts) that matches IP addresses to domain names, an Ansible inventory file matches servers (IP addresses or domain names) to groups. Inventory files can do a lot more, but for now, we'll just create a simple file with one server. Create a file at /etc/ansible/hosts (the default location for Ansible's inventory file), and add one server to it:

```
$ sudo mkdir /etc/ansible
$ sudo touch /etc/ansible/hosts
```

Edit this hosts file with nano, vim, or whatever editor you'd like, but note you'll need to edit it with sudo as root. Put the following into the file:

```
1  [example]
2  www.example.com
```

...where example is the group of servers you're managing and www.example.com is the domain name (or IP address) of a server in that group. If you're not using port 22 for SSH on this server, you will need to add it to the address, like www.example.com:2222, since Ansible defaults to port 22 and won't get this value from your ssh config file.

 This first example assumes you have a server set up that you can test with; if you don't already have a spare server somewhere that you can connect to, you might want to create a small VM using DigitalOcean, Amazon Web Services, Linode, or some other service that bills by the hour. That way you have a full server environment to work with when learning Ansible—and when you're finished testing, delete the server and you'll only be billed a few pennies!

Replace the www.example.com in the above example with the name or IP address of your server.

# Running your first Ad-Hoc Ansible command

Now that you've installed Ansible and created an inventory file, it's time to run a command to see if everything works! Enter the following in the terminal (we'll do something safe so it doesn't make any changes on the server):

```
$ ansible example -m ping -u [username]
```

...where [username] is the user you use to log into the server. If everything worked, you should see a message that shows `www.example.com | success >>`, then the result of your ping. If it didn't work, run the command again with `-vvvv` on the end to see verbose output. Chances are you don't have SSH keys configured properly—if you login with `ssh username@www.example.com` and that works, the above Ansible command should work, too.

Ansible assumes you're using passwordless (key-based) login for SSH (e.g. you login by entering `ssh username@example.com` and don't have to type a password). If you're still logging into your remote servers with a username and password, or if you need a primer on Linux remote authentication and security best practices, please read Chapter 10 - Server Security and Ansible. If you insist on using passwords, add the `--ask-pass` (`-k`) flag to Ansible commands (you may also need to install the `sshpass` package for this to work). This entire book is written assuming passwordless authentication, so you'll need to keep this in mind every time you run a command or playbook.

Need a primer on SSH key-based authentication? Please read through Ubuntu's community documentation on SSH/OpenSSH/Keys[30].

Let's run a more useful command:

---

[30]https://help.ubuntu.com/community/SSH/OpenSSH/Keys

```
$ ansible example -a "free -m" -u [username]
```

In this example, we quickly see memory usage (in a human readable format) on all the servers (for now, just one) in the `example` group. Commands like this are helpful for quickly finding a server that has a value out of a normal range. I often use commands like `free -m` (to see memory statistics), `df -h` (to see disk usage statistics), and the like to make sure none of my servers is behaving erratically. While it's good to track these details in an external tool like Nagios[31], Munin[32], or Cacti[33], it's also nice to check these stats on all your servers with one simple command and one terminal window!

# Summary

That's it! You've just learned about configuration management and Ansible, installed it, told it about your server, and ran a couple commands on that server through Ansible. If you're not impressed yet, that's okay—you've only seen the *tip* of the iceberg.

```
 _____
/ A doctor can bury his mistakes but an \
| architect can only advise his clients |
\ to plant vines. (Frank Lloyd Wright)  /
 ---------------------------------------
        \   ^__^
         \  (oo)_____
            (__)\       )\/\
                ||----w |
                ||     ||
```

---

[31]http://www.nagios.org/
[32]http://munin-monitoring.org/
[33]http://www.cacti.net/

# Chapter 2 - Local Infrastructure Development: Ansible and Vagrant

## Prototyping and testing with local virtual machines

Ansible works well with any server to which you can connect—remote *or* local. For speedier testing and development of Ansible playbooks, and for testing in general, it's a very good idea to work locally. Local development and testing of infrastructure is both safer and faster than doing it on remote/live machines—especially in production environments!

 In the past decade, test-driven development (TDD), in one form or another, has become the norm for much of the software industry. Infrastructure development hasn't been as organized until recently, and best practices dictate that infrastructure (which is becoming more and more important to the software that runs on it) should be thoroughly tested as well.

Changes to software are tested either manually or in some automated fashion; there are now systems that integrate both with Ansible and with other deployment and configuration management tools, to allow some amount of infrastructure testing as well. Even if it's just testing a configuration change locally before applying it to production, that approach is a thousand times better than what, in the software development world, would be called 'cowboy coding'—working directly in a production environment, not documenting or encapsulating changes in code, and not having a way to roll back to a previous version.

The past decade has seen the growth of many virtualization tools that allow for flexible and very powerful infrastructure emulation, all from your local workstation!

It's empowering to be able to play around with a config file, or to tweak the order of a server update to perfection, over and over again, with no fear of breaking an important server. If you use a local virtual machine, there's no downtime for a server rebuild; just re-run the provisioning on a new VM, and you're back up and running in minutes—with no one the wiser.

Vagrant[34], a server provisioning tool, and VirtualBox[35], a local virtualization environment, make a potent combination for testing infrastructure and individual server configurations locally. Both applications are free and open source, and work well on Mac, Linux, or Windows hosts.

We're going to set up Vagrant and VirtualBox for easy testing with Ansible to provision a new server.

# Your first local server: Setting up Vagrant

To get started with your first local virtual server, you need to download and install Vagrant and VirtualBox, and set up a simple Vagrantfile, which will describe the virtual server.

1. Download and install Vagrant and VirtualBox (whichever version is appropriate for your OS): - Download Vagrant[36] - Download VirtualBox[37] (when installing, make sure the command line tools are installed, so Vagrant work with it)
2. Create a new folder somewhere on your hard drive where you will keep your Vagrantfile and provisioning instructions.
3. Open a Terminal or PowerShell window, then navigate to the folder you just created.
4. Add a CentOS 7.x 64-bit 'box' using the `vagrant box add`[38] command: `vagrant box add geerlingguy/centos7` (note: HashiCorp's Atlas[39] has a comprehen-

---

[34]http://www.vagrantup.com/

[35]https://www.virtualbox.org/

[36]http://www.vagrantup.com/downloads.html

[37]https://www.virtualbox.org/wiki/Downloads

[38]http://docs.vagrantup.com/v2/boxes.html

[39]https://atlas.hashicorp.com/boxes/search

sive list of different pre-made Linux boxes. Also, check out the 'official' Vagrant Ubuntu boxes in Vagrant's Boxes documentation[40].

5. Create a default virtual server configuration using the box you just downloaded: `vagrant init geerlingguy/centos7`
6. Boot your CentOS server: `vagrant up`

Vagrant has downloaded a pre-built 64-bit CentOS 7 virtual machine (you can build your own[41] virtual machine 'boxes', if you so desire), loaded it into VirtualBox with the configuration defined in the default Vagrantfile (which is now in the folder you created earlier), and booted the virtual machine.

Managing this virtual server is extremely easy: `vagrant halt` will shut down the VM, `vagrant up` will bring it back up, and `vagrant destroy` will completely delete the machine from VirtualBox. A simple `vagrant up` again will re-create it from the base box you originally downloaded.

Now that you have a running server, you can use it just like you would any other server, and you can connect via SSH. To connect, enter `vagrant ssh` from the folder where the Vagrantfile is located. If you want to connect manually, or connect from another application, enter `vagrant ssh-config` to get the required SSH details.

## Using Ansible with Vagrant

Vagrant's ability to bring up preconfigured boxes is convenient on its own, but you could do similar things with the same efficiency using VirtualBox's (or VMWare's, or Parallels') GUI. Vagrant has some other tricks up its sleeve:

- **Network interface management**[42]: You can forward ports to a VM, share the public network connection, or use private networking for inter-VM and host-only communication.
- **Shared folder management**[43]: Vagrant sets up shares between your host machine and VMs using NFS or (much slower) native folder sharing in VirtualBox.

---

[40]https://www.vagrantup.com/docs/boxes.html

[41]https://www.vagrantup.com/docs/virtualbox/boxes.html

[42]https://www.vagrantup.com/docs/networking/index.html

[43]https://www.vagrantup.com/docs/synced-folders/index.html

- **Multi-machine management**[44]: Vagrant is able to configure and control multiple VMs within one Vagrantfile. This is important because, as stated in the documentation, "Historically, running complex environments was done by flattening them onto a single machine. The problem with that is that it is an inaccurate model of the production setup, which behaves far differently."
- **Provisioning**[45]: When running `vagrant up` the first time, Vagrant automatically *provisions* the newly-minted VM using whatever provisioner you have configured in the Vagrantfile. You can also run `vagrant provision` after the VM has been created to explicitly run the provisioner again.

It's this last feature that is most important for us. Ansible is one of many provisioners integrated with Vagrant (others include basic shell scripts, Chef, Docker, Puppet, and Salt). When you call `vagrant provision` (or `vagrant up`) the first time, Vagrant passes off the VM to Ansible, and tells Ansible to run a defined Ansible playbook. We'll get into the details of Ansible playbooks later, but for now, we're going to edit our Vagrantfile to use Ansible to provision our virtual machine.

Open the Vagrantfile that was created when we used the `vagrant init` command earlier. Add the following lines just before the final 'end' (Vagrantfiles use Ruby syntax, in case you're wondering):

```
1  # Provisioning configuration for Ansible.
2  config.vm.provision "ansible" do |ansible|
3    ansible.playbook = "playbook.yml"
4  end
```

This is a very basic configuration to get you started using Ansible with Vagrant. There are many other Ansible options[46] you can use once we get deeper into using Ansible. For now, we just want to set up a very basic playbook—a simple file you create to tell Ansible how to configure your VM.

---

[44]https://www.vagrantup.com/docs/multi-machine/index.html

[45]https://www.vagrantup.com/docs/provisioning/index.html

[46]https://www.vagrantup.com/docs/provisioning/ansible.html

# Your first Ansible playbook

Let's create the Ansible playbook.yml file now. Create an empty text file in the same folder as your Vagrantfile, and put in the following contents:

```
1   ---
2   - hosts: all
3     become: yes
4     tasks:
5     - name: Ensure NTP (for time synchronization) is installed.
6       yum: name=ntp state=present
7     - name: Ensure NTP is running.
8       service: name=ntpd state=started enabled=yes
```

I'll get into what this playbook is doing in a minute. For now, let's run the playbook on our VM. Make sure you're in the same directory as the Vagrantfile and new playbook.yml file, and enter vagrant provision. You should see status messages for each of the 'tasks' you defined, and then a recap showing what Ansible did on your VM—something like the following:

```
PLAY RECAP ***********************************************************
default                    : ok=3   changed=1   unreachable=0   failed=0
```

Ansible just took the simple playbook you defined, parsed the YAML syntax, and ran a bunch of commands via SSH to configure the server as you specified. Let's go through the playbook, step by step:

```
1   ---
```

This first line is a marker showing that the rest of the document will be formatted in YAML (read a getting started guide for YAML[47]).

---

[47]http://www.yaml.org/start.html

```
2  - hosts: all
```

This line tells Ansible to which hosts this playbook applies. `all` works here, since Vagrant is invisibly using its own Ansible inventory file (instead of the one we created earlier in `/etc/ansible/hosts`), which just defines the Vagrant VM.

```
3    become: yes
```

Since we need privileged access to install NTP and modify system configuration, this line tells Ansible to use `sudo` for all the tasks in the playbook (you're telling Ansible to 'become' the root user with `sudo`, or an equivalent).

```
4    tasks:
```

All the tasks after this line will be run on all hosts (or, in our case, our one VM).

```
5    - name: Ensure NTP daemon (for time synchronization) is installed.
6      yum: name=ntp state=present
```

This command is the equivalent of running `yum install ntp`, but is much more intelligent; it will check if ntp is installed, and, if not, install it. This is the equivalent of the following shell script:

```
if ! rpm -qa | grep -qw ntp; then
    yum install ntp
fi
```

However, the above script is still not quite as robust as Ansible's `yum` command. What if ntpdate is installed, but not ntp? This script would require extra tweaking and complexity to match the simple Ansible yum command, especially after we explore the yum module more intimately (or the `apt` module for Debian-flavored Linux, or `package` for OS-agnostic package installation).

```
7     - name: Ensure NTP is running.
8       service: name=ntpd state=started enabled=yes
```

This final task both checks and ensures that the ntpd service is started and running, and sets it to start at system boot. A shell script with the same effect would be:

```
# Start ntpd if it's not already running.
if ps aux | grep -v grep | grep "[n]tpd" > /dev/null
then
    echo "ntpd is running." > /dev/null
else
    systemctl start ntpd.service > /dev/null
    echo "Started ntpd."
fi
# Make sure ntpd is enabled on system startup.
systemctl enable ntpd.service
```

You can see how things start getting complex in the land of shell scripts! And this shell script is still not as robust as what you get with Ansible. To maintain idempotency and handle error conditions, you'll have to do a lot more extra work with basic shell scripts than you do with Ansible.

We could be even more terse (and really demonstrate Ansible's powerful simplicity) and not use Ansible's name module to give human-readable names to each command, resulting in the following playbook:

```
1   ---
2   - hosts: all
3     become: yes
4     tasks:
5     - yum: name=ntp state=present
6     - service: name=ntpd state=started enabled=yes
```

Just as with code and configuration files, documentation in Ansible (e.g. using the name function and/or adding comments to the YAML for complicated tasks) is not absolutely necessary. However, I'm a firm believer in thorough (but concise) documentation, so I almost always document what my tasks will do by providing a name for each one. This also helps when you're running the playbooks, so you can see what's going on in a human-readable format.

# Cleaning Up

Once you're finished experimenting with the CentOS Vagrant VM, you can remove it from your system by running vagrant destroy. If you want to rebuild the VM again, run vagrant up. If you're like me, you'll soon be building and rebuilding hundreds of VMs and containers per week using Vagrant and Ansible!

# Summary

Your workstation is on the path to becoming an "infrastructure-in-a-box," and you can now ensure your infrastructure is as well-tested as the code that runs on top if it. With one small example, you've got a glimpse at the simple-yet-powerful Ansible playbook. We'll dive deeper into Ansible playbooks later, and we'll also explore Vagrant a little more as we go.

```
 _____
/ I have not failed, I've just found  \
| 10,000 ways that won't work. (Thomas |
\ Edison)                              /
 -------------------------------------
        \   ^__^
         \  (oo)_____
            (__)\       )\/\
                ||----w |
                ||     ||
```

# Chapter 3 - Ad-Hoc Commands

In the previous chapter, we ended our exploration of local infrastructure testing with Vagrant by creating a very simple Ansible playbook. Earlier still, we used a simple ansible ad-hoc command to run a one-off command on a remote server.

We'll dive deeper into playbooks in coming chapters; for now, we'll explore how Ansible helps you quickly perform common tasks on, and gather data from, one or many servers with ad-hoc commands.

## Conducting an orchestra

The number of servers managed by an individual administrator has risen dramatically in the past decade, especially as virtualization and growing cloud application usage has become standard fare. As a result, admins have had to find new ways of managing servers in a streamlined fashion.

On any given day, a systems administrator has many tasks:

- Apply patches and updates via yum, apt, and other package managers.
- Check resource usage (disk space, memory, CPU, swap space, network).
- Check log files.
- Manage system users and groups.
- Manage DNS settings, hosts files, etc.
- Copy files to and from servers.
- Deploy applications or run application maintenance.
- Reboot servers.
- Manage cron jobs.

Nearly all of these tasks can be (and usually are) at least partially automated—but some often need a human touch, especially when it comes to diagnosing issues in real time. And in today's complex multi-server environments, logging into servers individually is not a workable solution.

Ansible allows admins to run ad-hoc commands on one or hundreds of machines at the same time, using the `ansible` command. In Chapter 1, we ran a couple of commands (`ping` and `free -m`) on a server that we added to our Ansible inventory file. This chapter will explore ad-hoc commands and multi-server environments in much greater detail. Even if you decide to ignore the rest of Ansible's powerful features, you will be able to manage your servers much more efficiently after reading this chapter.

 Some of the examples in this chapter will display how you can configure certain aspects of a server with ad-hoc commands. It is usually more appropriate to contain all configuration within playbooks and templates, so it's easier to provision your servers (running the playbook the first time) and then ensure their configuration is idempotent (you can run the playbooks over and over again, and your servers will be in the correct state).

The examples in this chapter are for illustration purposes only, and all might not be applicable to your environment. But even if you *only* used Ansible for server management and running individual tasks against groups of servers, and didn't use Ansible's playbook functionality at all, you'd still have a great orchestration and deployment tool in Ansible!

# Build infrastructure with Vagrant for testing

For the rest of this chapter, since we want to do a bunch of experimentation without damaging any production servers, we're going to use Vagrant's powerful multi-machine capabilities to configure a few servers which we'll manage with Ansible.

Earlier, we used Vagrant to boot up one virtual machine running CentOS 7. In that example, we used all of Vagrant's default configuration defined in the Vagrantfile. In this example, we'll use Vagrant's powerful multi-machine management features.

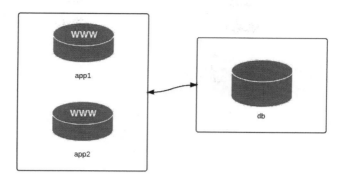

**Three servers: two application, one database.**

We're going to manage three VMs: two app servers and a database server. Many simple web applications and websites have a similar architecture, and even though this may not reflect the vast realm of infrastructure combinations that exist, it will be enough to highlight Ansible's server management abilities.

To begin, create a new folder somewhere on your local drive (I like using ~/VMs/[dir]), and create a new blank file named Vagrantfile (this is how we describe our virtual machines to Vagrant). Open the file in your favorite editor, add the following, and save the file:

```ruby
1   # -*- mode: ruby -*-
2   # vi: set ft=ruby :
3
4   VAGRANTFILE_API_VERSION = "2"
5
6   Vagrant.configure(VAGRANTFILE_API_VERSION) do |config|
7     # General Vagrant VM configuration.
8     config.vm.box = "geerlingguy/centos7"
9     config.ssh.insert_key = false
10    config.vm.synced_folder ".", "/vagrant", disabled: true
11    config.vm.provider :virtualbox do |v|
12      v.memory = 256
13      v.linked_clone = true
14    end
15
```

```
16    # Application server 1.
17    config.vm.define "app1" do |app|
18      app.vm.hostname = "orc-app1.dev"
19      app.vm.network :private_network, ip: "192.168.60.4"
20    end
21
22    # Application server 2.
23    config.vm.define "app2" do |app|
24      app.vm.hostname = "orc-app2.dev"
25      app.vm.network :private_network, ip: "192.168.60.5"
26    end
27
28    # Database server.
29    config.vm.define "db" do |db|
30      db.vm.hostname = "orc-db.dev"
31      db.vm.network :private_network, ip: "192.168.60.6"
32    end
33  end
```

This Vagrantfile defines the three servers we want to manage, and gives each one a unique hostname, machine name (for VirtualBox), and IP address. For simplicity's sake, all three servers will be running CentOS 7.

Open up a terminal window and change directory to the same folder where the Vagrantfile you just created exists. Enter vagrant up to let Vagrant begin building the three VMs. If you already downloaded the box while building the example from Chapter 2, this process shouldn't take too long—maybe 3-5 minutes.

While that's going on, we'll work on telling Ansible about the servers, so we can start managing them right away.

# Inventory file for multiple servers

There are many ways you can tell Ansible about the servers you manage, but the most standard, and simplest, is to add them to your system's main Ansible inventory file, which is located at /etc/ansible/hosts. If you didn't create the file in the previous chapter, go ahead and create the file now; make sure your user account has read permissions for the file.

Add the following to the file:

```
1   # Lines beginning with a # are comments, and are only included for
2   # illustration. These comments are overkill for most inventory files.
3
4   # Application servers
5   [app]
6   192.168.60.4
7   192.168.60.5
8
9   # Database server
10  [db]
11  192.168.60.6
12
13  # Group 'multi' with all servers
14  [multi:children]
15  app
16  db
17
18  # Variables that will be applied to all servers
19  [multi:vars]
20  ansible_ssh_user=vagrant
21  ansible_ssh_private_key_file=~/.vagrant.d/insecure_private_key
```

Let's step through this example, group by group:

1. The first block puts both of our application servers into an 'app' group.
2. The second block puts the database server into a 'db' group.
3. The third block tells ansible to define a new group 'multi', with child groups, and we add in both the 'app' and 'db' groups.
4. The fourth block adds variables to the multi group that will be applied to *all* servers within multi and all its children.

We'll dive deeper into variables, group definitions, group hierarchy, and other Inventory file topics later. For now, we just want Ansible to know about our servers, so we can start managing them quickly.

Save the updated inventory file, and then check to see if Vagrant has finished building the three VMs. Once Vagrant has finished, we can start managing the servers with Ansible.

# Your first ad-hoc commands

One of the first things you need to do is to check in on your servers. Let's make sure they're configured correctly, have the right time and date (we don't want any time synchronization-related errors in our application!), and have enough free resources to run an application.

 Many of the things we're manually checking here should also be monitored by an automated system on production servers; the best way to prevent disaster is to know when it could be coming, and to fix the problem *before* it happens. You should use tools like Munin, Nagios, Cacti, Hyperic, etc. to ensure you have a good idea of your servers' past and present resource usage! If you're running a website or web application available over the Internet, you should probably also use an external monitoring solution like Pingdom or Server Check.in.

## Discover Ansible's parallel nature

First, I want to make sure Vagrant configured the VMs with the right hostnames. Use ansible with the -a argument 'hostname' to run hostname against all the servers:

```
$ ansible multi -a "hostname"
```

Ansible will run this command against all three of the servers, and return the results (if Ansible can't reach one a server, it will show an error for that server, but continue running the command on the others).

If Ansible reports No hosts matched or returns some other inventory-related error, try setting the ANSIBLE_HOSTS environment variable explicitly: export ANSIBLE_HOSTS=/etc/ansible/hosts. Generally Ansible will read the file in /etc/ansible/hosts automatically, but depending on how you installed Ansible, you may need to explicitly set ANSIBLE_HOSTS for the ansible command to work correctly.

You may have noticed that the command was not run on each server in the order you'd expect. Go ahead and run the command a few more times, and see the order:

```
# First run results:
192.168.60.5 | success | rc=0 >>
orc-app2.dev

192.168.60.6 | success | rc=0 >>
orc-db.dev

192.168.60.4 | success | rc=0 >>
orc-app1.dev
```

```
# Second run results:
192.168.60.6 | success | rc=0 >>
orc-db.dev

192.168.60.5 | success | rc=0 >>
orc-app2.dev

192.168.60.4 | success | rc=0 >>
orc-app1.dev
```

By default, Ansible will run your commands in parallel, using multiple process forks, so the command will complete more quickly. If you're managing a few servers, this may not be much quicker than running the command serially, on one server after the other, but even managing 5-10 servers, you'll notice a dramatic speedup if you use Ansible's parallelism (which is enabled by default).

Run the same command again, but this time, add the argument -f 1 to tell Ansible to use only one fork (basically, to perform the command on each server in sequence):

```
$ ansible multi -a "hostname" -f 1
192.168.60.4 | success | rc=0 >>
orc-app1.dev

192.168.60.5 | success | rc=0 >>
orc-app2.dev

192.168.60.6 | success | rc=0 >>
orc-db.dev
```

Run the same command over and over again, and it will always return results in the same order. It's fairly rare that you will ever need to do this, but it's much more frequent that you'll want to *increase* the value (like -f 10, or -f 25... depending on how much your system and network connection can handle) to speed up the process of running commands on tens or hundreds of servers.

 Most people place the target of the action (multi) before the command/action itself ("on X servers, run Y command"), but if your brain works in the reverse order ("run Y command on X servers"), you could put the target *after* the other arguments (ansible -a "hostname" multi)—the commands are equivalent.

## Learning about your environment

Now that we trust Vagrant's ability to set hostnames correctly, let's make sure everything else is in order.

First, let's make sure the servers have disk space available for our application:

```
$ ansible multi -a "df -h"
192.168.60.6 | success | rc=0 >>
Filesystem                  Size  Used Avail Use% Mounted on
/dev/mapper/centos-root      19G 1014M   18G   6% /
devtmpfs                    111M     0  111M   0% /dev
tmpfs                       120M     0  120M   0% /dev/shm
tmpfs                       120M  4.3M  115M   4% /run
tmpfs                       120M     0  120M   0% /sys/fs/cgroup
/dev/sda1                   497M  124M  374M  25% /boot
none                        233G  217G   17G  94% /vagrant

192.168.60.5 | success | rc=0 >>
Filesystem                  Size  Used Avail Use% Mounted on
/dev/mapper/centos-root      19G 1014M   18G   6% /
devtmpfs                    111M     0  111M   0% /dev
tmpfs                       120M     0  120M   0% /dev/shm
tmpfs                       120M  4.3M  115M   4% /run
tmpfs                       120M     0  120M   0% /sys/fs/cgroup
/dev/sda1                   497M  124M  374M  25% /boot
none                        233G  217G   17G  94% /vagrant

192.168.60.4 | success | rc=0 >>
Filesystem                  Size  Used Avail Use% Mounted on
/dev/mapper/centos-root      19G 1014M   18G   6% /
devtmpfs                    111M     0  111M   0% /dev
tmpfs                       120M     0  120M   0% /dev/shm
tmpfs                       120M  4.3M  115M   4% /run
tmpfs                       120M     0  120M   0% /sys/fs/cgroup
/dev/sda1                   497M  124M  374M  25% /boot
none                        233G  217G   17G  94% /vagrant
```

It looks like we have plenty of room for now; our application is pretty lightweight.

Second, let's also make sure there is enough memory on our servers:

```
$ ansible multi -a "free -m"
192.168.60.4 | success | rc=0 >>
                total      used      free    shared   buffers    cached
Mem:              238       187        50         4         1        69
-/+ buffers/cache:          116       121
Swap:            1055         0      1055

192.168.60.6 | success | rc=0 >>
                total      used      free    shared   buffers    cached
Mem:              238       190        47         4         1        72
-/+ buffers/cache:          116       121
Swap:            1055         0      1055

192.168.60.5 | success | rc=0 >>
                total      used      free    shared   buffers    cached
Mem:              238       186        52         4         1        67
-/+ buffers/cache:          116       121
Swap:            1055         0      1055
```

Memory is pretty tight, but since we're running three VMs on our localhost, we need to be a little conservative.

Third, let's make sure the date and time on each server is in sync:

```
$ ansible multi -a "date"
192.168.60.5 | success | rc=0 >>
Sat Feb  1 20:23:08 UTC 2021

192.168.60.4 | success | rc=0 >>
Sat Feb  1 20:23:08 UTC 2021

192.168.60.6 | success | rc=0 >>
Sat Feb  1 20:23:08 UTC 2021
```

Most applications are written with slight tolerances for per-server time jitter, but it's always a good idea to make sure the times on the different servers are as close as possible, and the simplest way to do that is to use the Network Time Protocol, which is easy enough to configure. We'll do that next, using Ansible's modules to make the process painless.

 To get an exhaustive list of all the environment details ('facts', in Ansible's lingo) for a particular server (or for a group of servers), use the command `ansible [host-or-group] -m setup`. This will provide a list of every minute bit of detail about the server (including file systems, memory, OS, network interfaces... you name it, it's in the list).

## Make changes using Ansible modules

We want to install the NTP daemon on the server to keep the time in sync. Instead of running the command `yum install -y ntp` on each of the servers, we'll use ansible's `yum` module to do the same (just like we did in the playbook example earlier, but this time using an ad-hoc command).

```
$ ansible multi -s -m yum -a "name=ntp state=present"
```

You should see three simple 'success' messages, reporting no change, since NTP was already installed on the three machines; this confirms everything is in working order.

 The `-s` option (alias for `--sudo`) tells Ansible to run the command with sudo. This will work fine with our Vagrant VMs, but if you're running commands against a server where your user account requires a sudo password, you should also pass in `-K` (alias for `--ask-sudo-pass`), so you can enter your sudo password when Ansible needs it.

Now we'll make sure the NTP daemon is started and set to run on boot. We could use two separate commands, `service ntpd start` and `chkconfig ntpd on`, but we'll use Ansible's `service` module instead.

```
$ ansible multi -s -m service -a "name=ntpd state=started \
enabled=yes"
```

All three servers should show a success message like:

```
"changed": true,
"enabled": true,
"name": "ntpd",
"state": "started"
```

If you run the exact same command again, everything will be the same, but Ansible will report that nothing has changed, so the "changed" value becomes false.

When you use Ansible's modules instead of plain shell commands, you can use the powers of abstraction and idempotency offered by Ansible. Even if you're running shell commands, you could wrap them in Ansible's shell or command modules (like ansible multi -m shell -a "date"), but for these kind of commands, there's usually no need to use an Ansible module when running them ad-hoc.

The last thing we should do is check to make sure our servers are synced closely to the official time on the NTP server:

```
$ ansible multi -s -a "service ntpd stop"
$ ansible multi -s -a "ntpdate -q 0.rhel.pool.ntp.org"
$ ansible multi -s -a "service ntpd start"
```

For the ntpdate command to work, the ntpd service has to be stopped, so we stop the service, run the command to check our jitter, then start the service again.

In my test, I was within three one-hundredths of a second on all three servers—close enough for my purposes.

# Configure groups of servers, or individual servers

Now that we've been able to get all our servers to a solid baseline (e.g. all of them at least have the correct time), we need to set up the application servers, then the database server.

Since we set up two separate groups in our inventory file, app and db, we can target commands to just the servers in those groups.

## Configure the Application servers

Our hypothetical web application uses Django, so we need to make sure Django and its dependencies are installed. Django is not in the official CentOS yum repository, but we can install it using Python's easy_install (which, conveniently, has an Ansible module).

```
$ ansible app -s -m yum -a "name=MySQL-python state=present"
$ ansible app -s -m yum -a "name=python-setuptools state=present"
$ ansible app -s -m easy_install -a "name=django state=present"
```

You could also install django using pip, which can be installed via easy_install (since Ansible's easy_install module doesn't allow you to uninstall packages like pip does), but for simplicity's sake, we've installed it with easy_install.

Check to make sure Django is installed and working correctly.

```
$ ansible app -a "python -c 'import django; \
print django.get_version()'"
192.168.60.4 | success | rc=0 >>
1.10b1

192.168.60.5 | success | rc=0 >>
1.10b1
```

Things look like they're working correctly on our app servers. We can now move on to our database server.

 Almost all of the configuration we've done in this chapter would be much better off in an Ansible playbook (which will be explored in greater depth throughout the rest of this book). This chapter demonstrates how easy it is to manage multiple servers—for whatever purpose—using Ansible. Even if you set up and configure servers by hand using shell commands, using Ansible will save you a ton of time and help you do everything in the most secure and efficient manner possible.

## Configure the Database servers

We configured the application servers using the app group defined in Ansible's main inventory, and we can configure the database server (currently the only server in the db group) using the similarly-defined db group.

Let's install MariaDB, start it, and configure the server's firewall to allow access on MariaDB's default port, 3306.

```
$ ansible db -s -m yum -a "name=mariadb-server state=present"
$ ansible db -s -m service -a "name=mariadb state=started \
enabled=yes"
$ ansible db -s -a "iptables -F"
$ ansible db -s -a "iptables -A INPUT -s 192.168.60.0/24 -p tcp \
-m tcp --dport 3306 -j ACCEPT"
```

If you try connecting to the database from the app servers (or your host machine) at this point, you won't be able to connect, since MariaDB still needs to be set up. Typically, you'd do this by logging into the server and running mysql_secure_installation. Luckily, though, Ansible can control a MariaDB server with its assorted mysql_* modules. For now, we need to allow MySQL access for one user from our app servers. The MySQL modules require the MySQL-python module to be present on the managed server.

   Why MariaDB and not MySQL? RHEL 7 and CentOS 7 have MariaDB as the default supported MySQL-compatible database server. Some of the tooling around MariaDB still uses the old 'MySQL*' naming syntax, but if you're used to MySQL, things work similarly with MariaDB.

```
$ ansible db -s -m yum -a "name=MySQL-python state=present"
$ ansible db -s -m mysql_user -a "name=django host=% password=12345 \
priv=*.*:ALL state=present"
```

At this point, you should be able to create or deploy a Django application on the app servers, then point it at the database server with the username django and password 12345.

The MySQL configuration used here is for example/development purposes only! There are a few other things you should do to secure a production MySQL server, including removing the test database, adding a password for the root user account, restricting the IP addresses allowed to access port 3306 more closely, and some other minor cleanups. Some of these things will be covered later in this book, but, as always, you are responsible for securing your servers—make sure you're doing it correctly!

## Make changes to just one server

Congratulations! You now have a small web application environment running Django and MySQL. It's not much, and there's not even a load balancer in front of the app servers to spread out the requests; but we've configured everything pretty quickly, and without ever having to log into a server. What's even more impressive is that you could run any of the ansible commands again (besides a couple of the simple shell commands), and they wouldn't change anything—they would return `"changed"`: `false`, giving you peace of mind that the original configuration is intact.

Now that your local infrastructure has been running a while, you notice (hypothetically, of course) that the logs indicate one of the two app servers' time has gotten way out of sync with the others, likely because the NTP daemon has crashed or somehow been stopped. Quickly, you enter the following command to check the status of `ntpd`:

```
$ ansible app -s -a "service ntpd status"
```

Then, you restart the service on the affected app server:

```
$ ansible app -s -a "service ntpd restart" --limit "192.168.60.4"
```

In this command, we used the `--limit` argument to limit the command to a specific host in the specified group. `--limit` will match either an exact string or a regular expression (prefixed with $\sim$). The above command could be stated more simply if you want to apply the command to only the `.4` server (assuming you know there are no other servers with the an IP address ending in .4), the following would work exactly the same:

```
# Limit hosts with a simple pattern (asterisk is a wildcard).
$ ansible app -s -a "service ntpd restart" --limit "*.4"

# Limit hosts with a regular expression (prefix with a tilde).
$ ansible app -s -a "service ntpd restart" --limit ~".*\.4"
```

In these examples, we've been using IP addresses instead of hostnames, but in many real-world scenarios, you'll probably be using hostnames like nyc-dev-1.example.com; being able to match on regular expressions is often helpful.

 Try to reserve the --limit option for running commands on single servers. If you often find yourself running commands on the same set of servers using --limit, consider instead adding them to a group in your inventory file. That way you can enter ansible [my-new-group-name] [command], and save yourself a few keystrokes.

# Manage users and groups

One of the most common uses for Ansible's ad-hoc commands in my day-to-day usage is user and group management. I don't know how many times I've had to re-read the man pages or do a Google search just to remember which arguments I need to create a user with or without a home folder, add the user to certain groups, etc.

Ansible's user and group modules make things pretty simple and standard across any Linux flavor.

First, add an admin group on the app servers for the server administrators:

```
$ ansible app -s -m group -a "name=admin state=present"
```

The group module is pretty simple; you can remove a group by setting state=absent, set a group id with gid=[gid], and indicate that the group is a system group with system=yes.

Now add the user johndoe to the app servers with the group I just created and give him a home folder in /home/johndoe (the default location for most Linux distributions). Simple:

```
$ ansible app -s -m user -a "name=johndoe group=admin createhome=yes"
```

If you want to automatically create an SSH key for the new user (if one doesn't already exist), you can run the same command with the additional parameter `generate_ssh_key=yes`. You can also set the UID of the user by passing in `uid=[uid]`, set the user's shell with `shell=[shell]`, and the password with `password=[encrypted-password]`.

What if you want to delete the account?

```
$ ansible app -s -m user -a "name=johndoe state=absent remove=yes"
```

You can do just about anything you could do with `useradd`, `userdel`, and `usermod` using Ansible's `user` module, except you can do it more easily. The official documentation of the User module[48] explains all the possibilities in great detail.

# Manage packages

We've already used the `yum` module on our example CentOS infrastructure to ensure certain packages are installed. Ansible has a variety of package management modules for any flavor of Linux, but there's also a generic `package` module that can be used for easier cross-platform Ansible usage.

If you want to install a generic package like `git` on any Debian, RHEL, Fedora, Ubuntu, CentOS, FreeBSD, etc. system, you can use the command:

```
$ ansible app -s -m package -a "name=git state=present"
```

`package` works much the same as `yum`, `apt`, and other package management modules. Later in the book we'll explore ways of dealing with multi-platform package management where package names differ between OSes.

---

[48]http://docs.ansible.com/user_module.html

# Manage files and directories

Another common use for ad-hoc commands is remote file management. Ansible makes it easy to copy files from your host to remote servers, create directories, manage file and directory permissions and ownership, and delete files or directories.

## Get information about a file

If you need to check a file's permissions, MD5, or owner, use Ansible's stat module:

```
$ ansible multi -m stat -a "path=/etc/environment"
```

This gives the same information you'd get when running the stat command, but passes back information in JSON, which can be parsed a little more easily (or, later, used in playbooks to conditionally do or not do certain tasks).

## Copy a file to the servers

You probably use scp and/or rsync to copy files and directories to remote servers, and while Ansible has more advanced file copy modules like rsync, most file copy operations can be completed with Ansible's copy module:

```
$ ansible multi -m copy -a "src=/etc/hosts dest=/tmp/hosts"
```

The src can be a file or a directory. If you include a trailing slash, only the contents of the directory will be copied into the dest. If you omit the trailing slash, the contents *and* the directory itself will be copied into the dest.

The copy module is perfect for single-file copies, and works very well with small directories. When you want to copy hundreds of files, especially in very deeply-nested directory structures, you should consider either copying then expanding an archive of the files with Ansible's unarchive module, or using Ansible's synchronize or rsync modules.

# Retrieve a file from the servers

The fetch module works almost exactly the same as the copy module, except in reverse. The major difference is that files will be copied down to the local dest in a directory structure that matches the host from which you copied them. For example, use the following command to grab the hosts file from the servers:

```
$ ansible multi -s -m fetch -a "src=/etc/hosts dest=/tmp"
```

Fetch will, by default, put the /etc/hosts file from each server into a folder in the destination with the name of the host (in our case, the three IP addresses), then in the location defined by src. So, the db server's hosts file will end up in /tmp/192.168.60.6/etc/hosts.

You can add the parameter flat=yes, and set the dest to dest=/tmp/ (add a trailing slash), to make Ansible fetch the files directly into the /tmp directory. However, filenames must be unique for this to work, so it's not as useful when copying down files from multiple hosts. Only use flat=yes if you're copying files from a single host.

# Create directories and files

You can use the file module to create files and directories (like touch), manage permissions and ownership on files and directories, modify SELinux properties, and create symlinks.

Here's how to create a directory:

```
$ ansible multi -m file -a "dest=/tmp/test mode=644 state=directory"
```

Here's how to create a symlink (set state=link):

```
$ ansible multi -m file -a "src=/src/symlink dest=/dest/symlink \
owner=root group=root state=link"
```

# Delete directories and files

You can set the state to absent to delete a file or directory.

```
$ ansible multi -m file -a "dest=/tmp/test state=absent"
```

There are many simple ways to manage files remotely using Ansible. We've briefly covered the copy and file modules here, but be sure to read the documentation for the other file-management modules like lineinfile, ini_file, and unarchive. This book will cover these additional modules in depth in later chapters (when dealing with playbooks).

# Run operations in the background

Some operations take quite a while (minutes or even hours). For example, when you run yum update or apt-get update && apt-get dist-upgrade, it could be a few minutes before all the packages on your servers are updated.

In these situations, you can tell Ansible to run the commands asynchronously, and poll the servers to see when the commands finish. When you're only managing one server, this is not really helpful, but if you have many servers, Ansible starts the command *very* quickly on all your servers (especially if you set a higher --forks value), then polls the servers for status until they're all up to date.

To run a command in the background, you set the following options:

- -B <seconds>: the maximum amount of time (in seconds) to let the job run.
- -P <seconds>: the amount of time (in seconds) to wait between polling the servers for an updated job status.

## Update servers asynchronously, monitoring progress

Let's run yum -y update on all our servers to get them up to date. If we leave out -P, Ansible defaults to polling every 10 seconds:

```
$ ansible multi -s -B 3600 -a "yum -y update"
background launch...
```

```
192.168.60.6 | success >> {
    "ansible_job_id": "763350539037",
    "results_file": "/root/.ansible_async/763350539037",
    "started": 1
}
```

```
... [other hosts] ...
```

Wait a little while (or a *long* while, depending on how old the system image is we used to build our example VMs!), and eventually, you should see something like:

```
<job 763350539037> finished on 192.168.60.6 => {
    "ansible_job_id": "763350539037",
    "changed": true,
    "cmd": [
        "yum",
        "-y",
        "update"
    ],
    "delta": "0:13:13.973892",
    "end": "2021-02-09 04:47:58.259723",
    "finished": 1,
```

```
... [more info and stdout from job] ...
```

While a background task is running, you can also check on the status elsewhere using Ansible's async_status module, as long as you have the ansible_job_id value to pass in as jid:

```
$ ansible multi -s -m async_status -a "jid=763350539037"
```

## Fire-and-forget tasks

You may also need to run occasional long-running maintenance scripts, or other tasks
that take many minutes or hours to complete, and you'd rather not babysit the task.
In these cases, you can set the -B value as high as you want (be generous, so your
task will complete before Ansible kills it!), and set -P to '0', so Ansible fires off the
command then forgets about it:

```
$ ansible multi -B 3600 -P 0 -a "/path/to/fire-and-forget-script.sh"
background launch...


192.168.60.5 | success >> {
    "ansible_job_id": "204960925196",
    "results_file": "/root/.ansible_async/204960925196",
    "started": 1
}

... [other hosts] ...

$
```

Running the command this way doesn't allow status updates via async_status and a
jid, but you can still inspect the file ~/.ansible_async/<jid> on the remote server.
This option is usually more helpful for 'fire-and-forget' tasks.

 For tasks you don't track remotely, it's usually a good idea to log the
progress of the task *somewhere*, and also send some sort of alert on
failure—especially, for example, when running backgrounded tasks that
perform backup operations, or when running business-critical database
maintenance tasks.

You can also run tasks in Ansible playbooks in the background, asynchronously, by defining an `async` and `poll` parameter on the play. We'll discuss playbook task backgrounding in later chapters.

# Check log files

Sometimes, when debugging application errors, or diagnosing outages or other problems, you need to check server log files. Any common log file operation (like using `tail`, `cat`, `grep`, etc.) works through the `ansible` command, with a few caveats:

1. Operations that continuously monitor a file, like `tail -f`, won't work via Ansible, because Ansible only displays output after the operation is complete, and you won't be able to send the Control-C command to stop following the file. Someday, the async module might have this feature, but for now, it's not possible.
2. It's not a good idea to run a command that returns a huge amount of data via stdout via Ansible. If you're going to cat a file larger than a few KB, you should probably log into the server(s) individually.
3. If you redirect and filter output from a command run via Ansible, you need to use the `shell` module instead of Ansible's default `command` module (add `-m shell` to your commands).

As a simple example, let's view the last few lines of the messages log file on each of our servers:

```
$ ansible multi -s -a "tail /var/log/messages"
```

As stated in the caveats, if you want to filter the messages log with something like `grep`, you can't use Ansible's default `command` module, but instead, `shell`:

```
$ ansible multi -s -m shell -a "tail /var/log/messages | \
grep ansible-command | wc -l"

192.168.60.5 | success | rc=0 >>
12

192.168.60.4 | success | rc=0 >>
12

192.168.60.6 | success | rc=0 >>
14
```

This command shows how many ansible commands have been run on each server (the numbers you get may be different).

# Manage cron jobs

Periodic tasks run via cron are managed by a system's crontab. Normally, to change cron job settings on a server, you would log into the server, use crontab -e under the account where the cron jobs reside, and type in an entry with the interval and job.

Ansible makes managing cron jobs easy with its cron module. If you want to run a shell script on all the servers every day at 4 a.m., add the cron job with:

```
$ ansible multi -s -m cron -a "name='daily-cron-all-servers' \
hour=4 job='/path/to/daily-script.sh'"
```

Ansible will assume * for all values you don't specify (valid values are day, hour, minute, month, and weekday). You could also specify special time values like reboot, yearly, or monthly using special_time=[value]. You can also set the user the job will run under via user=[user], and create a backup of the current crontab by passing backup=yes.

What if we want to remove the cron job? Simple enough, use the same cron command, and pass the name of the cron job you want to delete, and state=absent:

```
$ ansible multi -s -m cron -a "name='daily-cron-all-servers' \
state=absent"
```

You can also use Ansible to manage custom crontab files; use the same syntax as you used earlier, but specify the location to the cron file with: `cron_file=cron_file_name` (where `cron_file_name` is a cron file located in `/etc/cron.d`).

 Ansible denotes Ansible-managed crontab entries by adding a comment on the line above the entry like `#Ansible: daily-cron-all-servers`. It's best to leave things be in the crontab itself, and always manage entries via ad-hoc commands or playbooks using Ansible's `cron` module.

# Deploy a version-controlled application

For simple application deployments, where you may need to update a git checkout, or copy a new bit of code to a group of servers, then run a command to finish the deployment, Ansible's ad-hoc mode can help. For more complicated deployments, use Ansible playbooks and rolling update features (which will be discussed in later chapters) to ensure successful deployments with zero downtime.

In the example below, I'll assume we're running a simple application on one or two servers, in the directory `/opt/myapp`. This directory is a git repository cloned from a central server or a service like GitHub, and application deployments and updates are done by updating the clone, then running a shell script at `/opt/myapp/scripts/update.sh`.

First, update the git checkout to the application's new version branch, 1.2.4, on all the app servers:

```
$ ansible app -s -m git -a "repo=git://example.com/path/to/repo.git \
dest=/opt/myapp update=yes version=1.2.4"
```

Ansible's git module lets you specify a branch, tag, or even a specific commit with the `version` parameter (in this case, we chose to checkout tag 1.2.4, but if you run the command again with a branch name, like prod, Ansible will happily do that instead). To force Ansible to update the checked-out copy, we passed in update=yes. The repo and dest options should be self-explanatory.

If you get a message saying "Failed to find required executable git", you will need to install Git on the server. To do so, run the ad-hoc command ansible package -s -m yum -a "name=git state=present".

If you get a message saying the Git server has an "unknown hostkey", add the option accept_hostkey=yes to the command, or add the hostkey to your server's known_hosts file before running this command.

Then, run the application's update.sh shell script:

```
$ ansible app -s -a "/opt/myapp/update.sh"
```

Ad-hoc commands are fine for the simple deployments (like our example above), but you should use Ansible's more powerful and flexible application deployment features described later in this book if you have complex application or infrastructure needs. See especially the 'Rolling Updates' section later in this book.

# Ansible's SSH connection history

One of Ansible's greatest features is its ability to function without running any extra applications or daemons on the servers it manages. Instead of using a proprietary protocol to communicate with the servers, Ansible uses the standard and secure SSH connection that is commonly used for basic administration on almost every Linux server running today.

Since a stable, fast, and secure SSH connection is the heart of Ansible's communication abilities, Ansible's implementation of SSH has continually improved throughout the past few years—and is still improving today.

One thing that is universal to all of Ansible's SSH connection methods is that Ansible uses the connection to transfer one or a few files defining a play or command to the remote server, then runs the play/command, then deletes the transferred file(s), and reports back the results. This sequence of events may change and become more simple/direct with later versions of Ansible (see the notes on Ansible 1.5 below), but a fast, stable, and secure SSH connection is of paramount importance to Ansible.

## Paramiko

In the beginning, Ansible used paramiko—an open source SSH2 implementation for Python—exclusively. However, as a single library for a single language (Python), development of paramiko doesn't keep pace with development of OpenSSH (the standard implementation of SSH used almost everywhere), and its performance and security is slightly worse than OpenSSH—at least to this writer's eyes.

Ansible continues to support the use of paramiko, and even chooses it as the default for systems (like RHEL 5/6) which don't support ControlPersist—an option present only in OpenSSH 5.6 or newer. (ControlPersist allows SSH connections to persist so frequent commands run over SSH don't have to go through the initial handshake over and over again until the `ControlPersist` timeout set in the server's SSH config is reached.)

## OpenSSH (default)

Beginning in Ansible 1.3, Ansible defaulted to using native OpenSSH connections to connect to servers supporting ControlPersist. Ansible had this ability since version 0.5, but didn't default to it until 1.3.

Most local SSH configuration parameters (like hosts, key files, etc.) are respected, but if you need to connect via a port other than port 22 (the default SSH port), you need to specify the port in an inventory file (`ansible_ssh_port` option) or when running `ansible` commands.

OpenSSH is faster, and a little more reliable, than paramiko, but there are ways to make Ansible faster still.

## Accelerated Mode

While not too helpful for ad-hoc commands, Ansible's Accelerated mode achieves greater performance for playbooks. Instead of connecting repeatedly via SSH, Ansible connects via SSH initially, then uses the AES key used in the initial connection to communicate further commands and transfers via a separate port (5099 by default, but this is configurable).

The only extra package required to use accelerated mode is `python-keyczar`, and almost everything in normal OpenSSH/Paramiko mode works in Accelerated mode, with two exceptions when using `sudo`:

- Your sudoers file needs to have `requiretty` disabled (comment out the line with it, or set it per user by changing the line to `Defaults:username !requiretty`).
- You must disable sudo passwords by setting `NOPASSWD` in the sudoers file.

Accelerated mode can offer 2-4 times faster performance (especially for things like file transfers) compared to OpenSSH, and you can enable it for a playbook by adding the option `accelerate: true` to your playbook, like so:

```
---
- hosts: all
  accelerate: true
  [...]
```

It goes without saying, if you use accelerated mode, you need to have the port through which it communicates open in your firewall (port 5099 by default, or whatever port you set with the `accelerate_port` option after `accelerate`).

Accelerate mode is a spiritual descendant of the now-deprecated 'Fireball' mode, which used a similar method for accelerating Ansible communications, but required ZeroMQ to be installed on the controlled server (which is at odds with Ansible's simple no-dependency, no-daemon philosophy), and didn't work with sudo commands at all.

## Faster OpenSSH in Ansible 1.5+

Ansible 1.5 and later contains a very nice improvement to Ansible's default OpenSSH implementation.

Instead of copying files, running them on the remote server, then removing them, the new method of OpenSSH transfer will send and execute commands for most Ansible modules directly over the SSH connection.

This method of connection is only available in Ansible 1.5+, and it can be enabled by adding `pipelining=True` under the `[ssh_connection]` section of the Ansible configuration file (`ansible.cfg`, which will be covered in more detail later).

> The `pipelining=True` configuration option won't help much unless you have removed or commented the `Defaults requiretty` option in `/etc/sudoers`. This is commented out in the default configuration for most OSes, but you might want to double-check this setting to make sure you're getting the fastest connection possible!

> If you're running a recent version of Mac OS X, Ubuntu, Windows with Cygwin, or most other OS for the host from which you run `ansible` and `ansible-playbook`, you should be running OpenSSH version 5.6 or later, which works perfectly with the `ControlPersist` setting used with all of Ansible's SSH connections settings.
>
> If the host on which Ansible runs has RHEL or CentOS, however, you might need to update your version of OpenSSH so it supports the faster/persistent connection method. Any OpenSSH version 5.6 or greater should work. To install a later version, either compile from source, or use a different repository (like CentALT[49] and `yum update openssh`.

# Summary

In this chapter, you learned how to build a multi-server infrastructure for testing on your local workstation using Vagrant, and you configured, monitored, and managed the infrastructure without ever logging in to an individual server. You also learned how Ansible connects to remote servers, and how to use the `ansible` command to perform tasks on many servers quickly in parallel, or one by one.

---

[49]http://mirror.neu.edu.cn/CentALT/readme.txt

By now, you should be getting familiar with the basics of Ansible, and you should
be able to start managing your own infrastructure more efficiently.

```
 _____
/ It's easier to seek forgiveness than \
\ ask for permission. (Proverb)         /
 ----------------------------------------
        \   ^__^
         \  (oo)_____
            (__)\       )\/\
                ||----w |
                ||     ||
```

# Chapter 4 - Ansible Playbooks

## Power plays

Like many other configuration management solutions, Ansible uses a metaphor to describe its configuration files. They are called 'playbooks', and they list a set of tasks ('plays' in Ansible parlance) that will be run against a particular server or set of servers. In American football, a team follows a set of pre-written playbooks as the basis for a bunch of plays they execute to try to win a game. In Ansible, you write playbooks (a list of instructions describing the steps to bring your server to a certain configuration state) that are then *play*ed on your servers.

Playbooks are written in YAML[50], a simple human-readable syntax popular for defining configuration. Playbooks may be included within other playbooks, and certain metadata and options cause different plays or playbooks to be run in different scenarios on different servers.

Ad-hoc commands alone make Ansible a powerful tool; playbooks turn Ansible into a top-notch server provisioning and configuration management tool.

What attracts most DevOps personnel to Ansible is the fact that it is easy to convert shell scripts (or one-off shell commands) directly into Ansible plays. Consider the following script, which installs Apache on a RHEL/CentOS server:

**Shell Script**

---

[50]https://docs.ansible.com/ansible/YAMLSyntax.html

```
1   # Install Apache.
2   yum install --quiet -y httpd httpd-devel
3   # Copy configuration files.
4   cp httpd.conf /etc/httpd/conf/httpd.conf
5   cp httpd-vhosts.conf /etc/httpd/conf/httpd-vhosts.conf
6   # Start Apache and configure it to run at boot.
7   service httpd start
8   chkconfig httpd on
```

To run the shell script (in this case, a file named shell-script.sh with the contents as above), you would call it directly from the command line:

```
# (From the same directory in which the shell script resides).
$ ./shell-script.sh
```

**Ansible Playbook**

```
1   ---
2   - hosts: all
3
4     tasks:
5       - name: Install Apache.
6         command: yum install --quiet -y httpd httpd-devel
7       - name: Copy configuration files.
8         command: >
9           cp httpd.conf /etc/httpd/conf/httpd.conf
10      - command: >
11          cp httpd-vhosts.conf /etc/httpd/conf/httpd-vhosts.conf
12      - name: Start Apache and configure it to run at boot.
13        command: service httpd start
14      - command: chkconfig httpd on
```

To run the Ansible Playbook (in this case, a file named playbook.yml with the contents as above), you would call it using the ansible-playbook command:

```
# (From the same directory in which the playbook resides).
$ ansible-playbook playbook.yml
```

Ansible is powerful in that you quickly transition to using playbooks if you know how to write standard shell commands—the same commands you've been using for years—and then as you get time, rebuild your configuration to take advantage of Ansible's helpful features.

In the above playbook, we use Ansible's command module to run standard shell commands. We're also giving each play a 'name', so when we run the playbook, the play has human-readable output on the screen or in the logs. The command module has some other tricks up its sleeve (which we'll see later), but for now, be assured shell scripts are translated directly into Ansible playbooks without much hassle.

> The greater-than sign (>) immediately following the command: module directive tells YAML "automatically quote the next set of indented lines as one long string, with each line separated by a space". It helps improve task readability in some cases. There are different ways of describing configuration using valid YAML syntax, and these methods are discussed in-depth in the YAML Conventions and Best Practices section in Appendix B.
>
> This book uses three different task-formatting techniques: For tasks which require one or two simple parameters, Ansible's shorthand syntax (e.g. yum: name=apache2 state=present) is used. For most uses of command or shell, where longer commands are entered, the > technique mentioned above is used. For tasks which require many parameters, YAML object notation is used—placing each key and variable on its own line. This assists with readability and allows for version control systems to easily distinguish changes line-by-line.

The above playbook will perform *exactly* like the shell script, but you can improve things greatly by using some of Ansible's built-in modules to handle the heavy lifting:

**Revised Ansible Playbook - Now with idempotence!**

```
1   ---
2   - hosts: all
3     become: yes
4
5     tasks:
6       - name: Install Apache.
7         yum: name={{ item }} state=present
8         with_items:
9           - httpd
10          - httpd-devel
11      - name: Copy configuration files.
12        copy:
13          src: "{{ item.src }}"
14          dest: "{{ item.dest }}"
15          owner: root
16          group: root
17          mode: 0644
18        with_items:
19          - src: "httpd.conf"
20            dest: "/etc/httpd/conf/httpd.conf"
21          - src: "httpd-vhosts.conf"
22            dest: "/etc/httpd/conf/httpd-vhosts.conf"
23      - name: Make sure Apache is started now and at boot.
24        service: name=httpd state=started enabled=yes
```

Now we're getting somewhere. Let me walk you through this simple playbook:

1. The first line, ---, is how we mark this document as using YAML syntax (like using <html> at the top of an HTML document, or <?php at the top of a block of PHP code).
2. The second line, - hosts: all defines the first (and in this case, only) *play*, and tells Ansible to run the play on all hosts that it knows about.
3. The third line, become: yes tells Ansible to run all the commands through sudo, so the commands will be run as the root user.

4. The fifth line, `tasks:`, tells Ansible that what follows is a list of tasks to run as part of this playbook.

5. The first task begins with `name: Install Apache`.. `name` is not a module that does something to your server; rather, it's a way of giving a human-readable description to the play that follows. Seeing "Install Apache" is more relevant than seeing "yum name=httpd state=present"... but if you drop the name line completely, that won't cause any problem.

   - We use the `yum` module to install Apache. Instead of the command `yum -y install httpd httpd-devel`, we can describe to Ansible exactly what we want. Ansible will take the `items` array we pass in (`{{ variable }}` references a variable in Ansible's playbooks). We tell yum to make sure the packages we define are installed with `state=present`, but we could also use `state=latest` to ensure the latest version is installed, or `state=absent` to make sure the package is *not* installed.

   - Ansible allows simple lists to be passed into tasks using `with_items:` Define a list of items below, and each line will be passed into the play, one by one. In this case, each of the items will be substituted for the `{{ item }}` variable.

6. The second task again starts with a human-readable name (which could be left out if you'd like).

   - We use the `copy` module to copy files from a source (on our local workstation) to a destination (the server being managed). We could also pass in more variables, like file metadata including ownership and permissions (`owner`, `group`, and `mode`).

   - In this case, we are using an array with multiple elements for variable substitution; you use the syntax `{var1: value, var2: value}` to define each element (it can have as many variables as you want within, or even nested levels of variables!). When you reference the variables in the play, you use a dot to access the variable within the item, so `{{ item.var1 }}` would access the first variable. In our example, `item.src` accesses the `src` in each item.

7. The third task also uses a name to describe it in a human-readable format.

   - We use the `service` module to describe the desired state of a particular service, in this case `httpd`, Apache's http daemon. We want it to be running, so we set `state=started`, and we want it to run at system startup, so we say `enabled=yes` (the equivalent of running `chkconfig httpd on`).

With this playbook format, Ansible can keep track of the state of everything on all our servers. If you run the playbook the first time, it will provision the server by ensuring Apache is installed and running, and your custom configuration is in place.

Even better, the *second* time you run it (if the server is in the correct state), it won't actually do anything besides tell you nothing has changed. So, with this one short playbook, you're able to provision and ensure the proper configuration for an Apache web server. Additionally, running the playbook with the `--check` option (see the next section below) verifies the configuration matches what's defined in the playbook, without actually running the tasks on the server.

If you ever want to update your configuration, or install another httpd package, either update the file locally or add the package to the `with_items` list and run the playbook again. Whether you have one or a thousand servers, all of their configurations will be updated to match your playbook—and Ansible will tell you if anything ever changes (you're not making ad-hoc changes on individual production servers, *are you?*).

# Running Playbooks with `ansible-playbook`

If we run the playbooks in the examples above (which are set to run on `all` hosts), then the playbook would be run against every host defined in your Ansible inventory file (see Chapter 1's basic inventory file example).

## Limiting playbooks to particular hosts and groups

You can limit a playbook to specific groups or individual hosts by changing the `hosts:` definition. The value can be set to `all` hosts, a `group` of hosts defined in your inventory, multiple groups of hosts (e.g. `webservers,dbservers`), individual hosts (e.g. `atl.example.com`), or a mixture of hosts. You can even do wild card matches, like `*.example.com`, to match all subdomains of a top-level domain.

You can also limit the hosts on which the playbook is run via the `ansible-playbook` command:

```
$ ansible-playbook playbook.yml --limit webservers
```

In this case (assuming your inventory file contains a webservers group), even if the playbook is set to hosts: all, or includes hosts in addition to what's defined in the webservers group, it will only be run on the hosts defined in webservers.

You could also limit the playbook to one particular host:

```
$ ansible-playbook playbook.yml --limit xyz.example.com
```

If you want to see a list of hosts that would be affected by your playbook before you actually run it, use --list-hosts:

```
$ ansible-playbook playbook.yml --list-hosts
```

Running this should give output like:

```
playbook: playbook.yml

  play #1 (all): host count=4
    127.0.0.1
    192.168.24.2
    foo.example.com
    bar.example.com
```

(Where count is the count of servers defined in your inventory, and following is a list of all the hosts defined in your inventory).

## Setting user and sudo options with ansible-playbook

If no remote_user is defined alongside the hosts in a playbook, Ansible assumes you'll connect as the user defined in your inventory file for a particular host, and then will fall back to your local user account name. You can explicitly define a remote user to use for remote plays using the --remote-user (-u) option:

```
$ ansible-playbook playbook.yml --remote-user=johndoe
```

In some situations, you will need to pass along your sudo password to the remote server to perform commands via sudo. In these situations, you'll need use the `--ask-become-pass` (-K) option. You can also explicitly force all tasks in a playbook to use sudo with `--become` (-b. Finally, you can define the sudo user for tasks run via sudo (the default is root) with the `--become-user` (-U) option.

For example, the following command will run our example playbook with sudo, performing the tasks as the sudo user janedoe, and Ansible will prompt you for the sudo password:

```
$ ansible-playbook playbook.yml --become --become-user=janedoe \
--ask-become-pass
```

If you're not using key-based authentication to connect to your servers (read my warning about the security implications of doing so in Chapter 1), you can use `--ask-pass`.

## Other options for `ansible-playbook`

The `ansible-playbook` command also allows for some other common options:

- `--inventory=PATH` (-i PATH): Define a custom inventory file (default is the default Ansible inventory file, usually located at /etc/ansible/hosts).
- `--verbose` (-v): Verbose mode (show all output, including output from successful options). You can pass in -vvvv to give every minute detail.
- `--extra-vars=VARS` (-e VARS): Define variables to be used in the playbook, in "key=value,key=value" format.
- `--forks=NUM` (-f NUM): Number for forks (integer). Set this to a number higher than 5 to increase the number of servers on which Ansible will run tasks concurrently.
- `--connection=TYPE` (-c TYPE): The type of connection which will be used (this defaults to ssh; you might sometimes want to use local to run a playbook on your local machine, or on a remote server via cron).

- `--check`: Run the playbook in Check Mode ('Dry Run'); all tasks defined in the playbook will be checked against all hosts, but none will actually be run.

There are some other options and configuration variables that are important to get the most out of `ansible-playbook`, but this should be enough to get you started running the playbooks in this chapter on your own servers or virtual machines.

 The rest of this chapter uses more realistic Ansible playbooks. All the examples in this chapter are in the Ansible for DevOps GitHub repository[51], and you can clone that repository to your computer (or browse the code online) to follow along more easily. The GitHub repository includes Vagrantfiles with each example, so you can build the servers on your local host using Vagrant.

# Real-world playbook: CentOS Node.js app server

The first example, while being helpful for someone who might want to post a simple static web page to a clunky old Apache server, is not a good representation of a real-world scenario. I'm going to run through more complex playbooks that do many different things, most of which are actually being used to manage production infrastructure today.

The first playbook will configure a CentOS server with Node.js, and install and start a simple Node.js application. The server will have a very simple architecture:

---

[51]https://github.com/geerlingguy/ansible-for-devops

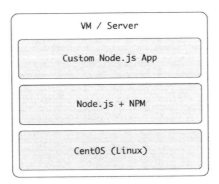

**Node.js app on CentOS.**

To start things off, we need to create a YAML file (playbook.yml in this example) to contain our playbook. Let's keep things simple:

```
1   ---
2   - hosts: all
3
4     tasks:
```

First, define a set of hosts (all) on which this playbook will be run (see the section above about limiting the playbook to particular groups and hosts), then tell Ansible that what follows will be a list of tasks to run on the hosts.

## Add extra repositories

Adding extra package repositories (yum or apt) is one thing many admins will do before any other work on a server to ensure that certain packages are available, or are at a later version than the ones in the base installation.

In the shell script below, we want to add both the EPEL and Remi repositories, so we can get some packages like Node.js or later versions of other necessary software (these examples presume you're running RHEL/CentOS 7.x):

```
1  # Import Remi GPG key.
2  wget http://rpms.famillecollet.com/RPM-GPG-KEY-remi \
3    -O /etc/pki/rpm-gpg/RPM-GPG-KEY-remi
4  rpm --import /etc/pki/rpm-gpg/RPM-GPG-KEY-remi
5
6  # Install Remi repo.
7  rpm -Uvh --quiet \
8    http://rpms.remirepo.net/enterprise/remi-release-7.rpm
9
10 # Install EPEL repo.
11 yum install epel-release
12
13 # Install Node.js (npm plus all its dependencies).
14 yum --enablerepo=epel install node
```

This shell script uses the rpm command to import the EPEL and Remi repository GPG keys, then adds the repositories, and finally installs Node.js. It works okay for a simple deployment (or by hand), but it's silly to run all these commands (some of which could take time or stop your script entirely if your connection is flaky or bad) if the result has already been achieved (namely, two repositories and their GPG keys have been added).

 If you wanted to skip a couple steps, you could skip adding the GPG keys, and just run your commands with --nogpgcheck (or, in Ansible, set the disable_gpg_check parameter of the yum module to yes), but it's a good idea to leave this enabled. GPG stands for *GNU Privacy Guard*, and it's a way that developers and package distributors can sign their packages (so you know it's from the original author, and hasn't been modified or corrupted). Unless you *really* know what you're doing, don't disable security settings like GPG key checks.

Ansible makes things a little more robust. Even though the following is slightly more verbose, it performs the same actions in a more structured way, which is simpler to understand, and works with variables other nifty Ansible features we'll discuss later:

```
 9        - name: Install Remi repo.
10          yum:
11            name: "http://rpms.remirepo.net/enterprise/remi-release-7.rp\
12   m"
13            state: present
14
15        - name: Import Remi GPG key.
16          rpm_key:
17            key: "http://rpms.remirepo.net/RPM-GPG-KEY-remi"
18            state: present
19
20        - name: Install EPEL repo.
21          yum: name=epel-release state=present
22
23        - name: Ensure firewalld is stopped (since this is for testing).
24          service: name=firewalld state=stopped
25
26        - name: Install Node.js and npm.
27          yum: name=npm state=present enablerepo=epel
28
29        - name: Install Forever (to run our Node.js app).
30          npm: name=forever global=yes state=present
```

Let's walk through this playbook step-by-step:

1. We can install extra yum repositories using the yum module. Just pass in the URL to the repo .rpm file, and Ansible will take care of the rest.

2. rpm_key is a very simple Ansible module that takes and imports an RPM key from a URL or file, or the key id of a key that is already present, and ensures the key is either present or absent (the state parameter). We're importing one key, for Remi's repository.

3. yum installs the EPEL repository (much simpler than the two-step process we had to follow to get Remi's repository installed!).

4. Since this server is being used only for test purposes, we disable the system firewall so it won't interfere with testing (using the service module).

5. `yum` installs Node.js (along with all the required packages for `npm`, Node's package manager) if it's not present, and allows the EPEL repo to be searched via the `enablerepo` parameter (you could also explicitly *disable* a repository using `disablerepo`).

6. Since NPM is now installed, we use Ansible's `npm` module to install a Node.js utility, `forever`, to launch our app and keep it running. Setting `global` to yes tells NPM to install the `forever` node module in `/usr/lib/node_modules/` so it will be available to all users and Node.js apps on the system.

We're beginning to have a nice little Node.js app server set up. Let's set up a little Node.js app that responds to HTTP requests on port 80.

## Deploy a Node.js app

The next step is to install a simple Node.js app on our server. First, we'll create a really simple Node.js app by creating a new folder, `app`, in the same folder as your playbook.yml. Create a new file, `app.js`, in this folder, with the following contents:

```
1   // Load the express module.
2   var express = require('express'),
3   app = express.createServer();
4
5   // Respond to requests for / with 'Hello World'.
6   app.get('/', function(req, res){
7       res.send('Hello World!');
8   });
9
10  // Listen on port 80 (like a true web server).
11  app.listen(80);
12  console.log('Express server started successfully.');
```

Don't worry about the syntax or the fact that this is Node.js. We just need a quick example to deploy. This example could've been written in Python, Perl, Java, PHP, or another language, but since Node is a simple language (JavaScript) that runs in a lightweight environment, it's an easy language to use when testing things or prodding your server.

Since this little app is dependent on Express (an http framework for Node), we also need to tell NPM about this dependency via a `package.json` file in the same folder as `app.js`:

```
1  {
2    "name": "examplenodeapp",
3    "description": "Example Express Node.js app.",
4    "author": "Jeff Geerling <geerlingguy@mac.com>",
5    "dependencies": {
6      "express": "3.x.x"
7    },
8    "engine": "node >= 0.10.6"
9  }
```

We need to copy the entire app to the server, and then have NPM download the required dependencies (in this case, express), so add these tasks to your playbook:

```
31      - name: Ensure Node.js app folder exists.
32        file: "path={{ node_apps_location }} state=directory"
33
34      - name: Copy example Node.js app to server.
35        copy: "src=app dest={{ node_apps_location }}"
36
37      - name: Install app dependencies defined in package.json.
38        npm: path={{ node_apps_location }}/app
```

First, we ensure the directory where our app will be installed exists, using the `file` module. The `{{ node_apps_location }}` variable used in each command can be defined under a `vars` section at the top of our playbook, in your inventory, or on the command line when calling `ansible-playbook`.

Second, we copy the entire app folder up to the server, using Ansible's `copy` command, which intelligently distinguishes between a single file or a directory of files, and recurses through the directory, similar to recursive scp or rsync.

Ansible's `copy` module works very well for single or small groups of files, and recurses through directories automatically. If you are copying hundreds of files, or deeply-nested directory structures, `copy` will get bogged down. In these situations, consider either using the `synchronize` or `rsync` module to copy a full directory, or `unarchive` to copy an archive and have it expanded in place on the server.

Third, we use `npm` again, this time, with no extra arguments besides the path to the app. This tells NPM to parse the package.json file and ensure all the dependencies are present.

We're *almost* finished! The last step is to start the app.

## Launch a Node.js app

We'll now use `forever` (which we installed earlier) to start the app.

```
40       - name: Check list of running Node.js apps.
41         command: forever list
42         register: forever_list
43         changed_when: false
44
45       - name: Start example Node.js app.
46         command: "forever start {{ node_apps_location }}/app/app.js"
47         when: "forever_list.stdout.find('{{ node_apps_location }}/\
48   app/app.js') == -1"
```

In the first play, we're doing two new things:

1. `register` creates a new variable, `forever_list`, to be used in the next play to determine when to run the play. `register` stashes the output (stdout, stderr) of the defined command in the variable name passed to it.
2. `changed_when` tells Ansible explicitly when this play results in a change to the server. In this case, we know the `forever list` command will never change the server, so we just say `false`—the server will never be changed when the command is run.

The second play actually starts the app, using Forever. We could also start the app by calling `node {{ node_apps_location }}/app/app.js`, but we would not be able to control the process easily, and we would also need to use `nohup` and `&` to avoid Ansible hanging on this play.

Forever tracks the Node apps it manages, and we use Forever's `list` option to print a list of running apps. The first time we run this playbook, the list will obviously be empty—but on future runs, if the app is running, we don't want to start another instance of it. To avoid that situation, we tell Ansible when we want to start the app with `when`. Specifically, we tell Ansible to start the app only when the app's path in *not* in the `forever list` output.

## Node.js app server summary

At this point, you have a complete playbook that will install a simple Node.js app which responds to HTTP requests on port 80 with "Hello World!".

To run the playbook on a server (in our case, we could just set up a new VirtualBox VM for testing, either via Vagrant or manually), use the following command (pass in the `node_apps_location` variable via the command):

```
$ ansible-playbook playbook.yml \
--extra-vars="node_apps_location=/usr/local/opt/node"
```

Once the playbook has finished configuring the server and deploying your app, visit `http://hostname/` in a browser (or use `curl` or `wget` to request the site), and you should see the following:

**Node.js Application home page.**

Simple, but very powerful. We've configured an entire Node.js application server In fewer than fifty lines of YAML!

The entire example Node.js app server playbook is in this book's code repository at https://github.com/geerlingguy/ansible-for-devops[52], in the `nodejs` directory.

# Real-world playbook: Ubuntu LAMP server with Drupal

At this point, you should be getting comfortable with Ansible playbooks and the YAML syntax used to define them. Up to this point, most examples have assumed you're working with a CentOS, RHEL, or Fedora server. Ansible plays nicely with other flavors of Linux and BSD-like systems as well. In the following example, we're going to set up a traditional LAMP (Linux, Apache, MySQL, and PHP) server using Ubuntu 14.04 to run a Drupal website.

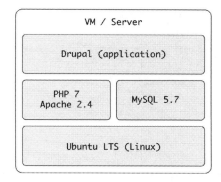

**Drupal LAMP server.**

## Include a variables file, and discover `pre_tasks` and `handlers`

To make our playbook more efficient and readable, let's begin the playbook (named `playbook.yml`) by instructing Ansible to load in variables from a separate `vars.yml` file:

---

[52]https://github.com/geerlingguy/ansible-for-devops

```
1    ---
2    - hosts: all
3
4      vars_files:
5        - vars.yml
```

Using one or more included variable files cleans up your main playbook file, and lets you organize all your configurable variables in one place. At the moment, we don't have any variables to add; we'll define the contents of vars.yml later. For now, create the empty file, and continue on to the next section of the playbook, pre_tasks:

```
7      pre_tasks:
8        - name: Update apt cache if needed.
9          apt: update_cache=yes cache_valid_time=3600
```

Ansible lets you run tasks before or after the main set of tasks using pre_tasks and post_tasks. In this case, we need to ensure that our apt cache is updated before we run the rest of the playbook, so we have the latest package versions on our server. We use Ansible's apt module and tell it to update the cache if it's been more than 3600 seconds (1 hour) since the last update.

With that out of the way, we'll add another new section to our playbook, handlers:

```
11     handlers:
12       - name: restart apache
13         service: name=apache2 state=restarted
```

handlers are special kinds of tasks you run at the end of a group of tasks by adding the notify option to any of the tasks in that group. The handler will only be called if one of the tasks notifying the handler makes a change to the server (and doesn't fail), and it will only be notified at the *end* of the group of tasks.

To call this handler, add the option notify: restart apache after defining the rest of a play. We've defined this handler so we can restart the apache2 service after a configuration change, which will be explained below.

ⓘ Just like variables, handlers and tasks may be placed in separate files and included in your playbook to keep things tidy (we'll discuss this in chapter 6). For simplicity's sake, though, the examples in this chapter are shown as in a single playbook file. We'll discuss different playbook organization methods later.

ⓘ By default, Ansible will stop all playbook execution when a task fails, and won't even notify any handlers that may need to be triggered. In some cases, this leads to unintended side effects. If you want to make sure handlers always run after a task uses `notify` to call the handler, even in case of playbook failure, add `--force-handlers` to your `ansible-playbook` command.

## Basic LAMP server setup

The first step towards building an application server that depends on the LAMP stack is to build the actual LAMP part of it. This is the simplest process, but still requires a little extra work for our particular server. We want to install Apache, MySQL and PHP, but we'll also need a couple other dependencies.

```
15    tasks:
16      - name: Get software for apt repository management.
17        apt: name={{ item }} state=present
18        with_items:
19          - python-apt
20          - python-pycurl
21
22      - name: "Install Apache, MySQL, PHP, and other dependencies."
23        apt: name={{ item }} state=present
24        with_items:
25          - git
26          - curl
27          - sendmail
```

```
28              - apache2
29              - php7.0-common
30              - php7.0-cli
31              - php7.0-dev
32              - php7.0-gd
33              - php7.0-curl
34              - php7.0-json
35              - php7.0-opcache
36              - php7.0-xml
37              - php7.0-mbstring
38              - php7.0-pdo
39              - php7.0-mysql
40              - php-apcu
41              - libpcre3-dev
42              - libapache2-mod-php7.0
43              - python-mysqldb
44              - mysql-server
45
46      - name: Disable the firewall (since this is for local dev only).
47        service: name=ufw state=stopped
48
49      - name: "Start Apache, MySQL, and PHP."
50        service: "name={{ item }} state=started enabled=yes"
51        with_items:
52          - apache2
53          - mysql
```

In this playbook, we begin with a common LAMP setup:

1. Install a couple helper libraries which allow Python to manage apt more pre-
   cisely (python-apt and python-pycurl are required for the apt_repository
   module to do its work).
2. Install all the required packages for our LAMP server (including all the PHP
   extensions Drupal requires).

3. Disable the firewall entirely, for testing purposes. If on a production server or any server exposed to the Internet, you should instead have a restrictive firewall only allowing access on ports 22, 80, 443, and other necessary ports.

4. Start up all the required services, and make sure they're enabled to start on system boot.

## Configure Apache

The next step is configuring Apache so it will work correctly with Drupal. Out of the box, Apache doesn't have mod_rewrite enabled on Ubuntu's current release. To remedy that situation, you could use the command `sudo a2enmod rewrite`, but Ansible has a handy `apache2_module` module that will do the same thing with idempotence.

We also need to add a VirtualHost entry to give Apache the site's document root and provide other options for the site.

```
58    - name: Enable Apache rewrite module (required for Drupal).
59      apache2_module: name=rewrite state=present
60      notify: restart apache
61
62    - name: Add Apache virtualhost for Drupal 8 development.
63      template:
64        src: "templates/drupal.dev.conf.j2"
65        dest: "/etc/apache2/sites-available/{{ domain }}.dev.conf"
66        owner: root
67        group: root
68        mode: 0644
69      notify: restart apache
70
71    - name: Symlink Drupal virtualhost to sites-enabled.
72      file:
73        src: "/etc/apache2/sites-available/{{ domain }}.dev.conf"
74        dest: "/etc/apache2/sites-enabled/{{ domain }}.dev.conf"
75        state: link
76      notify: restart apache
```

```
77
78      - name: Remove default virtualhost file.
79        file:
80          path: "/etc/apache2/sites-enabled/000-default.conf"
81          state: absent
82        notify: restart apache
```

The first command enables all the required Apache modules by symlinking them from /etc/apache2/mods-available to /etc/apache2/mods-enabled.

The second command copies a Jinja2 template we define inside a templates folder to Apache's sites-available folder, with the correct owner and permissions. Additionally, we notify the restart apache handler, because copying in a new VirtualHost means Apache needs to be restarted to pick up the change.

Let's look at our Jinja2 template (denoted by the extra .j2 on the end of the filename), drupal.dev.conf.j2:

```
1   <VirtualHost *:80>
2       ServerAdmin webmaster@localhost
3       ServerName {{ domain }}.dev
4       ServerAlias www.{{ domain }}.dev
5       DocumentRoot {{ drupal_core_path }}
6       <Directory "{{ drupal_core_path }}">
7           Options FollowSymLinks Indexes
8           AllowOverride All
9       </Directory>
10  </VirtualHost>
```

This is a fairly standard Apache VirtualHost definition, but we have a few Jinja2 template variables mixed in. The syntax for printing a variable in a Jinja2 template is the same syntax we use in our Ansible playbooks—two brackets around the variable's name (like so: {{ variable }}).

There are three variables we will need (drupal_core_version, drupal_core_path, and domain), so add them to the empty vars.yml file we created earlier:

```
1    ---
2    # The core version you want to use (e.g. 8.1.x, 8.2.x).
3    drupal_core_version: "8.1.x"
4
5    # The path where Drupal will be downloaded and installed.
6    drupal_core_path: "/var/www/drupal-{{ drupal_core_version }}-dev"
7
8    # The resulting domain will be [domain].dev (with .dev appended).
9    domain: "drupaltest"
```

Now, when Ansible reaches the play that copies this template into place, the Jinja2 template will have the variable names replaced with the values /var/www/drupal-8.1.x-dev and drupaltest (or whatever values you'd like!).

The last two tasks (lines 71-82) enable the VirtualHost we just added, and remove the default VirtualHost definition, which we no longer need.

At this point, you could start the server, but Apache will likely throw an error since the VirtualHost you've defined doesn't exist (there's no directory at {{ drupal_-core_path }} yet!). This is why using notify is important—instead of adding a task after these three steps to restart Apache (which will fail the first time you run the playbook), notify will wait until after we've finished all the other steps in our main group of tasks (giving us time to finish setting up the server), *then* restart Apache.

## Configure PHP with `lineinfile`

We briefly mentioned `lineinfile` earlier in the book, when discussing file management and ad-hoc task execution. Modifying PHP's configuration is a perfect way to demonstrate `lineinfile`'s simplicity and usefulness:

```
84    - name: Adjust OpCache memory setting.
85      lineinfile:
86        dest: "/etc/php/7.0/apache2/conf.d/10-opcache.ini"
87        regexp: "^opcache.memory_consumption"
88        line: "opcache.memory_consumption = 96"
89        state: present
90      notify: restart apache
```

Ansible's `lineinfile` module does a simple task: ensures that a particular line of text exists (or doesn't exist) in a file.

In this example, we need to adjust PHP's default `opcache.memory_consumption` option so the Drupal codebase can be compiled into PHP's system memory for much faster page load times.

First, we tell `lineinfile` the location of the file, in the `dest` parameter. Then, we give a regular expression (Python-style) to define what the line looks like (in this case, the line starts with the exact phrase "opcache.memory_consumption"). Next, we tell `lineinfile` exactly how the resulting line should look. Finally, we explicitly state that we want this line to be present (with the `state` parameter).

Ansible will take the regular expression, and see if there's a matching line. If there is, Ansible will make sure the line matches the `line` parameter. If not, Ansible will add the line as defined in the `line` parameter. Ansible will only report a change if it had to add or change the line to match `line`.

## Configure MySQL

The next step is to remove MySQL's default test database, and create a database and user (named for the domain we specified earlier) for our Drupal installation to use.

```
 92        - name: Remove the MySQL test database.
 93          mysql_db: db=test state=absent
 94
 95        - name: Create a database for Drupal.
 96          mysql_db: "db={{ domain }} state=present"
 97
 98        - name: Create a MySQL user for Drupal.
 99          mysql_user:
100            name: "{{ domain }}"
101            password: "1234"
102            priv: "{{ domain }}.*:ALL"
103            host: localhost
104            state: present
```

MySQL installs a database named test by default, and it is recommended that you remove the database as part of MySQL's included mysql_secure_installation tool. The first step in configuring MySQL is removing this database. Next, we create a database named {{ domain }}—the database is named the same as the domain we're using for the Drupal site, and a MySQL user for Drupal.

Ansible works with many databases out of the box (MongoDB, MySQL/-MariaDB, PostgreSQL, Redis and Riak as of this writing). In MySQL's case, Ansible uses the MySQLdb Python package (python-mysqldb) to manage a connection to the database server, and assumes the default root account credentials ('root' as the username with no password). Obviously, leaving this default would be a bad idea! On a production server, one of the first steps should be to change the root account password, limit the root account to localhost, and delete any nonessential database users.

If you use different credentials, you can add a .my.cnf file to your remote user's home directory containing the database credentials to allow Ansible to connect to the MySQL database without leaving passwords in your Ansible playbooks or variable files. Otherwise, you can prompt the user running the Ansible playbook for a MySQL username and password. This option, using prompts, will be discussed later in the book.

## Install Composer and Drush

Drupal has a command-line companion in the form of Drush. Drush is developed independently of Drupal, and provides a full suite of CLI commands to manage Drupal. Drush, like most modern PHP tools, integrates with external dependencies defined in a composer.json file which describes the dependencies to Composer.

We could just download Drupal and perform some setup in the browser by hand at this point, but the goal of this playbook is to have a fully-automated and idempotent Drupal installation. So, we need to install Composer, then Drush, and use both to install Drupal:

```
106    - name: Download Composer installer.
107      get_url:
108        url: https://getcomposer.org/installer
109        dest: /tmp/composer-installer.php
110        mode: 0755
111
112    - name: Run Composer installer.
113      command: >
114        php composer-installer.php
115        chdir=/tmp
116        creates=/usr/local/bin/composer
117
118    - name: Move Composer into globally-accessible location.
119      shell: >
120        mv /tmp/composer.phar /usr/local/bin/composer
121        creates=/usr/local/bin/composer
```

The first two commands download and run Composer's php-based installer, which generates a 'composer.phar' PHP application archive in /tmp. This archive is then copied (using the mv shell command) to the location /usr/local/bin/composer so we can use the composer command to install all of Drush's dependencies. The latter two commands are set to run only if the /usr/local/bin/composer file doesn't already exist (using the creates parameter).

Why use `shell` instead of `command`? Ansible's `command` module is the preferred option for running commands on a host (when an Ansible module won't suffice), and it works in most scenarios. However, `command` doesn't run the command via the remote shell `/bin/sh`, so options like `<`, `>`, `|`, and `&`, and local environment variables like `$HOME` won't work. `shell` allows you to pipe command output to other commands, access the local environment, etc.

There are two other modules which assist in executing shell commands remotely: `script` executes shell scripts (though it's almost always a better idea to convert shell scripts into idempotent Ansible playbooks!), and `raw` executes raw commands via SSH (it should only be used in circumstances where you can't use one of the other options).

It's best to use an Ansible module for every task. If you have to resort to a regular command-line command, try the the `command` module first. If you require the options mentioned above, use `shell`. Use of `script` or `raw` should be exceedingly rare, and won't be covered in this book.

Now, we'll install Drush using the latest version from GitHub:

```
123      - name: Check out drush master branch.
124        git:
125          repo: https://github.com/drush-ops/drush.git
126          dest: /opt/drush
127
128      - name: Install Drush dependencies with Composer.
129        shell: >
130          /usr/local/bin/composer install
131          chdir=/opt/drush
132          creates=/opt/drush/vendor/autoload.php
133
134      - name: Create drush bin symlink.
135        file:
136          src: /opt/drush/drush
137          dest: /usr/local/bin/drush
138          state: link
```

Earlier in the book, we cloned a git repository using an ad-hoc command. In this case, we're defining a play that uses the git module to clone Drush from its repository URL on GitHub. Since we want the master branch, pass in the repo (repository URL) and dest (destination path) parameters, and the git module will check out master by default.

After Drush is downloaded to /opt/drush, we use Composer to install all the required dependencies. In this case, we want Ansible to run composer install in the directory /opt/drush (this is so Composer finds Drush's composer.json file automatically), so we pass along the parameter chdir=/opt/drush. Once Composer is finished, the file /opt/drush/vendor/autoload.php will be created, so we use the creates parameter to tell Ansible to skip this step if the file already exists (for idempotency).

Finally, we create a symlink from /usr/local/bin/drush to the executable at /opt/drush/drush, so we can call the drush command anywhere on the system.

## Install Drupal with Git and Drush

We'll use git again to clone Drupal to the Apache document root we defined earlier in our virtual host configuration, install Drupal's dependencies with Composer, run Drupal's installation via Drush, and fix a couple other file permissions issues so Drupal loads correctly within our VM.

```
140    - name: Check out Drupal Core to the Apache docroot.
141      git:
142        repo: http://git.drupal.org/project/drupal.git
143        version: "{{ drupal_core_version }}"
144        dest: "{{ drupal_core_path }}"
145
146    - name: Install Drupal dependencies with Composer.
147      shell: >
148        /usr/local/bin/composer install
149        chdir={{ drupal_core_path }}
150        creates={{ drupal_core_path }}/sites/default/settings.php
151
152    - name: Install Drupal.
```

```
153        command: >
154          drush si -y --site-name="{{ drupal_site_name }}"
155          --account-name=admin
156          --account-pass=admin
157          --db-url=mysql://{{ domain }}:1234@localhost/{{ domain }}
158          chdir={{ drupal_core_path }}
159          creates={{ drupal_core_path }}/sites/default/settings.php
160        notify: restart apache
161
162      # SEE: https://drupal.org/node/2121849#comment-8413637
163      - name: Set permissions properly on settings.php.
164        file:
165          path: "{{ drupal_core_path }}/sites/default/settings.php"
166          mode: 0744
167
168      - name: Set permissions on files directory.
169        file:
170          path: "{{ drupal_core_path }}/sites/default/files"
171          mode: 0777
172          state: directory
173          recurse: yes
```

First, we clone Drupal's git repository, using the version defined in our vars.yml file as drupal_core_version. The git module's version parameter defines the branch (master, 8.1.x, etc.), tag (1.0.1, 8.1.5, etc.), or individual commit hash (50a1877, etc.) to clone.

Before installing Drupal, we must install Drupal's dependencies using Composer (just like with Drush). For both this and the next task, we only want to run them the first time we install Drupal, so we can use the creation of a settings.php file along with the creates parameter to let Ansible know if the dependencies and database have already been installed.

To install Drupal, we use Drush's si command (short for site-install) to run Drupal's installation (which configures the database, runs some maintenance, and sets some default configuration settings for the site). We passed in a few variables, like the `drupal_core_version` and `domain`; we also added a `drupal_site_name`, so add that variable to your `vars.yml` file:

```
10   # Your Drupal site name.
11   drupal_site_name: "Drupal Test"
```

Once the site is installed, we also restart Apache for good measure (using `notify` again, like we did when updating Apache's configuration).

The final two tasks set permissions on Drupal's settings.php and files folder to 744 and 777, respectively.

## Drupal LAMP server summary

To run the playbook on a server (either via a local VM for testing or on another server), use the following command:

```
$ ansible-playbook playbook.yml
```

After the playbook completes, if you access the server at http://drupaltest.dev/ (assuming you've pointed drupaltest.dev to your server or VM's IP address), you'll see Drupal's default home page, and you could login with 'admin'/'admin'. (Obviously, you'd set a secure password on a production server!).

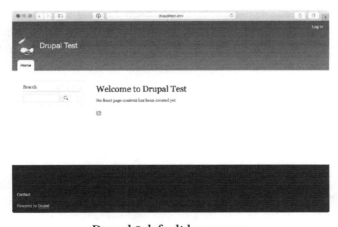

**Drupal 8 default home page.**

A similar server configuration, running Apache, MySQL, and PHP, can be used to run many popular web frameworks and CMSes besides Drupal, including Symfony, Wordpress, Joomla, Laravel, etc.

 The entire example Drupal LAMP server playbook is in this book's code repository at https://github.com/geerlingguy/ansible-for-devops[53], in the `drupal` directory.

# Real-world playbook: Ubuntu server with Solr

Apache Solr is a fast and scalable search server optimized for full-text search, word highlighting, faceted search, fast indexing, and more. It's a very popular search server, and it's pretty easy to install and configure using Ansible. In the following example, we're going to set up Apache Solr using Ubuntu 16.04 and Java.

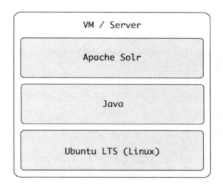

**Apache Solr Server.**

## Include a variables file, and more `pre_tasks` and `handlers`

Just like the previous LAMP server example, we'll begin this playbook (again named `playbook.yml`) by telling Ansible our variables will be in a separate `vars.yml` file:

---

[53]https://github.com/geerlingguy/ansible-for-devops

```
1   ---
2   - hosts: all
3
4     vars_files:
5       - vars.yml
```

Let's quickly create the vars.yml file, while we're thinking about it. Create the file in the same folder as your Solr playbook, and add the following contents:

```
1   download_dir: /tmp
2   solr_dir: /opt/solr
3   solr_version: 6.1.0
4   solr_checksum: sha1:41045799ed9b5f826b0dcab4b28b3b1986afa523
```

These variables define two paths we'll use while downloading and installing Apache Solr, and the version and file download checksum for downloading Apache Solr's source.

Back in our playbook, after the vars_files, we also need to make sure the apt cache is up to date, using pre_tasks like the previous example:

```
7     pre_tasks:
8       - name: Update apt cache if needed.
9         apt: update_cache=yes cache_valid_time=3600
```

Like the Drupal playbook, we again use handlers to define certain tasks that are notified by tasks in the tasks section. This time, we just need a handler to restart solr, a service that will be configured by the Apache Solr installation:

```
11    handlers:
12      - name: restart solr
13        service: name=solr state=restarted
```

We can call this handler with the option notify: restart solr in any play in our playbook.

## Install Java 8

It's easy enough to install Java 8 on Ubuntu, as it's in the default apt repositories. We just need to make sure the right package is installed:

```
15    tasks:
16      - name: Install Java.
17        apt: name=openjdk-8-jdk state=present
```

That was easy enough! We used the apt module to install openjdk-8-jdk.

## Install Apache Solr

Ubuntu's LTS release includes a package for Apache Solr, but it installs an older version, so we'll install the latest version of Solr from source. The first step is downloading the source:

```
19      - name: Download Solr.
20        get_url:
21          url: "https://archive.apache.org/dist/lucene/solr/\
22  {{ solr_version }}/solr-{{ solr_version }}.tgz"
23          dest: "{{ download_dir }}/solr-{{ solr_version }}.tgz"
24          checksum: "{{ solr_checksum }}"
```

When downloading files from remote servers, the get_url module provides more flexibility and convenience than raw wget or curl commands.

You have to pass get_url a url (the source of the file to be downloaded), and a dest (the location where the file will be downloaded). If you pass a directory to the dest parameter, Ansible will place the file inside, but will always re-download the file on subsequent runs of the playbook (and overwrite the existing download if it has changed). To avoid this extra overhead, we give the full path to the downloaded file.

We also use checksum, an optional parameter, for peace of mind; if you are downloading a file or archive that's critical to the functionality and security of your application, it's a good idea to check the file to make sure it is exactly what you're expecting.

checksum compares a hash of the data in the downloaded file to a hash that you specify (and which is provided alongside the downloads on the Apache Solr website). If the checksum doesn't match the supplied hash, Ansible will fail and discard the freshly-downloaded (and invalid) file.

We need to expand the Solr archive so we can run the installer inside, and we can use the creates option to make this operation idempotent:

```
25      - name: Expand Solr.
26        unarchive:
27          src: "{{ download_dir }}/solr-{{ solr_version }}.tgz"
28          dest: "{{ download_dir }}"
29          copy: no
30          creates: "{{ download_dir }}/solr-{{ solr_version }}/\
31  README.txt"
```

 If you read the unarchive module's documentation, you might notice you could consolidate both the get_url and unarchive tasks into one task by setting src to the file URL. Doing this saves a step in the playbook and is generally preferred, but in Apache Solr's case, the original .tgz archive must be present to complete installation, so we still need both tasks.

Now that the source is present, run the Apache Solr installation script (provided inside the Solr archive's bin directory) to complete Solr installation:

```
32      - name: Run Solr installation script.
33        shell: >
34          {{ download_dir }}/solr-{{ solr_version }}/bin/install_solr_\
35  service.sh
36          {{ download_dir }}/solr-{{ solr_version }}.tgz
37          -i /opt
38          -d /var/solr
39          -u solr
40          -s solr
41          -p 8983
42          creates={{ solr_dir }}/bin/solr
```

In this example, the options passed to the installer are hardcoded (e.g. the `-p 8983` tells Apache Solr to run on port 8983), and this works fine, but if you're going to reuse this playbook for many different types of Solr servers, you should probably configure many of these options with variables defined in `vars.yml`. This exercise is left to the reader.

Finally, we need a task that runs at the end of the playbook to make sure Apache Solr is started, and will start at system boot:

```
43    - name: Ensure solr is started and enabled on boot.
44        service: name=solr state=started enabled=yes
```

Run the playbook with $ `ansible-playbook playbook.yml`, and after a few minutes (depending on your server's Internet connection speed), you should be able to access the Solr admin interface at http://solr.dev:8983/solr (where 'solr.dev' is your server's hostname or IP address):

Solr Admin page.

## Apache Solr server summary

The configuration we used when deploying Apache Solr allows for a multi core setup, so you could add more 'search cores' via the admin interface (as long as the directories and core schema configuration is in place in the filesystem), and have multiple indexes for multiple websites and applications.

A playbook similar to the one above is used as part of the infrastructure for Hosted Apache Solr[54], a service I run which hosts Apache Solr search cores for Drupal websites.

 The entire example Apache Solr server playbook is in this book's code repository at https://github.com/geerlingguy/ansible-for-devops[55], in the solr directory.

## Summary

At this point, you should be getting comfortable with Ansible's *modus operandi*. Playbooks are the heart of Ansible's configuration management and provisioning functionality, and the same modules and similar syntax can be used with ad-hoc commands for deployments and general server management.

Now that you're familiar with playbooks, we'll explore more advanced concepts in building playbooks, like organization of tasks, conditionals, variables, and more. Later, we'll explore the use of playbooks with roles to make them infinitely more flexible and to save time setting up and configuring your infrastructure.

```
 _____
/ If everything is under control, you are \
\ going too slow. (Mario Andretti)        /
 -----------------------------------------
        \   ^__^
         \  (oo)_____
            (__)\       )\/\
                ||----w |
                ||     ||
```

---

[54]https://hostedapachesolr.com/
[55]https://github.com/geerlingguy/ansible-for-devops

# Chapter 5 - Ansible Playbooks - Beyond the Basics

The playbooks and simple playbook organization we used in the previous chapter cover many common use cases. When discussing the breadth of system administration needs, there are thousands more features of Ansible you need to know.

We'll cover how to run plays with more granularity, how to organize your tasks and playbooks for simplicity and usability, and other advanced playbook topics that will help you manage your infrastructure with even more confidence.

## Handlers

In chapter 4, the Ubuntu LAMP server example used a simple handler to restart Apache, and certain tasks that affected Apache's configuration notified the handler with the option `notify: restart apache`:

```
handlers:
  - name: restart apache
    service: name=apache2 state=restarted

tasks:
  - name: Enable Apache rewrite module.
    apache2_module: name=rewrite state=present
    notify: restart apache
```

In some circumstances you may want to notify multiple handlers, or even have handlers notify additionally handlers. Both are easy to do with Ansible. To notify multiple handlers from one task, use a list for the `notify` option:

```
- name: Rebuild application configuration.
  command: /opt/app/rebuild.sh
  notify:
    - restart apache
    - restart memcached
```

To have one handler notify another, add a notify option onto the handler—handlers are basically glorified tasks that can be called by the notify option, but since they act as tasks themselves, they can chain themselves to other handlers:

```
handlers:
  - name: restart apache
    service: name=apache2 state=restarted
    notify: restart memcached

  - name: restart memcached
    service: name=memcached state=restarted
```

There are a few other considerations when dealing with handlers:

- Handlers will only be run if a task notifies the handler; if a task that would've notified the handlers is skipped due to a when condition or something of the like, the handler will not be run.
- Handlers will run once, and only once, at the end of a play. If you absolutely need to override this behavior and run handlers in the middle of a playbook, you can use the meta module to do so (e.g. - meta: flush_handlers).
- If the play fails on a particular host (or all hosts) before handlers are notified, the handlers will never be run. If it's desirable to always run handlers, even after the playbook has failed, you can use the meta module as described above as a separate task in the playbook, or you use the command line flag --force-handlers when running your playbook. Handlers won't run on any hosts that became unreachable during the playbook's run.

# Environment variables

Ansible allows you to work with environment variables in a variety of ways. First of all, if you need to set some environment variables for your remote user account, you can do that by adding lines to the remote user's .bash_profile, like so:

```
- name: Add an environment variable to the remote user's shell.
  lineinfile: "dest=~/.bash_profile regexp=^ENV_VAR= \
  line=ENV_VAR=value"
```

All subsequent tasks will then have access to this environment variable (remember, of course, only the shell module will understand shell commands that use environment variables!). To use an environment variable in further tasks, it's recommended you use a task's register option to store the environment variable in a variable Ansible can use later, for example:

```
1  - name: Add an environment variable to the remote user's shell.
2    lineinfile: "dest=~/.bash_profile regexp=^ENV_VAR= \
3    line=ENV_VAR=value"
4
5  - name: Get the value of the environment variable we just added.
6    shell: 'source ~/.bash_profile && echo $ENV_VAR'
7    register: foo
8
9  - name: Print the value of the environment variable.
10   debug: msg="The variable is {{ foo.stdout }}"
```

We use source ~/.bash_profile in line 4 because Ansible needs to make sure it's using the latest environment configuration for the remote user. In some situations, the tasks all run over a persistent or quasi-cached SSH session, over which $ENV_VAR wouldn't yet be defined.

(This is also the first time the debug module has made an appearance. It will be explored more in-depth along with other debugging techniques later.).

Why ~/.bash_profile? There are many different places you can store environment variables, including .bashrc, .profile, and .bash_profile in a user's home folder. In our case, since we want the environment variable to be available to Ansible, which runs a pseudo-TTY shell session, in which case .bash_profile is used to configure the environment. You can read more about shell session configuration and these dotfiles in *Configuring your login sessions with dotfiles*[56].

Linux will also read global environment variables added to /etc/environment, so you can add your variable there:

```
- name: Add a global environment variable.
  lineinfile: "dest=/etc/environment regexp=^ENV_VAR= \
  line=ENV_VAR=value"
  become: yes
```

In any case, it's pretty simple to manage environment variables on the server with lineinfile. If your application requires many environment variables (as is the case in many Java applications), you might consider using copy or template with a local file instead of using lineinfile with a large list of items.

## Per-play environment variables

You can also set the environment for just one play, using the environment option for that play. As an example, let's say you need to set an http proxy for a certain file download. This can be done with:

```
- name: Download a file, using example-proxy as a proxy.
  get_url: url=http://www.example.com/file.tar.gz dest=~/Downloads/
  environment:
    http_proxy: http://example-proxy:80/
```

That could be rather cumbersome, though, especially if you have many tasks that require a proxy or some other environment variable. In this case, you can pass an environment in via a variable in your playbook's vars section (or via an included variables file), like so:

---

[56]http://mywiki.wooledge.org/DotFiles

```
vars:
  var_proxy:
    http_proxy: http://example-proxy:80/
    https_proxy: https://example-proxy:443/
    [etc...]

tasks:
- name: Download a file, using example-proxy as a proxy.
  get_url: url=http://www.example.com/file.tar.gz dest=~/Downloads/
  environment: var_proxy
```

If a proxy needs to be set system-wide (as is the case behind many corporate firewalls), I like to do so using the global /etc/environment file:

```
1  # In the 'vars' section of the playbook (set to 'absent' to disable \
2  proxy):
3  proxy_state: present
4
5  # In the 'tasks' section of the playbook:
6  - name: Configure the proxy.
7    lineinfile:
8      dest: /etc/environment
9      regexp: "{{ item.regexp }}"
10     line: "{{ item.line }}"
11     state: "{{ proxy_state }}"
12   with_items:
13     - regexp: "^http_proxy="
14       line: "http_proxy=http://example-proxy:80/"
15     - regexp: "^https_proxy="
16       line: "https_proxy=https://example-proxy:443/"
17     - regexp: "^ftp_proxy="
18       line: "ftp_proxy=http://example-proxy:80/"
```

Doing it this way allows me to configure whether the proxy is enabled per-server (using the proxy_state variable), and with one play, set the http, https, and ftp proxies. You can use a similar kind of play for any other types of environment variables you need to set system-wide.

 You can test remote environment variables using the `ansible` command: `ansible test -m shell -a 'echo $TEST'`. When doing so, be careful with your use of quotes and escaping—you might end up using double quotes where you meant to use single quotes, or vice-versa, and end up printing a local environment variable instead of one from the remote server!

# Variables

Variables in Ansible work just like variables in most other systems. Variables always begin with a letter (`[A-Za-z]`), and can include any number of underscores (`_`) or numbers (`[0-9]`).

Valid variable names include `foo`, `foo_bar`, `foo_bar_5`, and `fooBar`, though the standard is to use all lowercase letters, and typically avoid numbers in variable names (no `camelCase` or `UpperCamelCase`).

Invalid variable names include `_foo`, `foo-bar`, `5_foo_bar`, `foo.bar` and `foo bar`.

In an inventory file, a variable's value is assigned using an equals sign, like so:

```
foo=bar
```

In a playbook or variables include file, a variable's value is assigned using a colon, like so:

```
foo: bar
```

## Playbook Variables

There are many different ways you can define variables to use in tasks.

Variables can be passed in via the command line, when calling `ansible-playbook`, with the `--extra-vars` option:

```
ansible-playbook example.yml --extra-vars "foo=bar"
```

You can also pass in extra variables using quoted JSON, YAML, or even by passing a JSON or YAML file directly, like `--extra-vars "@even_more_vars.json"` or `--extra-vars "@even_more_vars.yml`, but at this point, you might be better off using one of the other methods below.

Variables may be included inline with the rest of a playbook, in a `vars` section:

```
1    ---
2    - hosts: example
3      vars:
4        foo: bar
5      tasks:
6        # Prints "Variable 'foo' is set to bar".
7        - debug: msg="Variable 'foo' is set to {{ foo }}"
```

Variables may also be included in a separate file, using the `vars_files` section:

```
1    ---
2    # Main playbook file.
3    - hosts: example
4      vars_files:
5        - vars.yml
6      tasks:
7        - debug: msg="Variable 'foo' is set to {{ foo }}"
```

```
1    ---
2    # Variables file 'vars.yml' in the same folder as the playbook.
3    foo: bar
```

Notice how the variables are all at the root level of the YAML file. They don't need to be under any kind of `vars` heading when they are included as a standalone file.

Variable files can also be imported conditionally. Say, for instance, you have one set of variables for your CentOS servers (where the Apache service is named `httpd`), and another for your Debian servers (where the Apache service is named `apache2`). In this case, you could use a conditional `vars_files` include:

```
1    ---
2    - hosts: example
3      vars_files:
4        - "apache_default.yml"
5        - "apache_{{ ansible_os_family }}.yml"
6      tasks:
7        - service: name={{ apache }} state=running
```

Then, add two files in the same folder as your example playbook, apache_CentOS.yml, and apache_default.yml. Define the variable apache: httpd in the CentOS file, and apache: apache2 in the default file.

As long as your remote server has facter or ohai installed, Ansible will be able to read the OS of the server, translate that to a variable (ansible_os_family), and include the vars file with the resulting name. If ansible can't find a file with that name, it will use the second option (apache_default.yml). So, on a Debian or Ubuntu server, Ansible would correctly use apache2 as the service name, even though there is no apache_Debian.yml or apache_Ubuntu.yml file available.

## Inventory variables

Variables may also be added via Ansible inventory files, either inline with a host definition, or after a group:

```
1    # Host-specific variables (defined inline).
2    [washington]
3    app1.example.com proxy_state=present
4    app2.example.com proxy_state=absent
5
6    # Variables defined for the entire group.
7    [washington:vars]
8    cdn_host=washington.static.example.com
9    api_version=3.0.1
```

If you need to define more than a few variables, especially variables that apply to more than one or two hosts, inventory files can be cumbersome. In fact, Ansible's documentation recommends *not* storing variables within the inventory. Instead, you can use `group_vars` and `host_vars` YAML variable files within a specific path, and Ansible will assign them to individual hosts and groups defined in your inventory.

For example, to apply a set of variables to the host `app1.example.com`, create a blank file named `app1.example.com` at the location `/etc/ansible/host_vars/app1.example.com`, and add variables as you would in an included `vars_files` YAML file:

```
---
foo: bar
baz: qux
```

To apply a set of variables to the entire `washington` group, create a similar file in the location `/etc/ansible/group_vars/washington` (substitute `washington` for whatever group name's variables you're defining).

You can also put these files (named the same way) in `host_vars` or `group_vars` directories in your playbook's directory. Ansible will use the variables defined in the inventory `/etc/ansible/[host|group]_vars` directory first (if the appropriate files exist), then it will use variables defined in the playbook directories.

Another alternative to using `host_vars` and `group_vars` is to use conditional variable file imports, as was mentioned above.

## Registered Variables

There are many times that you will want to run a command, then use its return code, stderr, or stdout to determine whether to run a later task. For these situations, Ansible allows you to use `register` to store the output of a particular command in a variable at runtime.

In the previous chapter, we used `register` to get the output of the `forever list` command, then used the output to determine whether we needed to start our Node.js app:

```
39  - name: "Node: Check list of Node.js apps running."
40    command: forever list
41    register: forever_list
42    changed_when: false
43
44  - name: "Node: Start example Node.js app."
45    command: forever start {{ node_apps_location }}/app/app.js
46    when: "forever_list.stdout.find('{{ node_apps_location}}/\
47  app/app.js') == -1"
```

In that example, we used a string function built into Python (find) to search for the path to our app, and if it was not present, the Node.js app was started.

We will explore the use of register further later in this chapter.

## Accessing Variables

Simple variables (gathered by Ansible, defined in inventory files, or defined in playbook or variable files) can be used as part of a task using syntax like {{ variable }}. For example:

```
- command: /opt/my-app/rebuild {{ my_environment }}
```

When the command is run, Ansible will substitute the contents of my_environment for {{ my_environment }}. So the resulting command would be something like /opt/my-app/rebuild dev.

Many variables you will use are structured as arrays (or 'lists'), and accessing the array foo would not give you enough information to be useful (except when passing in the array in a context where Ansible will use the entire array, like when using with_items).

If you define a list variable like so:

```
foo_list:
  - one
  - two
  - three
```

You could access the first item in that array with either of the following syntax:

```
foo[0]
foo|first
```

Note that the first line uses standard Python array access syntax ('retrieve the first (0-indexed) element of the array'), whereas the second line uses a convenient *filter* provided by Jinja2. Either way is equally valid and useful, and it's really up to you whether you like the first or second technique.

For larger and more structured arrays (for example, when retrieving the IP address of the server using the facts Ansible gathers from your server), you can access any part of the array by drilling through the array keys, either using bracket ([ ]) or dot (.) syntax. For example, if you would like to retrieve the information about the eth0 network interface, you could first take a look at the entire array using debug in your playbook:

```
# In your playbook.
tasks:
  - debug: var=ansible_eth0
```

```
TASK: [debug var=ansible_eth0]  ***************************************
ok: [webserver] => {
    "ansible_eth0": {
        "active": true,
        "device": "eth0",
        "ipv4": {
            "address": "10.0.2.15",
            "netmask": "255.255.255.0",
            "network": "10.0.2.0"
        },
        "ipv6": [
            {
                "address": "fe80::a00:27ff:feb1:589a",
                "prefix": "64",
                "scope": "link"
            }
        ],
        "macaddress": "08:00:27:b1:58:9a",
        "module": "e1000",
        "mtu": 1500,
        "promisc": false,
        "type": "ether"
    }
}
```

Now that you know the overall structure of the variable, you can use either of the following techniques to retrieve only the IPv4 address of the server:

```
{{ ansible_eth0.ipv4.address }}
{{ ansible_eth0['ipv4']['address'] }}
```

## Host and Group variables

Ansible conveniently lets you define or override variables on a per-host or per-group basis. As we learned earlier, your inventory file can define groups and hosts like so:

```
1  [group]
2  host1
3  host2
```

The simplest way to define variables on a per-host or per-group basis is to do so directly within the inventory file:

```
1  [group]
2  host1 admin_user=jane
3  host2 admin_user=jack
4  host3
5
6  [group:vars]
7  admin_user=john
```

In this case, Ansible will use the group default variable 'john' for `{{ admin_user }}`, but for `host1` and `host2`, the admin users defined alongside the hostname will be used.

This is convenient and works well when you need to define a variable or two per-host or per-group, but once you start getting into more involved playbooks, you might need to add a few (3+) host-specific variables. In these situations, you can define the variables in a different place to make maintenance and readability much easier.

### Automatically-loaded `group_vars` and `host_vars`

Ansible will search within the same directory as your inventory file (or inside `/etc/ansible` if you're using the default inventory file at `/etc/ansible/hosts`) for two specific directories: `group_vars` and `host_vars`.

You can place YAML files inside these directories named after the group name or hostname defined in your inventory file. Continuing our example above, let's move the specific variables into place:

```
1   ---
2   # File: /etc/ansible/group_vars/group
3   admin_user: john
```

```
1   ---
2   # File: /etc/ansible/host_vars/host1
3   admin_user: jane
```

Even if you're using the default inventory file (or an inventory file outside of your playbook's root directory), Ansible will also use host and group variables files located within your playbook's own group_vars and host_vars directories. This is convenient when you want to package together your entire playbook and infrastructure configuration (including all host/group-specific configuration) into a source-control repository.

You can also define a group_vars/all file that would apply to *all* groups, as well as a host_vars/all file that would apply to *all* hosts. Usually, though, it's best to provide defaults in your playbooks and roles (which will be discussed later).

## Magic variables with host and group variables and information

If you ever need to retrieve a specific host's variables from another host, Ansible provides a magic hostvars variable containing all the defined host variables (from inventory files and any discovered YAML files inside host_vars directories).

```
# From any host, returns "jane".
{{ hostvars['host1']['admin_user'] }}
```

There are a variety of other variables Ansible provides that you may need to use from time to time:

- groups: A list of all group names in the inventory.
- group_names: A list of all the groups of which the *current* host is a part.

- inventory_hostname: The hostname of the current host, according to the *inventory* (this can differ from ansible_hostname, which is the hostname reported by the system).
- inventory_hostname_short: The first part of inventory_hostname, up to the first period.
- play_hosts: All hosts on which the current play will be run.

Please see Magic Variables, and How To Access Information About Other Hosts[57] in Ansible's official documentation for the latest information and further usage examples.

## Facts (Variables derived from system information)

By default, whenever you run an Ansible playbook, Ansible first gathers information ("facts") about each host in the play. You may have noticed this whenever we ran playbooks in earlier chapters:

```
$ ansible-playbook playbook.yml

PLAY [group] ********************************************************

GATHERING FACTS ****************************************************
ok: [host1]
ok: [host2]
ok: [host3]
```

Facts can be extremely helpful when you're running playbooks; you can use gathered information like host IP addresses, CPU type, disk space, operating system information, and network interface information to change when certain tasks are run, or to change certain information used in configuration files.

To get a list of every gathered fact available, you can use the ansible command with the setup module:

---

[57]http://docs.ansible.com/playbooks_variables.html#magic-variables-and-how-to-access-information-about-other-hosts

```
$ ansible munin -m setup
munin.midwesternmac.com | success >> {
    "ansible_facts": {
        "ansible_all_ipv4_addresses": [
            "167.88.120.81"
        ],
        "ansible_all_ipv6_addresses": [
            "2604:180::a302:9076",
[...]
```

If you don't need to use facts, and would like to save a few seconds per-host when running playbooks (this can be especially helpful when running an Ansible playbook against dozens or hundreds of servers), you can set `gather_facts: no` in your playbook:

```
- hosts: db
  gather_facts: no
```

Many of my own playbooks and roles use facts like `ansible_os_family`, `ansible_-hostname`, and `ansible_memtotal_mb` to register new variables or in tandem with `when`, to determine whether to run certain tasks.

 If you have Facter[58] or Ohai[59] installed on a remote host, Ansible will also include their gathered facts as well, prefixed by `facter_` and `ohai_`, respectively. If you're using Ansible in tandem with Puppet or Chef, and are already familiar with those system-information-gathering tools, you can conveniently use them within Ansible as well. If not, Ansible's Facts are usually sufficient for whatever you need to do, and can be made even more flexible through the use of Local Facts.

---

[58]https://tickets.puppetlabs.com/browse/FACT
[59]http://docs.getchef.com/ohai.html

If you run a playbook against similar servers or virtual machines (e.g. all your servers are running the same OS, same hosting provider, etc.), facts are almost always consistent in their behavior. When running playbooks against a diverse set of hosts (for example, hosts with different OSes, virtualization stacks, or hosting providers), know that some facts may contain different information than you were expecting. For Server Check.in[60], I have servers from no less than five different hosting providers, running on vastly different hardware, so I am sure to monitor the output of my `ansible-playbook` runs for abnormalities, especially when adding new servers to the mix.

## Local Facts (Facts.d)

Another way of defining host-specific facts is to place `.fact` file in a special directory on remote hosts, `/etc/ansible/facts.d/`. These files can be either JSON or INI files, or you could use executables that return JSON. As an example, create the file `/etc/ansible/facts.d/settings.fact` on a remote host, with the following contents:

```
1  [users]
2  admin=jane,john
3  normal=jim
```

Next, use Ansible's `setup` module to display the new facts on the remote host:

---

[60]https://servercheck.in/

```
$ ansible hostname -m setup -a "filter=ansible_local"
munin.midwesternmac.com | success >> {
    "ansible_facts": {
        "ansible_local": {
            "settings": {
                "users": {
                    "admin": "jane,john",
                    "normal": "jim"
                }
            }
        }
    },
    "changed": false
}
```

If you are using a playbook to provision a new server, and part of that playbook adds a local .fact file which generates local facts that are used later, you can explicitly tell Ansible to reload the local facts using a task like the following:

```
1  - name: Reload local facts.
2    setup: filter=ansible_local
```

 While it may be tempting to use local facts rather than host_vars or other variable definition methods, remember that it's often better to build your playbooks in a way that doesn't rely (or care about) specific details of individual hosts. Sometimes it is necessary to use local facts (especially if you are using executables in facts.d to define the facts based on changing local environments), but it's almost always better to keep configuration in a central repository, and move away from host-specific facts.

 Note that setup module options (like filter) won't work on remote Windows hosts, as of this writing.

# Ansible Vault - Keeping secrets secret

If you use Ansible to fully automate the provisioning and configuration of your servers, chances are you will need to use passwords or other sensitive data for some tasks, whether it's setting a default admin password, synchronizing a private key, or authenticating to a remote service.

Some projects store such data in a normal variables file, in version control with the rest of the playbook, but in this case, the data is easily accessed by anyone with a copy of the project. It's better to treat passwords and sensitive data specially, and there are two primary ways to do this:

1. Use a separate secret management service, such as Vault[61] by HashiCorp, Keywhiz[62] by Square, or a hosted service like AWS's Key Management Service[63] or Microsoft Azure's Key Vault[64].
2. Use Ansible Vault, which is built into Ansible and stores encrypted passwords and other sensitive data alongside the rest of your playbook.

For most projects, Ansible's built-in Vault is adequate, but if you need some of the more advanced features found in the other projects listed in option #1 above, Ansible Vault might be too limiting.

Ansible Vault works much like a real-world vault:

1. You take any YAML file you would normally have in your playbook (e.g. a variables file, host vars, group vars, role default vars, or even task includes!), and store it in the vault.
2. Ansible encrypts the vault ('closes the door'), using a key (a password you set).
3. You store the key (your vault's password) separately from the playbook in a location only you control or can access.
4. You use the key to let Ansible decrypt the encrypted vault whenever you run your playbook.

---

[61]https://vaultproject.io/

[62]http://square.github.io/keywhiz/

[63]https://aws.amazon.com/kms/

[64]http://azure.microsoft.com/en-us/services/key-vault/

Let's see how it works in practice. Here's a playbook that connects to a service's API, and requires a secure API key to do so:

```
1   ---
2   - hosts: appserver
3
4     vars_files:
5       - vars/api_key.yml
6
7     tasks:
8       - name: Connect to service with our API key.
9         command: connect_to_service
10        environment:
11          SERVICE_API_KEY: "{{ myapp_service_api_key }}"
```

The vars_file, which is stored alongside the playbook, in plain text, looks like:

```
1   ---
2   myapp_service_api_key: "yJJvPqhqgxyPZMispRycaVMBmBWPqYDf3DFanPxAMAm4\
3   UZcw"
```

This is convenient, but it's not safe to store the API key in plain text. Even when running the playbook locally on an access-restricted computer, secrets should be encrypted. If you're running the playbook via a central server (e.g. using Ansible Tower or Jenkins), or if you have this playbook in a shared repository, it's even more important. *You* may follow best practices for physical and OS security, but can you guarantee *every* developer and sysadmin who has access to this file does the same?

For the best security, use Ansible Vault to encrypt the file. If you ever checked the original file into version control, it's also a good time to expire the old key and generate a new one, since the old key is part of the plaintext history of your project!

To encrypt the file with Vault, run:

```
$ ansible-vault encrypt api_key.yml
```

Enter a secure password for the file, and Ansible will encrypt it. If you open the file now, you should see something like:

```
1    $ANSIBLE_VAULT;1.1;AES256
2    6536353639636634393838653132623966653530636638396162666137376165393303
3    5303136633162643361336262663365376164633664656538623662313103a30633064
4    6332343063353337396236616331323762356665636531613532393838664613433663
5    1303132303566316232373865356237383539613437653563300a3263386336393866
6    3765356465623366643031373464323135633737353437326436383530373936362393
7    6396461376566336566303139333234643335633766626433366165343532346663332
8    6561383265303664343131616363562333639383864333635333766316161383832383
9    8316261666237626432303134363863393734373338303064386538336666364653164
10   66336131323237386633266363437
```

Next time you run the playbook, you will need to provide the password you used for the vault so Ansible can decrypt the playbook in memory for the brief period in which it will be used. If you don't specify the password, you'll receive an error:

```
$ ansible-playbook test.yml
ERROR: A vault password must be specified to decrypt vars/api_key.yml
```

There are a number of ways you can provide the password, depending on how you run playbooks. Providing the password at playbook runtime works well when running a playbook interactively:

```
# Use --ask-vault-pass to supply the vault password at runtime.
$ ansible-playbook test.yml --ask-vault-pass
Vault password:
```

After supplying the password, Ansible decrypts the vault (in memory) and runs the playbook with the decrypted data.

You can edit the encrypted file with `ansible-vault edit`. You can also `rekey` a file (change it's password), `create` a new file, `view` an existing file, or `decrypt` a file. All these commands work with one or multiple files (e.g. `ansible-vault create x.yml y.yml z.yml`).

For convenience, or for automated playbook runs (e.g. on a continuous integration server), you can supply vault passwords via a password file. Just like secure keys in your `~/.ssh` folder, you should treat these files carefully: never check them into source control, and set strict permissions (e.g. `600`) so only *you* can read or write this file. Create the file `~/.ansible/vault_pass.txt` with your password in it, set permissions to `600`, and tell Ansible the location of the file when you run the playbook:

```
# Use --vault-password-file to supply the password via file/script.
$ ansible-playbook test.yml --vault-password-file ~/.ansible/\
vault_pass.txt
```

You could also use an executable script (e.g. `~/.ansible/vault_pass.py` with execute permissions, `700`), as long as the script outputs a single line of text, the vault password.

 You can make Ansible's Vault operations slightly faster by installing Python's `cryptography` library, with `pip install cryptography`.

 Are you worried about the security of Vault-encrypted files? AES-256 encryption is extremely secure; it would take *billions of billions* of years to decrypt this single file, even if all of today's fastest supercomputer clusters were all put to the task 24x7. Of course, every vault is only as secure as its password, so make sure you use a secure password and store *it* securely!

More options and examples are available in the official documentation for Ansible Vault[65].

---

[65]http://docs.ansible.com/ansible/playbooks_vault.html

# Variable Precedence

It should be rare that you would need to dig into the details of which variable is used when you define the same variable in five different places, but since there are odd occasions where this is the case, Ansible's documentation provides the following ranking:

1. `--extra-vars` passed in via the command line (these always win, no matter what).
2. Task-level vars (in a task block).
3. Block-level vars (for all tasks in a block).
4. Role vars (e.g. `[role]/vars/main.yml`) and vars from `include_vars` module.
5. Vars set via `set_facts` modules.
6. Vars set via `register` in a task.
7. Individual play-level vars: 1. `vars_files` 2. `vars_prompt` 3. `vars`
8. Host facts.
9. Playbook `host_vars`.
10. Playbook `group_vars`.
11. Inventory: 1. `host_vars` 2. `group_vars` 3. `vars`
12. Role default vars (e.g. `[role]/defaults/main.yml`).

After lots of experience building playbooks, roles, and managing inventories, you'll likely find the right mix of variable definition for your needs, but there are a few general things that will mitigate any pain in setting and overriding variables on a per-play, per-host, or per-run basis:

- Roles (to be discussed in the next chapter) should provide sane default values via the role's 'defaults' variables. These variables will be the fallback in case the variable is not defined anywhere else in the chain.
- Playbooks should rarely define variables (e.g. via `set_fact`), but rather, variables should be defined either in included `vars_files` or, less often, via inventory.
- Only truly host- or group-specific variables should be defined in host or group inventories.

- Dynamic and static inventory sources should contain a minimum of variables, especially as these variables are often less visible to those maintaining a particular playbook.
- Command line variables (`-e`) should be avoided when possible. One of the main use cases is when doing local testing or running one-off playbooks where you aren't worried about the maintainability or idempotence of the tasks you're running.

See Ansible's Variable Precedence[66] documentation for more detail and examples, especially if you use older versions of Ansible (since older versions were not as strict about the precedence).

# If/then/when - Conditionals

Many tasks need only be run in certain circumstances. Some tasks use modules with built-in idempotence (as is the case when ensuring a yum or apt package is installed), and you usually don't need to define further conditional behaviors for these tasks.

However, there are many tasks—especially those using Ansible's `command` or `shell` modules—which require further input as to when they're supposed to run, whether they've changed anything after they've been run, or when they've failed to run.

We'll cover all the main conditionals behaviors you can apply to Ansible tasks, as well as how you can tell Ansible when a play has done something to a server or failed.

## Jinja2 Expressions, Python built-ins, and Logic

Before discussing all the different uses of conditionals in Ansible, it's worthwhile to cover a small part of Jinja2 (the syntax Ansible uses both for templates and for conditionals), and available Python functions (often referred to as 'built-ins'). Ansible uses expressions and built-ins with `when`, `changed_when`, and `failed_when` so you can describe these things to Ansible with as much precision as possible.

---

[66]http://docs.ansible.com/playbooks_variables.html#variable-precedence-where-should-i-put-a-variable

Jinja2 allows the definition of literals like strings ("string"), integers (42), floats (42.33), lists ([1, 2, 3]), tuples (like lists, but can't be modified) dictionaries ({key: value, key2: value2}), and booleans (true or false).

Jinja2 also allows basic math operations, like addition, subtraction, multiplication and division, and comparisons (== for equality, != for inequality, >= for greater than or equal to, etc.). Logical operators are and, or, and not, and you can group expressions by placing them within parenthesis.

If you're familiar with almost any programming language, you will probably pick up basic usage of Jinja2 expressions in Ansible very quickly.

For example:

```
# The following expressions evaluate to 'true':
1 in [1, 2, 3]
'see' in 'Can you see me?'
foo != bar
(1 < 2) and ('a' not in 'best')

# The following expressions evaluate to 'false':
4 in [1, 2, 3]
foo == bar
(foo != foo) or (a in [1, 2, 3])
```

Jinja2 also offers a helpful set of 'tests' you can use to test a given object. For example, if you define the variable foo for only a certain group of servers, but not others, you can use the expression foo is defined with a conditional to evaluate to 'true' if the variable is defined, or false if not.

There are many other checks you can perform as well, like undefined (the opposite of defined), equalto (works like ==), even (returns true if the variable is an even number), and iterable (if you can iterate over the object). We'll cover the full gamut later in the book, but for now, know that you can use Ansible conditionals with Jinja2 expressions to do some powerful things!

For the few cases where Jinja2 doesn't provide enough power and flexibility, you can invoke Python's built-in library functions (like string.split, [number].is_-

signed()) to manipulate variables and determine whether a given task should be run, resulted in a change, failed, etc.

As an example, I need to parse version strings from time to time, to find the major version of a particular project. Assuming the variable software_version is set to 4.6.1, I can get the major version by splitting the string on the . character, then using the first element of the array. I can check if the major version is 4 using when, and choose to run (or not run) a certain task:

```
1  - name: Do something only for version 4 of the software.
2    [task here]
3    when: software_version.split('.')[0] == '4'
```

It's generally best to stick with simpler Jinja2 filters and variables, but it's nice to be able to use Python when you're doing more advanced variable manipulation.

### register

In Ansible, any play can 'register' a variable, and once registered, that variable will be available to all subsequent tasks. Registered variables work just like normal variables or host facts.

Many times, you may need the output (stdout or stderr) of a shell command, and you can get that in a variable using the following syntax:

```
- shell: my_command_here
  register: my_command_result
```

Later, you can access stdout (as a string) with my_command_result.stdout, and stderr with my_command_result.stderr.

Registered facts are very helpful for many types of tasks, and can be used both with conditionals (defining when and how a play runs), and in any part of the play. As an example, if you have a command that outputs a version number string like "10.0.4", and you register the output as version, you can use the string later when doing a code checkout by printing the variable {{ version.stdout }}.

If you want to see the different properties of a particular registered variable, you can run a playbook with -v to inspect play output. Usually, you'll get access to values like changed (whether the play resulted in a change), delta (the time it took to run the play), stderr and stdout, etc. Some Ansible modules (like stat) add much more data to the registered variable, so always inspect the output with -v if you need to see what's inside.

## when

One of the most helpful extra keys you can add to a play is a when statement. Let's take a look at a simple use of when:

```
- yum: name=mysql-server state=present
  when: is_db_server
```

The above statement assumes you've defined the is_db_server variable as a boolean (true or false) earlier, and will run the play if the value is true, or skip the play when the value is false.

If you only define the is_db_server variable on database servers (meaning there are times when the variable may not be defined at all), you could run tasks conditionally like so:

```
- yum: name=mysql-server state=present
  when: (is_db_server is defined) and is_db_server
```

when is even more powerful if used in conjunction with variables registered by previous tasks. As an example, we want to check the status of a running application, and run a play only when that application reports it is 'ready' in its output:

```
- command: my-app --status
  register: myapp_result

- command: do-something-to-my-app
  when: "'ready' in myapp_result.stdout"
```

These examples are a little contrived, but they illustrate basic uses of when in your tasks. Here are some examples of uses of when in real-world playbooks:

```
# From our Node.js playbook - register a command's output, then see
# if the path to our app is in the output. Start the app if it's
# not present.
- command: forever list
  register: forever_list
- command: forever start /path/to/app/app.js
  when: "forever_list.stdout.find('/path/to/app/app.js') == -1"


# Run 'ping-hosts.sh' script if 'ping_hosts' variable is true.
- command: /usr/local/bin/ping-hosts.sh
  when: ping_hosts


# Run 'git-cleanup.sh' script if a branch we're interested in is
# missing from git's list of branches in our project.
- command: chdir=/path/to/project git branch
  register: git_branches
- command: /path/to/project/scripts/git-cleanup.sh
  when: "(is_app_server == true) and ('interesting-branch' not in \
  git_branches.stdout)"


# Downgrade PHP version if the current version contains '7.0'.
- shell: php --version
  register: php_version
- shell: yum -y downgrade php*
  when: "'7.0' in php_version.stdout"
```

```
# Copy a file to the remote server if the hosts file doesn't exist.
- stat: path=/etc/hosts
  register: hosts_file
- copy: src=path/to/local/file dest=/path/to/remote/file
  when: hosts_file.stat.exists == false
```

### changed_when **and** failed_when

Just like when, you can use changed_when and failed_when to influence Ansible's reporting of when a certain task results in changes or failures.

It is difficult for Ansible to determine if a given command results in changes, so if you use the command or shell module without also using changed_when, Ansible will always report a change. Most Ansible modules report whether they resulted in changes correctly, but you can also override this behavior by invoking changed_when yourself.

When using PHP Composer as a command to install project dependencies, it's useful to know when Composer installed something, or when nothing changed. Here's an example:

```
1  - name: Install dependencies via Composer.
2    command: "/usr/local/bin/composer global require phpunit/phpunit \
3    --prefer-dist"
4    register: composer
5    changed_when: "'Nothing to install' not in composer.stdout"
```

You can see we used register to store the results of the command, then we checked whether a certain string was in the registered variable's stdout. Only when Composer doesn't do anything will it print "Nothing to install or update", so we use that string to tell Ansible if the task resulted in a change.

Many command-line utilities print results to stderr instead of stdout, so failed_when can be used to tell Ansible when a task has *actually* failed and is not just reporting its results in the wrong way. Here's an example where we need to parse the stderr of a Jenkins CLI command to see if Jenkins did, in fact, fail to perform the command we requested:

```
1  - name: Import a Jenkins job via CLI.
2    shell: >
3      java -jar /opt/jenkins-cli.jar -s http://localhost:8080/
4      create-job "My Job" < /usr/local/my-job.xml
5    register: import
6    failed_when: "import.stderr and 'exists' not in import.stderr"
```

In this case, we only want Ansible to report a failure when the command returns an error, **and** that error doesn't contain 'exists'. It's debatable whether the command should report a job already exists via stderr, or just print the result to stdout... but it's easy to account for whatever the command does with Ansible!

### ignore_errors

Sometimes there are commands that should be run always, and they often report errors. Or there are scripts you might run that output errors left and right, and the errors don't actually indicate a problem, but they're just annoying (and they cause your playbooks to stop executing).

For these situations, you can add ignore_errors: true to the task, and Ansible will remain blissfully unaware of any problems running a particular task. Be careful using this, though; it's usually best if you can find a way to work with and around the errors generated by tasks so playbooks *do* fail if there are actual problems.

## Delegation, Local Actions, and Pauses

Some tasks, like sending a notification, communicating with load balancers, or making changes to DNS, networking, or monitoring servers, require Ansible to run the task on the host machine (running the playbook) or another host besides the one(s) being managed by the playbook. Ansible allows any task to be delegated to a particular host using delegate_to:

```
1  - name: Add server to Munin monitoring configuration.
2    command: monitor-server webservers {{ inventory_hostname }}
3    delegate_to: "{{ monitoring_master }}"
```

Delegation is often used to manage a server's participation in a load balancer or replication pool; you might either run a particular command locally (as in the example below), or you could use one of Ansible's built-in load balancer modules and delegate_to a specific load balancer host directly:

```
1  - name: Remove server from load balancer.
2    command: remove-from-lb {{ inventory_hostname }}
3    delegate_to: 127.0.0.1
```

If you're delegating a task to localhost, Ansible has a convenient shorthand you can use, local_action, instead of adding the entire delegate_to line:

```
1  - name: Remove server from load balancer.
2    local_action: command remove-from-lb {{ inventory_hostname }}
```

## Pausing playbook execution with `wait_for`

You might also use local_action in the middle of a playbook to wait for a freshly-booted server or application to start listening on a particular port:

```
1  - name: Wait for webserver to start.
2    local_action:
3      module: wait_for
4      host: "{{ inventory_hostname }}"
5      port: "{{ webserver_port }}"
6      delay: 10
7      timeout: 300
8      state: started
```

The above task waits until `webserver_port` is open on `inventory_hostname`, as checked from the host running the Ansible playbook, with a 5-minute timeout (and 10 seconds before the first check, and between checks).

`wait_for` can be used to pause your playbook execution to wait for many different things:

- Using `host` and `port`, wait a maximum of `timeout` seconds for the port to be available (or not).
- Using `path` (and `search_regex` if desired), wait a maximum of `timeout` seconds for the file to be present (or absent).
- Using `host` and `port` and `drained` for the `state` parameter, check if a given port has drained all it's active connections.
- Using `delay`, you can simply pause playbook execution for a given amount of time (in seconds).

## Running an entire playbook locally

When running playbooks on the server or workstation where the tasks need to be run (e.g. self-provisioning), or when a playbook should be otherwise run on the same host as the `ansible-playbook` command is run, you can use `--connection=local` to speed up playbook execution by avoiding the SSH connection overhead.

As a quick example, here's a short playbook that you can run with the command `ansible-playbook test.yml --connection=local`:

```
 1   ---
 2   - hosts: 127.0.0.1
 3     gather_facts: no
 4
 5     tasks:
 6       - name: Check the current system date.
 7         command: date
 8         register: date
 9
10       - name: Print the current system date.
11         debug: var=date.stdout
```

This playbook will run on localhost and output the current date in a debug message. It should run *very* fast (it took about .2 seconds on my Mac!) since it's running entirely over a local connection.

Running a playbook with `--connection=local` is also useful when you're either running a playbook with `--check` mode to verify configuration (e.g. on a cron job that emails you when changes are reported), or when testing playbooks on testing infrastructure (e.g. via Travis, Jenkins, or some other CI tool).

## Prompts

Under rare circumstances, you may require the user to enter the value of a variable that will be used in the playbook. If the playbook requires a user's personal login information, or if you prompt for a version or other values that may change depending on who is running the playbook, or where it's being run, and if there's no other way this information can be configured (e.g. using environment variables, inventory variables, etc.), use `vars_prompt`.

As a simple example, you can request a user to enter a username and password that could be used to login to a network share:

```
1  ---
2  - hosts: all
3
4    vars_prompt:
5      - name: share_user
6        prompt: "What is your network username?"
7
8      - name: share_pass
9        prompt: "What is your network password?"
10       private: yes
```

Before Ansible runs the play, Ansible prompts the user for a username and password, the latter's input being hidden on the command line for security purposes.

There are a few special options you can add to prompts:

- `private`: If set to yes, the user's input will be hidden on the command line.
- `default`: You can set a default value for the prompt, to save time for the end user.
- `encrypt` / `confirm` / `salt_size`: These values can be set for passwords so you can verify the entry (the user will have to enter the password twice if `confirm` is set to yes), and encrypt it using a salt (with the specified size and crypt scheme). See Ansible's Prompts[67] documentation for detailed information on prompted variable encryption.

Prompts are a simple way to gather user-specific information, but in most cases, you should avoid them unless absolutely necessary. It's preferable to use role or playbook variables, inventory variables, or even local environment variables, to maintain complete automation of the playbook run.

# Tags

Tags allow you to run (or exclude) subsets of a playbook's tasks.

You can tag roles, included files, individual tasks, and even entire plays. The syntax is simple, and below are examples of the different ways you can add tags:

```
 1  ---
 2  # You can apply tags to an entire play.
 3  - hosts: webservers
 4    tags: deploy
 5
 6    roles:
 7      # Tags applied to a role will be applied to tasks in the role.
 8      - { role: tomcat, tags: ['tomcat', 'app'] }
 9
10    tasks:
11      - name: Notify on completion.
12        local_action:
```

---

[67]http://docs.ansible.com/playbooks_prompts.html#prompts

```
13          module: osx_say
14          msg: "{{inventory_hostname}} is finished!"
15          voice: Zarvox
16        tags:
17          - notifications
18          - say
19
20      - include: foo.yml
21        tags: foo
```

Assuming we save the above playbook as `tags.yml`, you could run the command below to only run the `tomcat` role and the `Notify on completion` task:

```
1  $ ansible-playbook tags.yml --tags "tomcat,say"
```

If you want to exclude anything tagged with `notifications`, you can use `--skip-tags`.

```
1  $ ansible-playbook tags.yml --skip-tags "notifications"
```

This is incredibly handy if you have a decent tagging structure; when you want to only run a particular portion of a playbook, or one play in a series (or, alternatively, if you want to exclude a play or included tasks), then it's easy to do using `--tags` or `--skip-tags`.

There is one caveat when adding one or multiple tags using the `tags` option in a playbook: you can use the shorthand `tags: tagname` when adding just one tag, but if adding more than one tag, you have to use YAML's list syntax, for example:

```
# Shorthand list syntax.
tags: ['one', 'two', 'three']

# Explicit list syntax.
tags:
    - one
    - two
    - three

# Non-working example.
tags: one, two, three
```

In general, I tend to use tags for larger playbooks, especially with individual roles and plays, but unless I'm debugging a set of tasks, I generally avoid adding tags to individual tasks or includes (not adding tags everywhere reduces visual clutter). You will need to find a tagging style that suits your needs and lets you run (or *not* run) the specific parts of your playbooks you desire.

# Blocks

Introduced in Ansible 2.0.0, Blocks allow you to group related tasks together and apply particular task parameters on the block level. They also allow you to handle errors inside the blocks in a way similar to most programming languages' exception handling.

Here's an example playbook that uses blocks with when to run group of tasks specific to one platform without when parameters on each task:

```
1   ---
2   - hosts: web
3     tasks:
4       # Install and configure Apache on RHEL/CentOS hosts.
5       - block:
6           - yum: name=httpd state=present
7           - template: src=httpd.conf.j2 dest=/etc/httpd/conf/httpd.conf
8           - service: name=httpd state=started enabled=yes
9         when: ansible_os_family == 'RedHat'
10        become: yes
11
12      # Install and configure Apache on Debian/Ubuntu hosts.
13      - block:
14          - apt: name=apache2 state=present
15          - template: src=httpd.conf.j2 dest=/etc/apache2/apache2.conf
16          - service: name=apache2 state=started enabled=yes
17        when: ansible_os_family == 'Debian'
18        become: yes
```

If you want to perform a series of tasks with one set of task parameters (e.g. `with_items`, `when`, or `become`) applied, blocks are quite handy.

Blocks are also useful if you want to be able to gracefully handle failures in certain tasks. There might be a task that connects your app to a monitoring service that's not essential for a deployment to succeed, so it would be better to gracefully handle a failure than to bail out of the entire deployment!

Here's how to use a block to gracefully handle task failures:

```
 1  tasks:
 2    - block:
 3        - name: Script to connect the app to a monitoring service.
 4          script: monitoring-connect.sh
 5      rescue:
 6        - name: This will only run in case of an error in the block.
 7          debug: msg="There was an error in the block."
 8      always:
 9        - name: This will always run, no matter what.
10          debug: msg="This always executes."
```

Tasks inside the `block` will be run first. If there is a failure in any task in `block`, tasks inside `rescue` will be run. The tasks inside `always` will always be run, whether or not there were failures in either `block` or `rescue`.

Blocks can be very helpful for building reliable playbooks, but just like exceptions in programming languages, `block`/`rescue`/`always` failure handling can over-complicate things. If it's easier to maintain idempotence using `failed_when` per-task to define acceptable failure conditions, or to structure your playbook in a different way, it may not be necessary to use `block`/`rescue`/`always`.

# Summary

Playbooks are Ansible's primary means of automating infrastructure management. After reading this chapter, you should know how to use (and hopefully not abuse!) variables, inventories, handlers, conditionals, tags, and more.

The more you understand the fundamental components of a playbook, the more efficient you will be at building and expanding your infrastructure with Ansible.

```
   _____
 / Men have become the tools of their \
 \ tools. (Henry David Thoreau)        /
   -----------------------------------
          \     ^__^
           \   (oo)_____
              (__)\        )\/\
                  ||----w |
                  ||      ||
```

# Chapter 6 - Playbook Organization - Roles and Includes

So far, we've used fairly straightforward examples in this book. Most examples are created for a particular server, and are in one long playbook.

Ansible is flexible when it comes to organizing tasks in more efficient ways so you can make playbooks more maintainable, reusable, and powerful. We'll look at two ways to split up tasks more efficiently using includes and roles, and we'll explore Ansible Galaxy, a repository of some community-maintained roles that help configure common packages and applications.

## Includes

We've already seen one of the most basic ways of including other files in Chapter 4, when `vars_files` was used to place variables into a separate `vars.yml` file instead of inline with the playbook:

```
- hosts: all

  vars_files:
    - vars.yml
```

Tasks can easily be included in a similar way. In the `tasks:` section of your playbook, you can add `include` directives like so:

```
tasks:
  - include: included-playbook.yml
```

Just like with variable include files, tasks are formatted in a flat list in the included file. As an example, the `included-playbook.yml` could look like this:

```
---
- name: Add profile info for user.
  copy:
    src: example_profile
    dest: "/home/{{ username }}/.profile"
    owner: "{{ username }}"
    group: "{{ username }}"
    mode: 0744

- name: Add private keys for user.
  copy:
    src: "{{ item.src }}"
    dest: "/home/{{ username }}/.ssh/{{ item.dest }}"
    owner: "{{ username }}"
    group: "{{ username }}"
    mode: 0600
  with_items: ssh_private_keys

- name: Restart example service.
  service: name=example state=restarted
```

In this case, you'd probably want to name the file `user.yml`, since it's used to configure a user account and restart some service. Now, in this and any other playbook that provisions or configures a server, if you want to configure a particular user's account, add the following in your playbook's `tasks` section:

```
tasks:
  - include: user.yml
```

We used {{ username }} and {{ ssh_private_keys }} variables in this include file instead of hard-coded values so we could make this include file reusable. You could define the variables in your playbook's inline variables or an included variables file, but Ansible also lets you pass variables directly into includes using normal YAML syntax. For example:

```
tasks:
  - { include: user.yml, username: johndoe, ssh_private_keys: [] }
  - { include: user.yml, username: janedoe, ssh_private_keys: [] }
```

To make the syntax more readable, you can use structured variables, like so:

```
tasks:
  - include: user.yml
    vars:
      username: johndoe
      ssh_private_keys:
        - { src: /path/to/johndoe/key1, dest: id_rsa }
        - { src: /path/to/johndoe/key2, dest: id_rsa_2 }
  - include: user.yml
    vars:
      username: janedoe
      ssh_private_keys:
        - { src: /path/to/janedoe/key1, dest: id_rsa }
        - { src: /path/to/janedoe/key2, dest: id_rsa_2 }
```

Include files can even include other files, so you could have something like the following:

```
tasks:
  - include: user-config.yml
```

*inside* `user-config.yml`

```
- include: ssh-setup.yml
```

## Dynamic includes

Until Ansible 2.0.0, includes were processed when your playbook run started, so you couldn't do things like load a particular include when some condition was met. Ansible 2.0.0 evaluates includes during playbook execution, so you can do something like the following:

```
# Include extra tasks file, only if it's present at runtime.
- name: Check if extra_tasks.yml is present.
  stat: path=extras/extra-tasks.yml
  register: extra_tasks_file
  connection: local

- include: tasks/extra-tasks.yml
  when: extra_tasks_file.stat.exists
```

If the file `tasks/extra-tasks.yml` is not present, Ansible skips the `include`. You can even use a `with_items` loop (or any other `with_*` loop) with includes. Includes evaluated during playback execution can make your playbooks much more flexible!

## Handler includes

Handlers can be included just like tasks, within a playbook's `handlers` section. For example:

```
handlers:
  - include: included-handlers.yml
```

This can be helpful in limiting the noise in your main playbook, since handlers are usually used for things like restarting services or loading a configuration, and can distract from the playbook's primary purpose.

## Playbook includes

Playbooks can even be included in other playbooks, using the same `include` syntax in the top level of your playbook. For example, if you have two playbooks—one to set up your webservers (`web.yml`), and one to set up your database servers (`db.yml`), you could use the following playbook to run both at the same time:

```
- hosts: all
  remote_user: root

  tasks:
    [...]

- include: web.yml
- include: db.yml
```

This way, you can create playbooks to configure all the servers in your infrastructure, then create a master playbook that includes each of the individual playbooks. When you want to initialize your infrastructure, make changes across your entire fleet of servers, or check to make sure their configuration matches your playbook definitions, you can run one `ansible-playbook` command!

## Complete includes example

What if I told you we could remake the 137-line Drupal LAMP server playbook from Chapter 4 in just 21 lines? With includes, it's easy; just break out each of the sets of tasks into their own include files, and you'll end up with a main playbook like this:

```
1   ---
2   - hosts: all
3
4     vars_files:
5       - vars.yml
6
7     pre_tasks:
8       - name: Update apt cache if needed.
9         apt: update_cache=yes cache_valid_time=3600
10
11    handlers:
12      - include: handlers/handlers.yml
13
14    tasks:
15      - include: tasks/common.yml
16      - include: tasks/apache.yml
17      - include: tasks/php.yml
18      - include: tasks/mysql.yml
19      - include: tasks/composer.yml
20      - include: tasks/drush.yml
21      - include: tasks/drupal.yml
```

All you need to do is create two new folders in the same folder where you saved the Drupal playbook.yml file, handlers and tasks, then create files inside for each section of the playbook.

For example, inside handlers/handlers.yml, you'd have:

```
1   ---
2   - name: restart apache
3     service: name=apache2 state=restarted
```

And inside tasks/drush.yml:

```
 1  ---
 2  - name: Check out drush master branch.
 3    git:
 4      repo: https://github.com/drush-ops/drush.git
 5      dest: /opt/drush
 6
 7  - name: Install Drush dependencies with Composer."
 8    shell: >
 9      /usr/local/bin/composer install
10      chdir=/opt/drush
11      creates=/opt/drush/vendor/autoload.php
12
13  - name: Create drush bin symlink.
14    file:
15      src: /opt/drush/drush
16      dest: /usr/local/bin/drush
17      state: link
```

Separating all the tasks into separate includes files means you'll have more files to manage for your playbook, but it helps keep the main playbook more compact. It's easier to see all the installation and configuration steps the playbook contains, and it separates tasks into individual, maintainable groupings. Instead of having to browse one playbook with twenty-three separate tasks, you now maintain eight included files with two to five tasks, each.

It's much easier to maintain small groupings of related tasks than one long playbook. However, there's no reason to try to *start* writing a playbook with lots of individual includes. Most of the time, it's best to start with a monolithic playbook while you're working on the setup and configuration details, then move sets of tasks out to included files after you start seeing logical groupings.

You can also use tags (demonstrated in the previous chapter) to limit the playbook run to a certain include file. Using the above example, if you wanted to add a 'drush' tag to the included drush file (so you could run `ansible-playbook playbook.yml --tags=drush` and only run the drush tasks), you can change line 20 to the following:

```
20  - include: tasks/drush.yml tags=drush
```

 You can find the entire example Drupal LAMP server playbook using include files in this book's code repository at https://github.com/geerlingguy/ansible-for-devops[68], in the `includes` directory.

 You can't use variables for task include file names (like you could with `include_vars` directives, e.g. `include_vars`: "{{ `ansible_os_family` }}.yml" as a task, or with `vars_files`). There's usually a better way than conditional task includes to accomplish conditional task inclusion using a different playbook structure, or roles, which we will discuss next.

# Roles

Including playbooks inside other playbooks makes your playbook organization a little more sane, but once you start wrapping up your entire infrastructure's configuration in playbooks, you might end up with something resembling Russian nesting dolls.

Wouldn't it be nice if there were a way to take bits of related configuration, and package them together nicely? Additionally, what if we could take these packages (often configuring the same thing on many different servers) and make them flexible so that we can use the same package throughout our infrastructure, with slightly different settings on individual servers or groups of servers?

Ansible Roles can do all that and more!

Let's dive into what makes an Ansible role by taking one of the playbook examples from Chapter 4 and splitting it into a more flexible structure using roles.

---

[68]https://github.com/geerlingguy/ansible-for-devops

## Role scaffolding

Instead of requiring you to explicitly include certain files and playbooks in a role, Ansible automatically includes any `main.yml` files inside specific directories that make up the role.

There are only two directories required to make a working Ansible role:

```
role_name/
  meta/
  tasks/
```

If you create a directory structure like the one shown above, with a `main.yml` file in each directory, Ansible will run all the tasks defined in `tasks/main.yml` if you call the role from your playbook using the following syntax:

```
1  ---
2  - hosts: all
3    roles:
4      - role_name
```

Your roles can live in a couple different places: the default global Ansible role path (configurable in `/etc/ansible/ansible.cfg`), or a `roles` folder in the same directory as your main playbook file.

 Another simple way to build the scaffolding for a role is to use the command: `ansible-galaxy init role_name`. Running this command creates an example role in the current working directory, which you can modify to suit your needs. Using the `init` command also ensures the role is structured correctly in case you want to someday contribute the role to Ansible Galaxy.

# Building your first role

Let's clean up the Node.js server example from Chapter four, and break out one of the main parts of the configuration—installing Node.js and any required npm modules.

Create a roles folder in the same directory as the main playbook.yml file like, we created in Chapter 4's first example. Inside the roles folder, create a new folder: nodejs (which will be our role's name). Create two folders inside the nodejs role directory: meta and tasks.

Inside the meta folder, add a simple main.yml file with the following contents:

```
1   ---
2   dependencies: []
```

The meta information for your role is defined in this file. In basic examples and simple roles, you just need to list any role dependencies (other roles that are required to be run before the current role can do its work). You can add more to this file to describe your role to Ansible and to Ansible Galaxy, but we'll dive deeper into meta information later. For now, save the file and head over to the tasks folder.

Create a main.yml file in this folder, and add the following contents (basically copying and pasting the configuration from the Chapter 4 example):

```
1   ---
2   - name: Install Node.js (npm plus all its dependencies).
3     yum: name=npm state=present enablerepo=epel
4
5   - name: Install forever module (to run our Node.js app).
6     npm: name=forever global=yes state=present
```

The Node.js directory structure should now look like the following:

```
 1  nodejs-app/
 2    app/
 3      app.js
 4      package.json
 5    playbook.yml
 6    roles/
 7      nodejs/
 8        meta/
 9          main.yml
10        tasks/
11          main.yml
```

You now have a complete Ansible role that you can use in your node.js server configuration playbook. Delete the Node.js app installation lines from playbook.yml, and reformat the playbook so the other tasks run first (in a pre_tasks: section instead of tasks:), then the role, then the rest of the tasks (in the main tasks: section). Something like:

```
pre_tasks:
  # EPEL/GPG setup, firewall configuration...

roles:
  - nodejs

tasks:
  # Node.js app deployment tasks...
```

 You can view the full example of this playbook in the ansible-for-devops code repository[69].

Once you finish reformatting the main playbook, everything will run exactly the same during an ansible-playbook run, with the exception of the tasks inside the nodejs role being prefixed with nodejs | [Task name here].

---

[69]https://github.com/geerlingguy/ansible-for-devops/blob/master/nodejs-role/

This little bit of extra data shown during playbook runs is useful because it automatically prefixes tasks with the role that provides them, without you having to add in descriptions as part of the name values of the tasks.

Our role isn't all that helpful at this point, though, because it still does only one thing, and it's not really flexible enough to be used on other servers that might need different Node.js modules to be installed.

## More flexibility with role vars and defaults

To make our role more flexible, we can make it use a list of npm modules instead of a hardcoded value, then allow playbooks using the role to provide their own module list variable to override our role's default list.

When running a role's tasks, Ansible picks up variables defined in a role's vars/-main.yml file and defaults/main.yml (I'll get to the differences between the two later), but will allow your playbooks to override the defaults or other role-provided variables if you want.

Modify the tasks/main.yml file to use a list variable and iterate through the list to install as many packages as your playbook wants:

```
1   ---
2   - name: Install Node.js (npm plus all its dependencies).
3     yum: name=npm state=present enablerepo=epel
4
5   - name: Install npm modules required by our app.
6     npm: name={{ item }} global=yes state=present
7     with_items: node_npm_modules
```

Let's provide a sane default for the new node_npm_modules variable in defaults/-main.yml:

```
1  ---
2  node_npm_modules:
3    - forever
```

Now, if you run the playbook as-is, it will still do the exact same thing—install the forever module. But since the role is more flexible, we could create a new playbook like our first, but add a variable (either in a vars section or in an included file via vars_files) to override the default, like so:

```
1  node_npm_modules:
2    - forever
3    - async
4    - request
```

When you run the playbook with this custom variable (we didn't change *anything* with our nodejs role), all three of the above npm modules will be installed.

Hopefully you're beginning to see how this can be powerful!

Imagine if you had a playbook structure like:

```
1  ---
2  - hosts: appservers
3    roles:
4      - yum-repo-setup
5      - firewall
6      - nodejs
7      - app-deploy
```

Each one of the roles lives in its own isolated world, and can be shared with other servers and groups of servers in your infrastructure.

- A yum-repo-setup role could enable certain repositories and import their GPG keys.
- A firewall role could have per-server or per-inventory-group options for ports and services to allow or deny.

- An app-deploy role could deploy your app to a directory (configurable per-server) and set certain app options per-server or per-group.

These things are easy to manage when you have small bits of functionality separated into different roles. Instead of managing 100+ lines of playbook tasks, and manually prefixing every name: with something like "Common |" or "App Deploy |", you now manage a few roles with 10-20 lines of YAML each.

On top of that, when you're building your main playbooks, they can be extremely simple (like the above example), enabling you to see *everything* being configured and deployed on a particular server without scrolling through dozens of included playbook files and hundreds of tasks.

 **Variable precedence**: Note that Ansible handles variables placed in included files in defaults with less precedence than those placed in vars. If you have certain variables you need to allow hosts/playbooks to easily override, you should probably put them into defaults. If they are common variables that should almost always be the values defined in your role, put them into vars. For more on variable precedence, see the aptly-named "Variable Precedence" section in the previous chapter.

## Other role parts: handlers, files, and templates

### Handlers

In one of the prior examples, we introduced handlers—tasks that could be called via the notify option after any playbook task resulted in a change—and an example handler for restarting Apache was given:

```
1  handlers:
2    - name: restart apache
3      service: name=apache2 state=restarted
```

In Ansible roles, handlers are first-class citizens, alongside tasks, variables, and other configuration. You can store handlers directly inside a main.yml file inside a role's handlers directory. So if we had a role for Apache configuration, our handlers/main.yml file could look like this:

```
1   ---
2   - name: restart apache
3     service: name=apache2 state=restarted
```

You can call handlers defined in a role's handlers folder just like those included directly in your playbooks (e.g. `notify: restart apache`).

## Files and Templates

For the following examples, let's assume our role is structured with files and templates inside `files` and `templates` directories, respectively:

```
1   roles/
2     example/
3       files/
4         example.conf
5       meta/
6         main.yml
7       templates/
8         example.xml.j2
9       tasks/
10        main.yml
```

when copying a file directly to the server, add the filename or the full path from within a role's `files` directory, like so:

```
- name: Copy configuration file to server directly.
  copy:
    src: example.conf
    dest: /etc/myapp/example.conf
    mode: 0644
```

Similarly, when specifying a template, add the filename or the full path from within a role's `templates` directory, like so:

```
- name: Copy configuration file to server using a template.
  template:
    src: example.xml.j2
    dest: /etc/myapp/example.xml
    mode: 0644
```

The copy module copies files from within the module's files folder, and the template module runs given template files through the Jinja2 templating engine, merging in any variables available during your playbook run before copying the file to the server.

## Organizing more complex and cross-platform roles

For simple package installation and configuration roles, you can get by with placing all tasks, variables, and handlers directly in the respective main.yml file Ansible automatically loads. But you can also *include* other files from within a role's main.yml files if needed.

As a rule of thumb, I keep my playbook and role task files under 100 lines of YAML if at all possible. It's easier to keep the entire set of tasks in my head while making changes or fixing bugs. If I start nearing that limit, I usually split the tasks into logical groupings, and include files from the main.yml file.

Let's take a look at the way my geerlingguy.apache role is set up (it's available on Ansible Galaxy[70] and can be downloaded to your roles directory with the command ansible-galaxy install geerlingguy.apache; we'll discuss Ansible Galaxy itself later).

Initially, the role's main tasks/main.yml file looked something like the following (generally speaking):

---

```
1  - name: Ensure Apache is installed (via apt).
2
3  - name: Configure Apache with lineinfile.
4
5  - name: Enable Apache modules.
```

Soon after creating the role, though, I wanted to make the role work with both Debian and RHEL hosts. I could've added two sets of tasks in the main.yml file, resulting in twice the number of tasks and a bunch of extra when statements:

```
 1  - name: Ensure Apache is installed (via apt).
 2    when: ansible_os_family == 'Debian'
 3
 4  - name: Ensure Apache is installed (via yum).
 5    when: ansible_os_family == 'RedHat'
 6
 7  - name: Configure Apache with lineinfile (Debian).
 8    when: ansible_os_family == 'Debian'
 9
10  - name: Configure Apache with lineinfile (RHEL).
11    when: ansible_os_family == 'RedHat'
12
13  - name: Enable Apache modules (Debian).
14    when: ansible_os_family == 'Debian'
15
16  - name: Other OS-agnostic tasks...
```

If I had gone this route, and continued with the rest of the playbook tasks in one file, I would've quickly surpassed my informal 100-line limit. So I chose to use includes in my main tasks file:

```
1  - name: Include OS-specific variables.
2    include_vars: "{{ ansible_os_family }}.yml"
3
4  - include: setup-RedHat.yml
5    when: ansible_os_family == 'RedHat'
6
7  - include: setup-Debian.yml
8    when: ansible_os_family == 'Debian'
9
10 - name: Other OS-agnostic tasks...
```

Two important things to notice about this style of distribution-specific inclusion:

1. When including vars files (with include_vars), you can actually *use variables in the name of the file*. This is handy in many situations, and here we're including a vars file in the format distribution_name.yml. For our purposes, since the role will be used on Debian and RHEL-based hosts, we can create Debian.yml and RedHat.yml files in our role's defaults and vars folders, and put distribution-specific variables there.

2. When including playbook files (with include), you can't use variables in the name of the file, but you can do the next best thing: include the files by name explicitly, and use a condition to tell Ansible whether to run the tasks inside (the when condition will be applied to every task inside the included playbook).

After setting things up this way, I put RHEL and CentOS-specific tasks (like yum tasks) into tasks/setup-RedHat.yml, and Debian and Ubuntu-specific tasks (like apt tasks) into tasks/setup-Debian.yml. There are other ways of making roles work cross-platform, but using distribution-specific variables files and included playbooks is one of the simplest.

Now this Apache role can be used across different distributions, and with clever usage of variables in tasks and in configuration templates, it can be used in a wide variety of infrastructure that needs Apache installed.

# Ansible Galaxy

Ansible roles are powerful and flexible; they allow you to encapsulate sets of configuration and deployable units of playbooks, variables, templates, and other files, so you can easily reuse them across different servers.

It's annoying to have to start from scratch every time, though; wouldn't it be better if people could share roles for commonly-installed applications and services?

Enter Ansible Galaxy[71].

Ansible Galaxy, or just 'Galaxy', is a repository of community-contributed roles for common Ansible content. There are already hundreds of roles available which can configure and deploy common applications, and they're all available through the ansible-galaxy command, introduced in Ansible 1.4.2.

Galaxy offers the ability to add, download, and rate roles. With an account, you can contribute your own roles or rate others' roles (though you don't need an account to use roles).

## Getting roles from Galaxy

One of the primary functions of the ansible-galaxy command is retrieving roles from Galaxy. Roles must be downloaded before they can be used in playbooks.

Remember the basic LAMP (Linux, Apache, MySQL and PHP) server we installed earlier in the book? Let's create it again, but this time, using a few roles from Galaxy:

```
$ ansible-galaxy install geerlingguy.apache geerlingguy.mysql geerli\
ngguy.php
```

 The latest version or a role will be downloaded if no version is specified. To specify a version, add the version after the role name, for example: $ ansible-galaxy install geerlingguy.apache,1.0.0.

---

[71]https://galaxy.ansible.com/

Ansible Galaxy is still evolving rapidly, and has seen many improvements. There are a few areas where Galaxy could use some improvement (like browsing for roles by Operating System in the online interface, or automatically downloading roles that are included in playbooks), but most of these little bugs or rough spots will be fixed in time. Please check Ansible Galaxy's About[72] page and stay tuned to Ansible's blog for the latest updates.

## Using role requirements files to manage dependencies

If your infrastructure configuration requires five, ten, fifteen or more Ansible roles, installing them all via `ansible-galaxy install` commands can be exhausting. Additionally, if you host roles internally (e.g. via an internal Git or Mercurial repository), you can't install the roles through Ansible Galaxy. You can, however, pass the `ansible-galaxy` command a "requirements" file with the `-r` option to automatically download all dependencies.

Ansible allows a simple `.txt` format that is very basic (though this format is deprecated and may be removed), but you should generally use the more standard and expressive YAML format, which allows you to install roles from Ansible Galaxy, GitHub, an HTTP download, BitBucket, or your own repository. It also allows you to specify the path into which the roles should be downloaded. An example `requirements.yml` file looks like this:

```
1  ---
2  # From Ansible Galaxy, latest version.
3  - src: geerlingguy.firewall
4
5  # From Ansible Galaxy, specifying the version.
6  - src: geerlingguy.php
7    version: 1.4.1
8
9  # From GitHub, to a given path, with a custom name and version.
10 - src: https://github.com/geerlingguy/ansible-role-passenger
```

[72]https://galaxy.ansible.com/intro

```
11    path: /etc/ansible/roles/
12    name: passenger
13    version: 1.0.2
14
15  # From a web server, with a custom name.
16  - src: https://www.example.com/ansible/roles/my-role-name.tar.gz
17    name: my-role
```

To install the roles defined in a requirements file, use the command `ansible-galaxy install -r requirements.yml`. For more documentation on Ansible requirements files, see the official documentation: Advanced Control over Role Requirements Files[73].

## A LAMP server in nine lines of YAML

With the Apache, MySQL, and PHP roles installed, we can quickly create a LAMP server. This example assumes you already have an Ubuntu-based linux VM or server booted and can connect to it or run Ansible as a provisioner via Vagrant on it, and that you've run the `ansible-galaxy install` command above to download the required roles.

First, create an Ansible playbook named `lamp.yml` with the following contents:

```
1  ---
2  - hosts: all
3    become: yes
4
5    roles:
6      - geerlingguy.mysql
7      - geerlingguy.apache
8      - geerlingguy.php
9      - geerlingguy.php-mysql
```

Now, run the playbook against a host:

---

[73]http://docs.ansible.com/ansible/galaxy.html#advanced-control-over-role-requirements-files

```
$ ansible-playbook -i path/to/custom-inventory lamp.yml
```

After a few minutes, an entire LAMP server should be set up and running. If you add in a few variables, you can configure virtualhosts, PHP configuration options, MySQL server settings, etc.

We've effectively reduced about thirty lines of YAML (from previous examples dealing with LAMP or LAMP-like servers) down to four. Obviously, the roles have extra code in them, but the power here is in abstraction. Since most companies have many servers using similar software, but with slightly different configurations, having centralized, flexible roles saves a lot of repetition.

You could think of Galaxy roles as glorified packages; they not only install software, but they configure it *exactly* how you want it, every time, with minimal adjustment. Additionally, many of these roles work across different flavors of Linux and UNIX, so you have better configuration portability!

## A Solr server in eight lines of YAML

Let's grab a few more roles and build an Apache Solr search server, which requires Java and Apache Tomcat to be installed and configured.

```
$ ansible-galaxy install geerlingguy.java geerlingguy.tomcat6 \
geerlingguy.solr
```

Then create a playbook named solr.yml with the following contents:

```
1  ---
2  - hosts: all
3    become: yes
4
5    roles:
6      - geerlingguy.java
7      - geerlingguy.tomcat6
8      - geerlingguy.solr
```

Now we have a fully-functional Solr server, and we could add some variables to configure it exactly how we want, by using a non-default port, or changing the memory allocation for Tomcat6.

I could've also left out the `java` and `tomcat6` roles, since they'll be automatically picked up during installation of the `geerlingguy.solr` role (they're listed in the `solr` role's dependencies).

A role's page on the Ansible Galaxy website highlights available variables for setting things like what version of Solr to install, where to install it, etc. For an example, view the geerlingguy.solr Galaxy page[74].

You can build a wide variety of servers with minimal effort with existing contributed roles on Galaxy. Instead of having to maintain lengthy playbooks and roles unique to each server, Galaxy lets you build a list of the required roles, and a few variables that set up the servers with the proper versions and paths. Configuration management with Ansible Galaxy becomes *true* configuration management—you get to spend more time managing your server's configuration, and less time on packaging and building individual services!

## Helpful Galaxy commands

Some other helpful `ansible-galaxy` commands you might use from time to time:

- `ansible-galaxy list` displays a list of installed roles, with version numbers
- `ansible-galaxy remove [role]` removes an installed role

---

[74]https://galaxy.ansible.com/list#/roles/445

- `ansible-galaxy init` can be used to create a role template suitable for submission to Ansible Galaxy

You can configure the default path where Ansible roles will be downloaded by editing your `ansible.cfg` configuration file (normally located in `/etc/ansible/ansible.cfg`), and setting a `roles_path` in the `[defaults]` section.

## Contributing to Ansible Galaxy

If you've been working on some useful Ansible roles, and you'd like to share them with others, all you need to do is make sure they follow Ansible Galaxy's basic template (especially within the `meta/main.yml` and `README.md` files). To get started, use `ansible-galaxy init` to generate a basic Galaxy template, and make your own role match the Galaxy template's structure.

Then push your role up to a new project on GitHub (I usually name my Galaxy roles like `ansible-role-[rolename]`, so I can easily see them when browsing my repos on GitHub), and add a new role while logged into galaxy.ansible.com.

# Summary

Using includes and Ansible roles organizes Playbooks and makes them maintainable. This chapter introduced different ways of using `include`, the power and flexible structure of roles, and how you can utilize Ansible Galaxy, the community repository of configurable Ansible roles that do just about anything.

```
  _____
 / When the only tool you own is a hammer, \
 | every problem begins to resemble a       |
 \ nail. (Abraham Maslow)                   /
  ----------------------------------------
            \    ^__^
             \  (oo)_____
                (__)\       )\/\
                    ||----w |
                    ||     ||
```

# Chapter 7 - Inventories

Earlier in the book, a basic inventory file example was given (see Chapter 1's basic inventory file example). For the simplest of purposes, an inventory file at the default location (/etc/ansible/hosts) will suffice to describe to Ansible how to reach the servers you want to manage.

Later, a slightly more involved inventory file was introduced (see Chapter 3's inventory file for multiple servers), which allowed us to tell Ansible about multiple servers, and even group them into role-related groups, so we could run certain playbooks against certain groups.

Let's jump back to a basic inventory file example and build from there:

```
1   # Inventory file at /etc/ansible/hosts
2
3   # Groups are defined using square brackets (e.g. [groupname]).
4   # Each server in the group is defined on its own line.
5   [myapp]
6   www.myapp.com
```

If you want to run an ansible playbook on all the myapp servers in this inventory (so far, just one, www.myapp.com), you can set up the playbook like so:

```
---
- hosts: myapp

  tasks:
    [...]
```

If you want to run an ad-hoc command against all the myapp servers in the inventory, you can run a command like so:

```
# Use ansible to check memory usage on all the myapp servers.
$ ansible myapp -a "free -m"
```

# A real-world web application server inventory

The example above might be adequate for single-server services and tiny apps or websites, but most real-world applications require many more servers, and usually separate servers per application concern (database, caching, application, queuing, etc.). Let's take a look at a real-world inventory file for a small web application that monitors server uptime, Server Check.in[75].

```
1   # Individual Server Check.in servers.
2   [servercheck-web]
3   www1.servercheck.in
4   www2.servercheck.in
5
6   [servercheck-web:vars]
7   ansible_ssh_user=servercheck_svc
8
9   [servercheck-db]
10  db1.servercheck.in
11
12  [servercheck-log]
13  log.servercheck.in
14
15  [servercheck-backup]
16  backup.servercheck.in
17
18  [servercheck-nodejs]
19  atl1.servercheck.in
20  atl2.servercheck.in
21  nyc1.servercheck.in
22  nyc2.servercheck.in
```

---

[75]https://servercheck.in/

```
23  nyc3.servercheck.in
24  ned1.servercheck.in
25  ned2.servercheck.in
26
27  [servercheck-nodejs:vars]
28  ansible_ssh_user=servercheck_svc
29  foo=bar
30
31  # Server Check.in distribution-based groups.
32  [centos:children]
33  servercheck-web
34  servercheck-db
35  servercheck-nodejs
36  servercheck-backup
37
38  [ubuntu:children]
39  servercheck-log
```

This inventory may look a little overwhelming at first, but if you break it apart into simple groupings (web app servers, database servers, logging server, and node.js app servers), it describes a straightforward architecture.

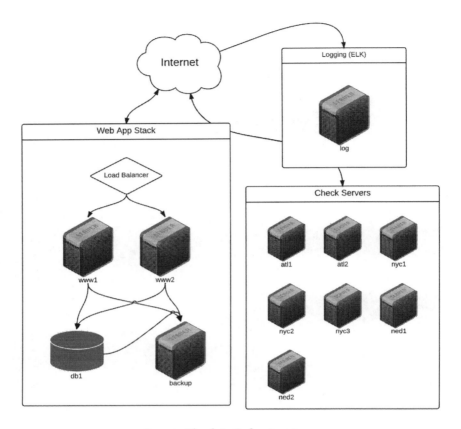

**Server Check.in Infrastructure**.

Lines 1-29 describe a few groups of servers (some with only one server), so playbooks and `ansible` commands can refer to the group by name. Lines 6-7 and 27-29 set variables that will apply only to the servers in the group (e.g. variables below `[servercheck-nodejs:vars]` will only apply to the servers in the `servercheck-nodejs` group).

Lines 31-39 describe groups of groups (using `groupname:children` to describe 'child' groups) that allow for some helpful abstractions.

Describing infrastructure in such a way affords a lot of flexibility when using Ansible. Consider the task of patching a vulnerability on all your CentOS servers; instead of having to log into each of the servers, or even having to run an `ansible` command against all the groups, using the above structure allows you to easily run an ansible command or playbook against all centos servers.

As an example, when the Shellshock[76] vulnerability was disclosed in 2014, patched bash packages were released for all the major distributions within hours. To update all the Server Check.in servers, all that was needed was:

```
$ ansible centos -m yum -a "name=bash state=latest"
```

You could even go further and create a small playbook that would patch the vulnerability, then run tests to make sure the vulnerability was no longer present, as illustrated in this playbook[77]. This would also allow you to run the playbook in check mode or run it through a continuous integration system to verify the fix works in a non-prod environment.

This infrastructure inventory is also nice in that you could create a top-level playbook that runs certain roles or tasks against all your infrastructure, others against all servers of a certain Linux flavor, and another against all servers in your entire infrastructure.

Consider, for example, this example master playbook to completely configure all the servers:

```
1  ---
2  # Set up basic, standardized components across all servers.
3  - hosts: all
4    become: yes
5    roles:
6      - security
7      - logging
8      - firewall
9
10 # Configure web application servers.
11 - hosts: servercheck-web
12   roles:
```

---

[76]https://en.wikipedia.org/wiki/Shellshock_(software_bug)

[77]https://raymii.org/s/articles/Patch_CVE-2014-6271_Shellshock_with_Ansible.html

```
13        - nginx
14        - php
15        - servercheck-web
16
17   # Configure database servers.
18   - hosts: servercheck-db
19     roles:
20       - pgsql
21       - db-tuning
22
23   # Configure logging server.
24   - hosts: servercheck-log
25     roles:
26       - java
27       - elasticsearch
28       - logstash
29       - kibana
30
31   # Configure backup server.
32   - hosts: servercheck-backup
33     roles:
34       - backup
35
36   # Configure Node.js application servers.
37   - hosts: servercheck-nodejs
38     roles:
39       - servercheck-node
```

There are a number of different ways you can structure your infrastructure-management playbooks and roles, and we'll explore some in later chapters, but for a simple infrastructure, something like this is adequate and maintainable.

## Non-prod environments, separate inventory files

Using the above playbook and the globally-configured Ansible inventory file is great for your production infrastructure, but what happens when you want to configure a separate but similar infrastructure for, say a development or user certification environment?

In this case, it's easiest to use individual inventory files, rather than the central Ansible inventory file. For typical team-managed infrastructure, I would recommend including an inventory file for each environment in the same version-controlled repository as your Ansible playbooks, perhaps within an 'inventories' directory.

For example, I could take the entire contents of /etc/ansible/hosts above, and stash that inside an inventory file named inventory-prod, then duplicate it, changing server names where appropriate (e.g. the [servercheck-web] group would only have www-dev1.servercheck.in for the development environment), and naming the files for the environments:

```
servercheck/
  inventories/
    inventory-prod
    inventory-cert
    inventory-dev
  playbook.yml
```

Now, when running playbook.yml to configure the development infrastructure, I would pass in the path to the dev inventory (assuming my current working directory is servercheck/):

```
$ ansible-playbook playbook.yml -i inventories/inventory-dev
```

Using inventory variables (which will be explored further), and well-constructed roles and/or tasks that use the variables effectively, you could architect your entire infrastructure, with environment-specific configurations, by changing some things in your inventory files.

# Inventory variables

Chapter 5 introduced basic methods of managing variables for individual hosts or groups of hosts through your inventory in the inventory variables section, but it's worth exploring the different ways of defining and overriding variables through inventory here.

For extremely simple use cases—usually when you need to define one or two connection-related variables (like `ansible_ssh_user` or `ansible_ssh_port`)—you can place variables directly inside an inventory file.

Assuming we have a standalone inventory file for a basic web application, here are some examples of variable definition inside the file:

```
1   [www]
2   # You can define host-specific variables inline with the host.
3   www1.example.com ansible_ssh_user=johndoe
4   www2.example.com
5
6   [db]
7   db1.example.com
8   db2.example.com
9
10  # You can add a '[group:vars]' heading to create variables that will\
11   apply
12  # to an entire inventory group.
13  [db:vars]
14  ansible_ssh_port=5222
15  database_performance_mode=true
```

It's usually better to avoid throwing too many variables inside static inventory files, because not only are these variables typically less visible, they are also mixed in with your architecture definition. Especially for host-specific vars (which appear on one long line per host), this is an unmaintainable, low-visibility approach to host and group-specific variables.

Fortunately, Ansible provides a more flexible way of declaring host and group variables.

## host_vars

For Hosted Apache Solr[78], different servers in a `solr` group have different memory requirements. The simplest way to tell Ansible to override a default variable in our Ansible playbook (in this case, the `tomcat_xmx` variable) is to use a `host_vars` directory (which can be placed either in the same location as your inventory file, or in a playbook's root directory), and place a YAML file named after the host which needs the overridden variable.

As an illustration of the use of `host_vars`, we'll assume we have the following directory layout:

```
hostedapachesolr/
  host_vars/
    nyc1.hostedapachesolr.com
  inventory/
    hosts
  main.yml
```

The `inventory/hosts` file contains a simple definition of all the servers by group:

```
1  [solr]
2  nyc1.hostedapachesolr.com
3  nyc2.hostedapachesolr.com
4  jap1.hostedapachesolr.com
5  ...
6
7  [log]
8  log.hostedapachesolr.com
```

Ansible will search for a file at either:

---

[78]https://hostedapachesolr.com/

`hostedapachesolr/host_vars/nyc1.hostedapachesolr.com`

Or:

`hostedapachesolr/inventory/host_vars/nyc1.hostedapachesolr.com`

If there are any variables defined in the file (in YAML format), those variables will override all other playbook and role variables and gathered facts, *only for the single host.*

The `nyc1.hostedapachesolr.com` host_vars file looks like:

```
1   ---
2   tomcat_xmx: "1024m"
```

The default for `tomcat_xmx` may normally be 640m, but when Ansible runs a playbook against nyc1.hostedapachesolr.com, the value of `tomcat_xmx` will be 1024m instead.

Overriding host variables with `host_vars` is much more maintainable than doing so directly in static inventory files, and also provides greater visibility into what hosts are getting what overrides.

**group_vars**

Much like `host_vars`, Ansible will automatically load any files named after inventory groups in a `group_vars` directory placed inside the playbook or inventory file's location.

Using the same example as above, we'll override one particular variable for an entire group of servers. First, we add a `group_vars` directory with a file named after the group needing the overridden variable:

```
hostedapachesolr/
  group_vars/
    solr
  host_vars/
    nyc1.hostedapachesolr.com
  inventory/
    hosts
  main.yml
```

Then, inside group_vars/solr, use YAML to define a list of variables that will be applied to servers in the solr group:

```
1  ---
2  do_something_amazing=true
3  foo=bar
```

Typically, if your playbook is only being run on one group of hosts, it's easier to define the variables in the playbook via an included vars file. However, in many cases you will be running a playbook or applying a set of roles to multiple inventory groups. In these situations, you may need to use group_vars to override specific variables for one or more groups of servers.

# Ephemeral infrastructure: Dynamic inventory

In many circumstances, static inventories are adequate for describing your infrastructure. When working on small applications, low-traffic web applications, and individual workstations, it's simple enough to manage an inventory file by hand.

However, in the age of cloud computing and highly scalable application architecture, it's often necessary to add dozens or hundreds of servers to an infrastructure in a short period of time—or to add and remove servers continuously, to scale as traffic grows and subsides. In this circumstance, it would be tedious (if not impossible) to manage a single inventory file by hand, especially if you're using auto-scaling infrastructure new instances are provisioned and need to be configured in minutes or seconds.

Even in the case of container-based infrastructure, new instances need to be configured correctly, with the proper port mappings, application settings, and filesystem configuration.

For these situations, Ansible allows you to define inventory *dynamically*. If you're using one of the larger cloud-based hosting providers, chances are there is already a dynamic inventory script (which Ansible uses to build an inventory) for you to use. Ansible core already includes scripts for Amazon Web Services, Cobbler, DigitalOcean, Linode, OpenStack, and other large providers, and later we'll explore creating our own dynamic inventory script (if you aren't using one of the major hosting providers or cloud management platforms).

# Dynamic inventory with DigitalOcean

DigitalOcean is one of the world's top five hosting companies, and has grown rapidly since it's founding in 2011. One of the reasons for the extremely rapid growth is the ease of provisioning new 'droplets' (cloud VPS servers), and the value provided; as of this writing, you could get a fairly speedy VPS with 512MB of RAM and a generous portion of fast SSD storage for $5 USD per month.

DigitalOcean's API and simple developer-friendly philosophy has made it easy for Ansible to interact with DigitalOcean droplets; you can create, manage, and delete droplets with Ansible, as well as use droplets with your playbooks using dynamic inventory.

## DigitalOcean account prerequisites

Before you can follow the rest of the examples in this section, you will need:

1. A DigitalOcean account (sign up at www.digitalocean.com).
2. dopy, a Python wrapper for DigitalOcean API interaction (you can install it with pip: sudo pip install dopy).
3. A DigitalOcean API Personal Access Token. Follow this guide[79] to generate a Personal Access Token for use with Ansible (grant Read and Write access when you create the token).

---

[79]https://www.digitalocean.com/community/tutorials/how-to-use-the-digitalocean-api-v2

4. An SSH key pair, which will be used to connect to your DigitalOcean servers. Follow this guide[80] to create a key pair and add the public key to your DigitalOcean account.

Once you have these four things set up and ready to go, you should be able to communicate with your DigitalOcean account through Ansible.

## Connecting to your DigitalOcean account

There are a few different ways you can specify your DigitalOcean Personal Access Token (including passing it via `api_token` to each DigitalOcean-related task, or exporting it in your local environment as `DO_API_TOKEN` or `DO_API_KEY`). For our example, we'll use environment variables (since these are easy to configure, and work both with Ansible's `digital_ocean` module and the dynamic inventory script). Open up a terminal session, and enter the following command:

```
$ export DO_API_TOKEN=YOUR_API_TOKEN_HERE
```

Before we can use a dynamic inventory script to discover our DigitalOcean droplets, let's use Ansible to provision a new droplet.

 Creating cloud instances ('Droplets', in DigitalOcean parlance) will incur minimal charges for the time you use them (currently less than $0.01/hour for the size in this example). For the purposes of this tutorial (and in general, for any testing), make sure you shut down and destroy your instances when you're finished using them, or you will be charged through the next billing cycle! Even so, using low-priced instances (like a $5/month DigitalOcean droplet with hourly billing) means that, even in the worst case, you won't have to pay much. If you create and destroy an instance in a few hours, you'll be charged a few pennies.

## Creating a droplet with Ansible

Create a new playbook named `provision.yml`, with the following contents:

---

[80]https://www.digitalocean.com/community/tutorials/how-to-use-ssh-keys-with-digitalocean-droplets

```
1    ---
2    - hosts: localhost
3      connection: local
4      gather_facts: false
5
6      tasks:
7        - name: Create new Droplet.
8          digital_ocean:
9            state: present
10           command: droplet
11           name: ansible-test
12           private_networking: yes
13           size_id: 512mb
14           image_id: centos-7-0-x64
15           region_id: nyc2
16           ssh_key_ids: 138954
17           # Required for idempotence/only one droplet creation.
18           unique_name: yes
19         register: do
```

The digital_ocean module lets you create, manage, and delete droplets with ease.
You can read the documentation for all the options, but the above is an overview of
the main options. name sets the hostname for the droplet, state can also be set to
deleted if you want the droplet to be destroyed, and other options tell DigitalOcean
where to set up the droplet, and with what OS and configuration.

You can use DigitalOcean's API, along with your Personal Access Token, to get the IDs for `size_id` (the size of the Droplet), `image_id` (the system or distro image to use), `region_id` (the data center in which your droplet will be created), and `ssh_key_ids` (a comma separate list of SSH keys to be included in the root account's `authorized_keys` file).

As an example, to get all the available images, use `curl --silent` `"https://api.digitalocean.com/v2/images?per_page=999" -H` `"Authorization: Bearer $DO_API_TOKEN" | python -m json.tool`, and you'll receive a JSON listing of all available values. Browse the DigitalOcean API[81] for information on how to query SSH key information, size information, etc.

We used `register` as part of the `digital_ocean` task so we could immediately start using and configuring the new host if needed. Running the above playbook returns the following output (using `debug: var=do` in an additional task to dump the contents of our registered variable, `do`):

```
$ ansible-playbook do_test.yml

PLAY [localhost] ********************************************\
***********

TASK [Create new Droplet.] *********************************\
***********
changed: [localhost]

TASK [debug] ***********************************************\
***********
ok: [localhost] => {
    "do": {
        "changed": true,
        "droplet": {
            "backup_ids": [],
            "created_at": "2017-07-22T00:58:51Z",
```

---

[81]https://developers.digitalocean.com/

```
        "disk": 20,
        "features": [
            "private_networking",
            "virtio"
        ],
        "id": 20203631,
        "image": {
            ...
        },
        "ip_address": "162.243.20.29",
        "kernel": null,
        "locked": false,
        "memory": 512,
        "name": "ansible-test",
        "networks": {
            ...
        },
        "next_backup_window": null,
        "private_ip_address": "10.1.1.2",
        "region": {
            ...
        },
        "size": {
            ...
        },
        "size_slug": "512mb",
        "snapshot_ids": [],
        "status": "active",
        "tags": [],
        "vcpus": 1,
        "volume_ids": []
      }
    }
}
```

```
PLAY RECAP *******************************************************
localhost                : ok=2    changed=1   unreachable=0   failed=0
```

Since do contains the new droplet's IP address (alongside other relevant information), you can place your freshly-created droplet in an existing inventory group using Ansible's add_host module. Adding to the playbook we started above, you could set up your playbook to provision an instance and immediately configure it (after waiting for port 22 to become available) with something like:

```
21      - name: Add new host to our inventory.
22        add_host:
23          name: "{{ do.droplet.ip_address }}"
24          groups: do
25        when: do.droplet is defined
26
27  - hosts: do
28    remote_user: root
29    gather_facts: false
30
31    tasks:
32      - name: Wait for port 22 to become available.
33        local_action: "wait_for port=22 host={{ inventory_hostname }}"
34
35      - name: Install tcpdump.
36        yum: name=tcpdump state=present
```

At this point, if you run the playbook ($ ansible-playbook provision.yml), it should create a new droplet (if it has not already been created), then add that droplet to the do inventory group, and finally, run a new play on all the do hosts (including the new droplet). Here are the results:

```
$ ansible-playbook provision.yml

PLAY [localhost] *************************************************

TASK: [Create new Droplet.] *************************************
changed: [localhost]

TASK: [Add new host to our inventory.] *************************
ok: [localhost]

PLAY [do] *******************************************************

TASK [Wait for port 22 to become available.] ******************\
***********
ok: [162.243.20.29 -> localhost]

TASK: [Install tcpdump.] ***************************************
changed: [162.243.20.29]

PLAY RECAP ****************************************************
162.243.20.29         : ok=2    changed=1    unreachable=0    failed=0
localhost             : ok=2    changed=1    unreachable=0    failed=0
```

If you run the same playbook again, it should report no changes—the entire playbook is idempotent! You might be starting to see just how powerful it is to have a tool as flexible as Ansible at your disposal; not only can you configure servers, you can create them (singly, or dozens at a time), and configure them at once. And even if a ham-fisted sysadmin jumps in and deletes an entire server, you can run the playbook again, and rest assured your server will be recreated and reconfigured exactly as it was when it was first set up.

Note that you might need to disable strict host key checking to get provisioning and instant configuration to work correctly, otherwise you may run into an error stating that Ansible can't connect to the new droplet during the second play. To do this, add the line `host_key_-checking=False` under the `[defaults]` section in your `ansible.cfg` file (located in `/etc/ansible` by default).

You should normally leave `host_key_checking` enabled, but when rapidly building and destroying VMs for testing purposes, it is simplest to disable it temporarily.

## DigitalOcean dynamic inventory with `digital_ocean.py`

Once you have some DigitalOcean droplets, you need a way for Ansible to dynamically build an inventory of your servers so you can build playbooks and use the servers in logical groupings (or run playbooks and `ansible` commands directly on all droplets).

There are a few steps to getting DigitalOcean's official dynamic inventory script working:

1. Install `dopy` via pip (the DigitalOcean Python library):

   ```
   $ pip install dopy
   ```

2. Download the DigitalOcean dynamic inventory script[82] from Ansible on GitHub:

   ```
   $ curl -O https://raw.githubusercontent.com/ansible/ansible/devel/\
   contrib/inventory/digital_ocean.py
   ```

3. Make the inventory script executable:

   ```
   $ chmod +x digital_ocean.py
   ```

4. Make sure you have `DO_API_TOKEN` set in your environment.

---

[82]https://raw.githubusercontent.com/ansible/ansible/devel/contrib/inventory/digital_ocean.py

5. Make sure the script is working by running the script directly (with the command below). After a second or two, you should see all your droplets (likely just the one you created earlier) listed by IP address and dynamic group as JSON.

```
$ ./digital_ocean.py --pretty
```

6. Ping all your DigitalOcean droplets:

```
$ ansible all -m ping -i digital_ocean.py -u root
```

Now that you have all your hosts being loaded through the dynamic inventory script, you can use add_hosts to build groups of the Droplets for use in your playbooks. Alternatively, if you want to fork the digital_ocean.py inventory script, you can modify it to suit your needs; exclude certain servers, build groups based on certain criteria, etc.

 Ansible < 1.9.5 only supported DigitalOcean's legacy v1 API, which is no longer supported. If you need to use Ansible with DigitalOcean, you should use the latest version of Ansible.

## Dynamic inventory with AWS

Many of this book's readers are familiar with Amazon Web Services (especially EC2, S3, ElastiCache, and Route53), and likely have managed or currently manage an infrastructure within Amazon's cloud. Ansible has very strong support for managing AWS-based infrastructure, and includes a dynamic inventory script[83] to help you run playbooks on your hosts in a variety of ways.

There are a few excellent guides to using Ansible with AWS, for example:

- Ansible - Amazon Web Services Guide[84]

---

[83]https://raw.githubusercontent.com/ansible/ansible/devel/plugins/inventory/ec2.py
[84]http://docs.ansible.com/guide_aws.html

- Ansible for AWS[85]

I won't be covering dynamic inventory in this chapter, but will mention that the
ec2.py dynamic inventory script, along with Ansible's extensive support for AWS
infrastructure through ec2_* modules, makes Ansible the best and most simple tool
for managing a broad AWS infrastructure.

In the next chapter, one of the examples will include a guide for provisioning
infrastructure on AWS, along with a quick overview of dynamic inventory on AWS.

## Inventory on-the-fly: add_host and group_by

Sometimes, especially when provisioning new servers, you will need to modify the
in-memory inventory during the course of a playbook run. Ansible offers the add_-
host and group_by modules to help you manage inventory for these scenarios.

In the DigitalOcean example above, add_host was used to add the new droplet to
the do group:

```
[...]
    - name: Add new host to our inventory.
      add_host:
        name: "{{ do.droplet.ip_address }}"
        groups: do
      when: do.droplet is defined

- hosts: do
  remote_user: root

  tasks:
[...]
```

You could add multiple groups with add_host, and you can also add other variables
for the host inline with add_host. As an example, let's say you created a VM using
an image that exposes SSH on port 2288 and requires an application-specific memory
limit specific to this VM:

[85]https://leanpub.com/ansible-for-aws

```
- name: Add new host to our inventory.
  add_host:
    name: "{{ do.droplet.ip_address }}"
    ansible_ssh_port: 2288
    myapp_memory_maximum: "1G"
  when: do.droplet is defined
```

The custom port will be used when Ansible connects to this host, and the myapp_mem-ory_maximum will be passed into the playbooks just as any other inventory variable.

The group_by module is even simpler, and allows you to create dynamic groups during the course of a playbook run. Usage is extremely simple:

```
- hosts: all
  gather_facts: yes
  tasks:
    - name: Create an inventory group for each architecture.
      group_by: "key=architecture-{{ ansible_machine }}"

    - debug: var=groups
```

After running the above playbook, you'd see all your normal inventory groups, plus groups for architecture-x86_64, i386, etc. (depending on what kind of server architectures you use).

## Multiple inventory sources - mixing static and dynamic inventories

If you need to combine static and dynamic inventory, or even if you wish to use multiple dynamic inventories (for example, if you are managing servers hosted by two different cloud providers), you can pass a directory to ansible or ansible-playbook, and Ansible will combine the output of all the inventories (both static and dynamic) inside the directory:

```
`ansible-playbook -i path/to/inventories main.yml`
```

One caveat: Ansible ignores .ini and backup files in the directory, but will attempt to parse every text file and execute every executable file in the directory—don't leave random files in mixed inventory folders!

## Creating custom dynamic inventories

Most infrastructure can be managed with a custom inventory file or an off-the-shelf cloud inventory script, but there are many situations where more control is needed. Ansible will accept any kind of executable file as an inventory file, so you can build your own dynamic inventory however you like, as long as you can pass it to Ansible as JSON.

You could create an executable binary, a script, or anything else that can be run and will output JSON to stdout, and Ansible will call it with the argument --list when you run, as an example, ansible all -i my-inventory-script -m ping.

Let's start working our own custom dynamic inventory script by outlining the basic JSON format Ansible expects:

```
1  {
2      "group": {
3          "hosts": [
4              "192.168.28.71",
5              "192.168.28.72"
6          ],
7          "vars": {
8              "ansible_ssh_user": "johndoe",
9              "ansible_ssh_private_key_file": "~/.ssh/mykey",
10             "example_variable": "value"
11         }
12     },
13     "_meta": {
14         "hostvars": {
15             "192.168.28.71": {
```

```
16              "host_specific_var": "bar"
17            },
18            "192.168.28.72": {
19              "host_specific_var": "foo"
20            }
21          }
22        }
23      }
```

Ansible expects a dictionary of groups (with each group having a list of hosts, and group variables in the group's vars dictionary), and a _meta dictionary that stores host variables for all hosts individually inside a hostvars dictionary.

 When you return a _meta dictionary in your inventory script, Ansible stores that data in its cache and doesn't call your inventory script *N* times for all the hosts in the inventory. You can leave out the _meta variables if you'd rather structure your inventory file to return host variables one host at a time (Ansible will call your script with the arguments --host [hostname] for each host), but it's often faster and easier to simply return all variables in the first call. In this book, all the examples will use the _meta dictionary.

The dynamic inventory script can do anything to get the data (call an external API, pull information from a database or file, etc.), and Ansible will use it as an inventory source, so long as it returns a JSON structure like the one above when the script is called with the --list.

## Building a Custom Dynamic Inventory in Python

To create a test dynamic inventory script for demonstration purposes, let's set up a quick set of two VMs using Vagrant. Create the following Vagrantfile in a new directory:

```
1   VAGRANTFILE_API_VERSION = "2"
2
3   Vagrant.configure(VAGRANTFILE_API_VERSION) do |config|
4     config.ssh.insert_key = false
5     config.vm.provider :virtualbox do |v|
6       v.memory = 256
7       v.linked_clone = true
8     end
9
10    # Application server 1.
11    config.vm.define "inventory1" do |inventory|
12      inventory.vm.hostname = "inventory1.dev"
13      inventory.vm.box = "geerlingguy/ubuntu1404"
14      inventory.vm.network :private_network, ip: "192.168.28.71"
15    end
16
17    # Application server 2.
18    config.vm.define "inventory2" do |inventory|
19      inventory.vm.hostname = "inventory2.dev"
20      inventory.vm.box = "geerlingguy/ubuntu1404"
21      inventory.vm.network :private_network, ip: "192.168.28.72"
22    end
23  end
```

Run vagrant up to boot two VMs running Ubuntu 14.04, with the IP addresses 192.168.28.71, and 192.168.28.72. A simple inventory file could be used to control the VMs with Ansible:

```
1   [group]
2   192.168.28.71 host_specific_var=foo
3   192.168.28.72 host_specific_var=bar
4
5   [group:vars]
6   ansible_ssh_user=vagrant
7   ansible_ssh_private_key_file=~/.vagrant.d/insecure_private_key
8   example_variable=value
```

However, let's assume the VMs were provisioned by another system, and you need to get the information through a dynamic inventory script. Here's a simple implementation of a dynamic inventory script in Python:

```python
1   #!/usr/bin/env python
2
3   '''
4   Example custom dynamic inventory script for Ansible, in Python.
5   '''
6
7   import os
8   import sys
9   import argparse
10
11  try:
12      import json
13  except ImportError:
14      import simplejson as json
15
16  class ExampleInventory(object):
17
18      def __init__(self):
19          self.inventory = {}
20          self.read_cli_args()
21
22          # Called with `--list`.
```

```
23        if self.args.list:
24            self.inventory = self.example_inventory()
25        # Called with `--host [hostname]`.
26        elif self.args.host:
27            # Not implemented, since we return _meta info `--list`.
28            self.inventory = self.empty_inventory()
29        # If no groups or vars are present, return empty inventory.
30        else:
31            self.inventory = self.empty_inventory()
32
33        print json.dumps(self.inventory);
34
35    # Example inventory for testing.
36    def example_inventory(self):
37        return {
38            'group': {
39                'hosts': ['192.168.28.71', '192.168.28.72'],
40                'vars': {
41                    'ansible_ssh_user': 'vagrant',
42                    'ansible_ssh_private_key_file':
43                        '~/.vagrant.d/insecure_private_key',
44                    'example_variable': 'value'
45                }
46            },
47            '_meta': {
48                'hostvars': {
49                    '192.168.28.71': {
50                        'host_specific_var': 'foo'
51                    },
52                    '192.168.28.72': {
53                        'host_specific_var': 'bar'
54                    }
55                }
56            }
57        }
```

```
58
59        # Empty inventory for testing.
60        def empty_inventory(self):
61            return {'_meta': {'hostvars': {}}}
62
63        # Read the command line args passed to the script.
64        def read_cli_args(self):
65            parser = argparse.ArgumentParser()
66            parser.add_argument('--list', action = 'store_true')
67            parser.add_argument('--host', action = 'store')
68            self.args = parser.parse_args()
69
70   # Get the inventory.
71   ExampleInventory()
```

Save the above as inventory.py in the same folder as the Vagrantfile you created earlier (make sure you booted the two VMs with vagrant up), and make the file executable chmod +x inventory.py.

Run the inventory script manually to verify it returns the proper JSON response when run with --list:

```
$ ./inventory.py --list
{"group": {"hosts": ["192.168.28.71", "192.168.28.72"], "vars":
{"ansible_ssh_user": "vagrant", "ansible_ssh_private_key_file":
"~/.vagrant.d/insecure_private_key", "example_variable": "value
"}}, "_meta": {"hostvars": {"192.168.28.72": {"host_specific_va
r": "bar"}, "192.168.28.71": {"host_specific_var": "foo"}}}}
```

Test Ansible's ability to use the inventory script to contact the two VMs:

```
$ ansible all -i inventory.py -m ping
192.168.28.71 | success >> {
    "changed": false,
    "ping": "pong"
}

192.168.28.72 | success >> {
    "changed": false,
    "ping": "pong"
}
```

Since Ansible can connect, verify the configured host variables (foo and bar) are set correctly on their respective hosts:

```
$ ansible all -i inventory.py -m debug -a "var=host_specific_var"
192.168.28.71 | success >> {
    "var": {
        "host_specific_var": "foo"
    }
}

192.168.28.72 | success >> {
    "var": {
        "host_specific_var": "bar"
    }
}
```

The only alteration for real-world usage you'd need to make to the above inventory.py script would be changing the example_inventory() method to something that incorporates the business logic you would need for your own inventory, whether it would be calling an external API with all the server data or pulling in the information from a database or other data store.

## Building a Custom Dynamic Inventory in PHP

You can build an inventory script in whatever language you'd like. For example, the Python script from above can be ported to functional PHP as follows:

```php
 1   #!/usr/bin/php
 2   <?php
 3
 4   /**
 5    * @file
 6    * Example custom dynamic inventory script for Ansible, in PHP.
 7    */
 8
 9   /**
10    * Example inventory for testing.
11    *
12    * @return array
13    *   An example inventory with two hosts.
14    */
15   function example_inventory() {
16     return [
17       'group' => [
18         'hosts' => ['192.168.28.71', '192.168.28.72'],
19         'vars' => [
20           'ansible_ssh_user' => 'vagrant',
21           'ansible_ssh_private_key_file' => '~/.vagrant.d/\
22   insecure_private_key',
23           'example_variable' => 'value',
24         ],
25       ],
26       '_meta' => [
27         'hostvars' => [
28           '192.168.28.71' => [
29             'host_specific_var' => 'foo',
30           ],
31           '192.168.28.72' => [
32             'host_specific_var' => 'bar',
33           ],
34         ],
35       ],
```

```
36      ];
37    }
38
39    /**
40     * Empty inventory for testing.
41     *
42     * @return array
43     *   An empty inventory.
44     */
45    function empty_inventory() {
46      return ['_meta' => ['hostvars' => new stdClass()]];
47    }
48
49    /**
50     * Get inventory.
51     *
52     * @param array $argv
53     *   Array of command line arguments (as in $_SERVER['argv']).
54     *
55     * @return array
56     *   Inventory of groups or vars, depending on arguments.
57     */
58    function get_inventory($argv = []) {
59      $inventory = new stdClass();
60
61      // Called with `--list`.
62      if (!empty($argv[1]) && $argv[1] == '--list') {
63        $inventory = example_inventory();
64      }
65      // Called with `--host [hostname]`.
66      elseif ((!empty($argv[1]) && $argv[1] == '--host') && \
67    !empty($argv[2])) {
68        // Not implemented, since we return _meta info `--list`.
69        $inventory = empty_inventory();
70      }
```

```
71    // If no groups or vars are present, return an empty inventory.
72    else {
73      $inventory = empty_inventory();
74    }
75
76    print json_encode($inventory);
77  }
78
79  // Get the inventory.
80  get_inventory($_SERVER['argv']);
81
82  ?>
```

If you were to save the code above into the file inventory.php, mark it executable
(chmod +x inventory.php), and run the same Ansible command as earlier (referencing inventory.php instead of inventory.py), the command should succeed, just as
with the previous Python example.

 All the files mentioned in these dynamic inventory examples are available
in the Ansible for DevOps GitHub repository[86], in the dynamic-inventory
folder.

## Managing a PaaS with a Custom Dynamic Inventory

Hosted Apache Solr[87]'s infrastructure is built using a custom dynamic inventory to
allow for centrally-controlled server provisioning and configuration. Here's how the
server provisioning process works on Hosted Apache Solr:

1. A Drupal website holds a 'Server' content type that stores metadata about
   each server (e.g. chosen hostname, data center location, choice of OS image,
   and memory settings).

---

[86]https://github.com/geerlingguy/ansible-for-devops
[87]https://hostedapachesolr.com/

2. When a new server is added, a remote Jenkins job is triggered, which: 1. Builds a new cloud server on DigitalOcean using an Ansible playbook. 2. Runs a provisioning playbook on the server to initialize the configuration. 3. Adds a new DNS entry for the server. 4. Posts additional server metadata (like the IP address) back to the Drupal website via a private API.

3. When a server is updated, or there is new configuration to be deployed to the server(s), a different Jenkins job is triggered, which: 1. Runs the same provisioning playbook on all the DigitalOcean servers. This playbook uses an inventory script which calls back to an inventory API endpoint that returns all the server information as JSON (the inventory script on the Jenkins server passes the JSON through to stdout). 2. Reports back success or failure of the ansible playbook to the REST API.

The above process transformed the management of the entire Hosted Apache Solr platform. Instead of taking twenty to thirty minutes to build a new server (even when using an Ansible playbook with a few manual steps), the process can be completed in just a few minutes, with no manual intervention.

 The security of your server inventory and infrastructure management should be a top priority; Hosted Apache Solr uses HTTPS everywhere, and has a hardened private API for inventory access and server metadata. If you have any automated processes that run over a network, you should take extra care to audit these processes and all the involved systems thoroughly!

# Summary

From the most basic infrastructure consisting of one server to a multi-tenant, dynamic infrastructure with thousands of them, Ansible offers many options for describing your servers and overriding playbook and role variables for specific hosts or groups. With Ansible's flexible inventory system, you should be able to describe all your servers, however they're managed and wherever they're hosted.

```
 _____
/ A pint of sweat saves a gallon of \
\ blood. (General Patton)           /
 --------------------------------
        \    ^__^
         \  (oo)_____
            (__)\       )\/\
               ||----w |
               ||     ||
```

# Chapter 8 - Ansible Cookbooks

Until now, most of this book has demonstrated individual aspects of Ansible—inventory, playbooks, ad-hoc tasks, etc. But this chapter synthesizes everything we've gone over in the previous chapters and shows how Ansible is applied to real-world infrastructure management scenarios.

## Highly-Available Infrastructure with Ansible

Real-world web applications require redundancy and horizontal scalability with multi-server infrastructure. In the following example, we'll use Ansible to configure a complex infrastructure on servers provisioned either locally (via Vagrant and VirtualBox) or on a set of automatically-provisioned instances (running on either DigitalOcean or Amazon Web Services):

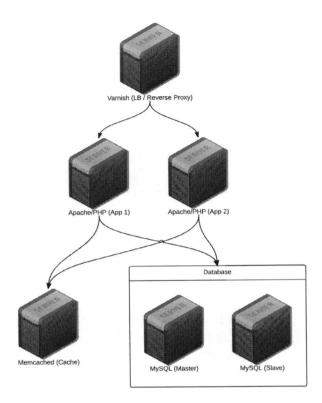

**Highly-Available Infrastructure**.

**Varnish** acts as a load balancer and reverse proxy, fronting web requests and routing them to the application servers. We could just as easily use something like **Nginx** or **HAProxy**, or even a proprietary cloud-based solution like an Amazon's **Elastic Load Balancer** or Linode's **NodeBalancer**, but for simplicity's sake and for flexibility in deployment, we'll use Varnish.

**Apache** and mod_php run a PHP-based application that displays the entire stack's current status and outputs the current server's IP address for load balancing verification.

A **Memcached** server provides a caching layer that can be used to store and retrieve frequently-accessed objects in lieu of slower database storage.

Two **MySQL** servers, configured as a master and slave, offer redundant and performant database access; all data will be replicated from the master to the slave, and in addition, the slave can be used as a secondary server for read-only queries to take some load off the master.

## Directory Structure

In order to keep our configuration organized, we'll use the following structure for our playbooks and configuration:

```
lamp-infrastructure/
  inventories/
  playbooks/
    db/
    memcached/
    varnish/
    www/
  provisioners/
  configure.yml
  provision.yml
  requirements.yml
  Vagrantfile
```

Organizing things this way allows us to focus on each server configuration individually, then build playbooks for provisioning and configuring instances on different hosting providers later. This organization also keeps server playbooks completely independent, so we can modularize and reuse individual server configurations.

## Individual Server Playbooks

Let's start building our individual server playbooks (in the playbooks directory). To make our playbooks more efficient, we'll use some contributed Ansible roles on Ansible Galaxy rather than install and configure everything step-by-step. We're going to target CentOS 6.x servers in these playbooks, but only minimal changes would be required to use the playbooks with Ubuntu, Debian, or later versions of CentOS.

**Varnish**

Create a main.yml file within the the playbooks/varnish directory, with the following contents:

```
1   ---
2   - hosts: lamp-varnish
3     become: yes
4
5     vars_files:
6       - vars.yml
7
8     roles:
9       - geerlingguy.firewall
10      - geerlingguy.repo-epel
11      - geerlingguy.varnish
12
13    tasks:
14      - name: Copy Varnish default.vcl.
15        template:
16          src: "templates/default.vcl.j2".
17          dest: "/etc/varnish/default.vcl"
18        notify: restart varnish
```

We're going to run this playbook on all hosts in the lamp-varnish inventory group (we'll create this later), and we'll run a few simple roles to configure the server:

- geerlingguy.firewall configures a simple iptables-based firewall using a couple variables defined in vars.yml.
- geerlingguy.repo-epel adds the EPEL repository (a prerequisite for varnish).
- geerlingguy.varnish installs and configures Varnish.

Finally, a task copies over a custom default.vcl that configures Varnish, telling it where to find our web servers and how to load balance requests between the servers.

Let's create the two files referenced in the above playbook. First, vars.yml, in the same directory as main.yml:

```
1   ---
2   firewall_allowed_tcp_ports:
3     - "22"
4     - "80"
5
6   varnish_use_default_vcl: false
```

The first variable tells the `geerlingguy.firewall` role to open TCP ports 22 and 80 for incoming traffic. The second variable tells the `geerlingguy.varnish` we will supply a custom `default.vcl` for Varnish configuration.

Create a `templates` directory inside the `playbooks/varnish` directory, and inside, create a `default.vcl.j2` file. This file will use Jinja2 syntax to build Varnish's custom `default.vcl` file:

```
1   vcl 4.0;
2
3   import directors;
4
5   {% for host in groups['lamp-www'] %}
6   backend www{{ loop.index }} {
7     .host = "{{ host }}";
8     .port = "80";
9   }
10  {% endfor %}
11
12  sub vcl_init {
13    new vdir = directors.random();
14  {% for host in groups['lamp-www'] %}
15    vdir.add_backend(www{{ loop.index }}, 1);
16  {% endfor %}
17  }
18
19  sub vcl_recv {
20    set req.backend_hint = vdir.backend();
21
```

```
22    # For testing ONLY; makes sure load balancing is working correctly.
23    return (pass);
24  }
```

We won't study Varnish's VCL syntax in depth but we'll run through `default.vcl` and highlight what is being configured:

1. (1-3) Indicate that we're using the 4.0 version of the VCL syntax and import the `directors` varnish module (which is used to configure load balancing).
2. (5-10) Define each web server as a new backend; give a host and a port through which varnish can contact each host.
3. (12-17) `vcl_init` is called when Varnish boots and initializes any required varnish modules. In this case, we're configuring a load balancer `vdir`, and adding each of the `www[#]` backends we defined earlier as backends to which the load balancer will distribute requests. We use a `random` director so we can easily demonstrate Varnish's ability to distribute requests to both app backends, but other load balancing strategies are also available.
4. (19-24) `vcl_recv` is called for each request, and routes the request through Varnish. In this case, we route the request to the `vdir` backend defined in `vcl_init`, and indicate that Varnish should *not* cache the result.

According to #4, we're actually *bypassing Varnish's caching layer*, which is not helpful in a typical production environment. If you only need a load balancer without any reverse proxy or caching capabilities, there are better options. However, we need to verify our infrastructure is working as it should. If we used Varnish's caching, Varnish would only ever hit one of our two web servers during normal testing.

In terms of our caching/load balancing layer, this should suffice. For a true production environment, you should remove the final `return (pass)` and customize `default.vcl` according to your application's needs.

**Apache / PHP**

Create a `main.yml` file within the the `playbooks/www` directory, with the following contents:

```
1   ---
2   - hosts: lamp-www
3     become: yes
4
5     vars_files:
6       - vars.yml
7
8     roles:
9       - geerlingguy.firewall
10      - geerlingguy.repo-epel
11      - geerlingguy.apache
12      - geerlingguy.php
13      - geerlingguy.php-mysql
14      - geerlingguy.php-memcached
15
16    tasks:
17      - name: Remove the Apache test page.
18        file:
19          path: /var/www/html/index.html
20          state: absent
21      - name: Copy our fancy server-specific home page.
22        template:
23          src: templates/index.php.j2
24          dest: /var/www/html/index.php
```

As with Varnish's configuration, we'll configure a firewall and add the EPEL repository (required for PHP's memcached integration), and we'll also add the following roles:

- geerlingguy.apache installs and configures the latest available version of the Apache web server.
- geerlingguy.php installs and configures PHP to run through Apache.
- geerlingguy.php-mysql adds MySQL support to PHP.
- geerlingguy.php-memcached adds Memcached support to PHP.

Two final tasks remove the default `index.html` home page included with Apache, and replace it with our PHP app.

As in the Varnish example, create the two files referenced in the above playbook. First, `vars.yml`, alongside `main.yml`:

```
1  ---
2  firewall_allowed_tcp_ports:
3    - "22"
4    - "80"
```

Create a `templates` directory inside the `playbooks/www` directory, and inside, create an `index.php.j2` file. This file will use Jinja2 syntax to build a (relatively) simple PHP script to display the health and status of all the servers in our infrastructure:

```
1  <?php
2  /**
3   * @file
4   * Infrastructure test page.
5   *
6   * DO NOT use this in production. It is simply a PoC.
7   */
8
9  $mysql_servers = array(
10 {% for host in groups['lamp-db'] %}
11   '{{ host }}',
12 {% endfor %}
13 );
14 $mysql_results = array();
15 foreach ($mysql_servers as $host) {
16   if ($result = mysql_test_connection($host)) {
17     $mysql_results[$host] = '<span style="color: green;">PASS\
18 </span>';
19     $mysql_results[$host] .= ' (' . $result['status'] . ')';
20   }
21   else {
```

```
22        $mysql_results[$host] = '<span style="color: red;">FAIL</span>';
23      }
24    }
25
26    // Connect to Memcached.
27    $memcached_result = '<span style="color: red;">FAIL</span>';
28    if (class_exists('Memcached')) {
29      $memcached = new Memcached;
30      $memcached->addServer('{{ groups['lamp-memcached'][0] }}', 11211);
31
32      // Test adding a value to memcached.
33      if ($memcached->add('test', 'success', 1)) {
34        $result = $memcached->get('test');
35        if ($result == 'success') {
36          $memcached_result = '<span style="color: green;">PASS</span>';
37          $memcached->delete('test');
38        }
39      }
40    }
41
42    /**
43     * Connect to a MySQL server and test the connection.
44     *
45     * @param string $host
46     *     IP Address or hostname of the server.
47     *
48     * @return array
49     *     Array with 'success' (bool) and 'status' ('slave' or 'master').
50     *     Empty if connection failure.
51     */
52    function mysql_test_connection($host) {
53      $username = 'mycompany_user';
54      $password = 'secret';
55      try {
56        $db = new PDO(
```

```php
57        'mysql:host=' . $host . ';dbname=mycompany_database',
58        $username,
59        $password,
60        array(PDO::ATTR_ERRMODE => PDO::ERRMODE_EXCEPTION));
61
62      // Query to see if the server is configured as a master or slave.
63      $statement = $db->prepare("SELECT variable_value
64        FROM information_schema.global_variables
65        WHERE variable_name = 'LOG_BIN';");
66      $statement->execute();
67      $result = $statement->fetch();
68
69      return array(
70        'success' => TRUE,
71        'status' => ($result[0] == 'ON') ? 'master' : 'slave',
72      );
73    }
74    catch (PDOException $e) {
75      return array();
76    }
77  }
78  ?>
79  <!DOCTYPE html>
80  <html>
81  <head>
82    <title>Host {{ inventory_hostname }}</title>
83    <style>* { font-family: Helvetica, Arial, sans-serif }</style>
84  </head>
85  <body>
86    <h1>Host {{ inventory_hostname }}</h1>
87    <?php foreach ($mysql_results as $host => $result): ?>
88      <p>MySQL Connection (<?php print $host; ?>):
89      <?php print $result; ?></p>
90    <?php endforeach; ?>
91    <p>Memcached Connection: <?php print $memcached_result; ?></p>
```

```
92  </body>
93  </html>
```

 Don't try transcribing this example manually; you can get the code from this book's repository on GitHub. Visit the ansible-for-devops[88] repository and download the source for index.php.j2[89]

As this is the heart of the example application we're deploying to the infrastructure, it's necessarily a bit more complex than most examples in the book, but a quick run through follows:

- (9-23) Iterate through all the `lamp-db` MySQL hosts defined in the playbook inventory and test the ability to connect to them—as well as whether they are configured as master or slave, using the `mysql_test_connection()` function defined later (40-73).
- (25-39) Check the first defined `lamp-memcached` Memcached host defined in the playbook inventory, confirming the ability to connect with the cache and to create, retrieve, or delete a cached value.
- (41-76) Define the `mysql_test_connection()` function, which tests the the ability to connect to a MySQL server and also returns its replication status.
- (78-91) Print the results of all the MySQL and Memcached tests, along with `{{ inventory_hostname }}` as the page title, so we can easily see which web server is serving the viewed page.

At this point, the heart of our infrastructure—the application that will test and display the status of all our servers—is ready to go.

**Memcached**

Compared to the earlier playbooks, the Memcached playbook is quite simple. Create `playbooks/memcached/main.yml` with the following contents:

---

[88]https://github.com/geerlingguy/ansible-for-devops
[89]https://github.com/geerlingguy/ansible-for-devops/blob/master/lamp-infrastructure/playbooks/www/templates/index.php.j2

```
1   ---
2   - hosts: lamp-memcached
3     become: yes
4
5     vars_files:
6       - vars.yml
7
8     roles:
9       - geerlingguy.firewall
10      - geerlingguy.memcached
```

As with the other servers, we need to ensure only the required TCP ports are open using the simple geerlingguy.firewall role. Next we install Memcached using the geerlingguy.memcached role.

In our vars.yml file (again, alongside main.yml), add the following:

```
1   ---
2   firewall_allowed_tcp_ports:
3     - "22"
4   firewall_additional_rules:
5     - "iptables -A INPUT -p tcp --dport 11211 -s \
6     {{ groups['lamp-www'][0] }} -j ACCEPT"
7     - "iptables -A INPUT -p tcp --dport 11211 -s \
8     {{ groups['lamp-www'][1] }} -j ACCEPT"
9
10  memcached_listen_ip: "{{ groups['lamp-memcached'][0] }}"
```

We need port 22 open for remote access, and for Memcached, we're adding manual iptables rules to allow access on port 11211 for the web servers *only*. We add one rule per lamp-www server by drilling down into each item in the the generated groups variable that Ansible uses to track all inventory groups currently available. We also bind Memcached to the server's IP address so it will accept connections through IP.

The **principle of least privilege** "requires that in a particular abstraction layer of a computing environment, every module ... must be able to access only the information and resources that are necessary for its legitimate purpose" (Source: Wikipedia[90]). Always restrict services and ports to only those servers or users that need access!

## MySQL

The MySQL configuration is more complex than the other servers because we need to configure MySQL users per-host and configure replication. Because we want to maintain an independent and flexible playbook, we also need to dynamically create some variables so MySQL will get the right server addresses in any potential environment.

Let's first create the main playbook, `playbooks/db/main.yml`:

```
1   ---
2   - hosts: lamp-db
3     become: yes
4
5     vars_files:
6       - vars.yml
7
8     pre_tasks:
9       - name: Create dynamic MySQL variables.
10        set_fact:
11          mysql_users:
12            - name: mycompany_user
13              host: "{{ groups['lamp-www'][0] }}"
14              password: secret
15              priv: "*.*:SELECT"
16            - name: mycompany_user
17              host: "{{ groups['lamp-www'][1] }}"
18              password: secret
19              priv: "*.*:SELECT"
```

---

[90]http://en.wikipedia.org/wiki/Principle_of_least_privilege

```
20          mysql_replication_master: "{{ groups['a4d.lamp.db.1'][0] }}"
21
22      roles:
23        - geerlingguy.firewall
24        - geerlingguy.mysql
```

Most of the playbook is straightforward, but in this instance, we're using set_fact as a pre_task (to be run before the geerlingguy.firewall and geerlingguy.mysql roles) to dynamically create variables for MySQL configuration.

set_fact allows us to define variables at runtime, so we can are guaranteed to have all server IP addresses available, even if the servers were freshly provisioned at the beginning of the playbook's run. We'll create two variables:

- mysql_users is a list of users the geerlingguy.mysql role will create when it runs. This variable will be used on all database servers so both of the two lamp-www servers get SELECT privileges on all databases.
- mysql_replication_master is used to indicate to the geerlingguy.mysql role which database server is the master; it will perform certain steps differently depending on whether the server being configured is a master or slave, and ensure that all the slaves are configured to replicate data from the master.

We'll need a few other normal variables to configure MySQL, so we'll add them alongside the firewall variable in playbooks/db/vars.yml:

```
1   ---
2   firewall_allowed_tcp_ports:
3     - "22"
4     - "3306"
5
6   mysql_replication_user: {name: 'replication', password: 'secret'}
7   mysql_databases:
8     - name: mycompany_database
9       collation: utf8_general_ci
10      encoding: utf8
```

We're opening port 3306 to anyone, but according to the **principle of least privilege** discussed earlier, you would be justified in restricting this port to only the servers and users that need access to MySQL (similar to the memcached server configuration). In this case, the attack vector is mitigated because MySQL's own authentication layer is used through the `mysql_user` variable generated in `main.yml`.

We are defining two MySQL variables: `mysql_replication_user` to be used for master and slave replication, and `mysql_databases` to define a list of databases that will be created (if they don't already exist) on the database servers.

With the configuration of the database servers complete, the server-specific play-books are ready to go.

## Main Playbook for Configuring All Servers

A simple playbook including each of the group-specific playbooks is all we need for the overall configuration to take place. Create `configure.yml` in the project's root directory, with the following contents:

```
1  ---
2  - include: playbooks/varnish/main.yml
3  - include: playbooks/www/main.yml
4  - include: playbooks/db/main.yml
5  - include: playbooks/memcached/main.yml
```

At this point, if you had some already-booted servers and statically defined inventory groups like `lamp-www`, `lamp-db`, etc., you could run `ansible-playbook config-ure.yml` and have a full HA infrastructure at the ready!

But we're going to continue to make our playbooks more flexible and useful.

## Getting the required roles

As mentioned in the Chapter 6, Ansible allows you to define all the required Ansible Galaxy roles for a given project in a `requirements.yml` file. Instead of having to remember to run `ansible-galaxy install -y [role1] [role2] [role3]` for each of the roles we're using, we can create `requirements.yml` in the root of our project, with the following contents:

```
1   ---
2   - src: geerlingguy.firewall
3   - src: geerlingguy.repo-epel
4   - src: geerlingguy.varnish
5   - src: geerlingguy.apache
6   - src: geerlingguy.php
7   - src: geerlingguy.php-mysql
8   - src: geerlingguy.php-memcached
9   - src: geerlingguy.mysql
10  - src: geerlingguy.memcached
```

To make sure all the required dependencies are installed, run `ansible-galaxy install -r requirements.yml` from within the project's root.

## Vagrantfile for Local Infrastructure via VirtualBox

As with many other examples in this book, we can use Vagrant and VirtualBox to build and configure the infrastructure locally. This lets us test things as much as we want with zero cost, and usually results in faster testing cycles, since everything is orchestrated over a local private network on a (hopefully) beefy workstation.

Our basic Vagrantfile layout will be something like the following:

1. Define a base box (in this case, CentOS 6.x) and VM hardware defaults.
2. Define all the VMs to be built, with VM-specific IP addresses and hostname configurations.
3. Define the Ansible provisioner along with the last VM, so Ansible can run once at the end of Vagrant's build cycle.

Here's the Vagrantfile in all its glory:

```ruby
1   # -*- mode: ruby -*-
2   # vi: set ft=ruby :
3
4   Vagrant.configure("2") do |config|
5     # Base VM OS configuration.
6     config.vm.box = "geerlingguy/centos6"
7     config.ssh.insert_key = false
8     config.vm.synced_folder '.', '/vagrant', disabled: true
9
10    # General VirtualBox VM configuration.
11    config.vm.provider :virtualbox do |v|
12      v.memory = 512
13      v.cpus = 1
14      v.linked_clone = true
15      v.customize ["modifyvm", :id, "--natdnshostresolver1", "on"]
16      v.customize ["modifyvm", :id, "--ioapic", "on"]
17    end
18
19    # Varnish.
20    config.vm.define "varnish" do |varnish|
21      varnish.vm.hostname = "varnish.dev"
22      varnish.vm.network :private_network, ip: "192.168.2.2"
23    end
24
25    # Apache.
26    config.vm.define "www1" do |www1|
27      www1.vm.hostname = "www1.dev"
28      www1.vm.network :private_network, ip: "192.168.2.3"
29
30      www1.vm.provision "shell",
31        inline: "sudo yum update -y"
32
33      www1.vm.provider :virtualbox do |v|
34        v.customize ["modifyvm", :id, "--memory", 256]
35      end
```

```
36    end
37
38    # Apache.
39    config.vm.define "www2" do |www2|
40      www2.vm.hostname = "www2.dev"
41      www2.vm.network :private_network, ip: "192.168.2.4"
42
43      www2.vm.provision "shell",
44        inline: "sudo yum update -y"
45
46      www2.vm.provider :virtualbox do |v|
47        v.customize ["modifyvm", :id, "--memory", 256]
48      end
49    end
50
51    # MySQL.
52    config.vm.define "db1" do |db1|
53      db1.vm.hostname = "db1.dev"
54      db1.vm.network :private_network, ip: "192.168.2.5"
55    end
56
57    # MySQL.
58    config.vm.define "db2" do |db2|
59      db2.vm.hostname = "db2.dev"
60      db2.vm.network :private_network, ip: "192.168.2.6"
61    end
62
63    # Memcached.
64    config.vm.define "memcached" do |memcached|
65      memcached.vm.hostname = "memcached.dev"
66      memcached.vm.network :private_network, ip: "192.168.2.7"
67
68      # Run Ansible provisioner once for all VMs at the end.
69      memcached.vm.provision "ansible" do |ansible|
70        ansible.playbook = "configure.yml"
```

```
71          ansible.inventory_path = "inventories/vagrant/inventory"
72          ansible.limit = "all"
73          ansible.extra_vars = {
74            ansible_ssh_user: 'vagrant',
75            ansible_ssh_private_key_file: \
76      "~/.vagrant.d/insecure_private_key"
77              }
78        end
79      end
80    end
```

Most of the Vagrantfile is straightforward, and similar to other examples used in this book. The last block of code, which defines the `ansible` provisioner configuration, contains three extra values that are important for our purposes:

```
1          ansible.inventory_path = "inventories/vagrant/inventory"
2          ansible.limit = "all"
3          ansible.extra_vars = {
4            ansible_ssh_user: 'vagrant',
5            ansible_ssh_private_key_file: \
6      "~/.vagrant.d/insecure_private_key"
7              }
```

1. `ansible.inventory_path` defines an inventory file to be used with the `ansible.playbook`. You could certainly create a dynamic inventory script for use with Vagrant, but because we know the IP addresses ahead of time, and are expecting a few specially-crafted inventory group names, it's simpler to build the inventory file for Vagrant provisioning by hand (we'll do this next).

2. `ansible.limit` is set to `all` so Vagrant knows it should run the Ansible playbook connected to all VMs, and not just the current VM. You could technically use `ansible.limit` with a provisioner configuration for each of the individual VMs, and just run the VM-specific playbook through Vagrant, but our live production infrastructure will be using one playbook to configure all the servers, so we'll do the same locally.

3. `ansible.extra_vars` contains the vagrant SSH user configuration for Ansible. It's more standard to include these settings in a static inventory file or use Vagrant's automatically-generated inventory file, but it's easiest to set them once for all servers here.

Before running `vagrant up` to see the fruits of our labor, we need to create an inventory file for Vagrant at `inventories/vagrant/inventory`:

```
1   [lamp-varnish]
2   192.168.2.2
3
4   [lamp-www]
5   192.168.2.3
6   192.168.2.4
7
8   [a4d.lamp.db.1]
9   192.168.2.5
10
11  [lamp-db]
12  192.168.2.5
13  192.168.2.6
14
15  [lamp-memcached]
16  192.168.2.7
```

Now `cd` into the project's root directory, run `vagrant up`, and after ten or fifteen minutes, load `http://192.168.2.2/` in your browser. Voila!

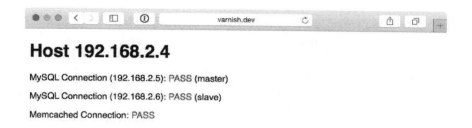

**Host 192.168.2.4**

MySQL Connection (192.168.2.5): PASS (master)

MySQL Connection (192.168.2.6): PASS (slave)

Memcached Connection: PASS

**Highly Available Infrastructure - Success!**

You should see something like the above screenshot. The PHP app displays the current app server's IP address, the individual MySQL servers' status, and the Memcached server status. Refresh the page a few times to verify Varnish is distributing requests randomly between the two app servers.

We now have local infrastructure development covered, and Ansible makes it easy to use the exact same configuration to build our infrastructure in the cloud.

## Provisioner Configuration: DigitalOcean

In Chapter 7, we learned provisioning and configuring DigitalOcean droplets in an Ansible playbook is fairly simple. But we need to take provisioning a step further by provisioning multiple droplets (one for each server in our infrastructure) and dynamically grouping them so we can configure them after they are booted and online.

For the sake of flexibility, let's create a playbook for our DigitalOcean droplets in `provisioners/digitalocean.yml`. This will allow us to add other provisioner configurations later, alongside the `digitalocean.yml` playbook. As with our example in Chapter 7, we will use a local connection to provision cloud instances. Begin the playbook with:

```
1  ---
2  - hosts: localhost
3    connection: local
4    gather_facts: false
```

Next we need to define some metadata to describe each of our droplets. For simplicity's sake, we'll inline the `droplets` variable in this playbook:

```
 6    vars:
 7      droplets:
 8        - { name: a4d.lamp.varnish, group: "lamp-varnish" }
 9        - { name: a4d.lamp.www.1, group: "lamp-www" }
10        - { name: a4d.lamp.www.2, group: "lamp-www" }
11        - { name: a4d.lamp.db.1, group: "lamp-db" }
12        - { name: a4d.lamp.db.2, group: "lamp-db" }
13        - { name: a4d.lamp.memcached, group: "lamp-memcached" }
```

Each droplet is an object with two keys:

- name: The name of the Droplet for DigitalOcean's listings and Ansible's host inventory.
- group: The Ansible inventory group for the droplet.

Next we need to add a task to create the droplets, using the droplets list as a guide, and as part of the same task, register each droplet's information in a separate dictionary, created_droplets:

```
15    tasks:
16      - name: Provision DigitalOcean droplets.
17        digital_ocean:
18          state: "{{ item.state | default('present') }}"
19          command: droplet
20          name: "{{ item.name }}"
21          private_networking: yes
22          size_id: "{{ item.size | default('512mb') }}"
23          image_id: "{{ item.image | default('centos-6-5-x32') }}"
24          region_id: "{{ item.region | default('nyc2') }}"
25          ssh_key_ids: "{{ item.ssh_key | default('138954') }}"
26          unique_name: yes
27        register: created_droplets
28        with_items: "{{ droplets }}"
```

Many of the options (e.g. `size_id`) are defined as `{{ item.property | default('default_-value') }}`, which allows us to use optional variables per droplet. For any of the defined droplets, we could add `size_id: 72` (or another valid value), and it would override the default value set in the task.

 You could specify an SSH public key per droplet, or use the same key for all hosts by providing a default (as I did above). In this example, I added an SSH key to my DigitalOcean account, then used the DigitalOcean API to retrieve the key's numeric ID (as described in the previous chapter).

It's best to use key-based authentication and add at least one SSH key to your DigitalOcean account so Ansible can connect using secure keys instead of insecure passwords—especially since these instances will be created with only a root account.

We loop through all the defined `droplets` using `with_items: droplets`, and after each droplet is created, we add the droplet's metadata (name, IP address, etc.) to the `created_droplets` variable. Next, we'll loop through that variable to build our inventory on-the-fly so our configuration applies to the correct servers:

```
30    - name: Add DigitalOcean hosts to inventory groups.
31      add_host:
32        name: "{{ item.1.droplet.ip_address }}"
33        groups: "do,{{ droplets[item.0].group }},\
34  {{ item.1.droplet.name }}"
35        # You can dynamically add inventory variables per-host.
36        ansible_ssh_user: root
37        mysql_replication_role: >
38          "{{ 'master' if (item.1.droplet.name == 'a4d.lamp.db.1')
39          else 'slave' }}"
40        mysql_server_id: "{{ item.0 }}"
41      when: item.1.droplet is defined
42      with_indexed_items: "{{ created_droplets.results }}"
```

You'll notice a few interesting things happening in this task:

- This is the first time we've used `with_indexed_items`. Though less common, this is a valuable loop feature because it adds a sequential and unique `mysql_-server_id`. Though only the MySQL servers need a server ID set, it's more simple to dynamically create the variable for every server so each is available when needed. `with_indexed_items` sets `item.0` to the key of the item and `item.1` to the value of the item.
- In addition to helping us create server IDs, `with_indexed_items` also helps us to reliably set each droplet's group. Because the v1 DigitalOcean API doesn't support features like tags for Droplets, we have to set up the groups on our own. By using the `droplets` variable we manually created earlier, we can set the proper group for a particular droplet.
- Finally, we add inventory variables per-host in `add_host`. To do this, we add the variable name as a key and the variable value as that key's value. Simple, but powerful!

 There are a few different ways you can approach dynamic provisioning and inventory management for your infrastructure. There are ways to avoid using more exotic features of Ansible (e.g. `with_indexed_items`) and complex if/else conditions, especially if you only use one cloud infrastructure provider. This example is slightly more complex because the playbook is being created to be interchangeable with similar provisioning playbooks.

The final step in our provisioning is to make sure all the droplets are booted and can be reached via SSH. So at the end of the `digitalocean.yml` playbook, add another play to be run on hosts in the `do` group we just defined:

```
43  - hosts: do
44    remote_user: root
45    gather_facts: no
46
47    tasks:
48      - name: Wait for port 22 to become available.
49        local_action: "wait_for port=22 host={{ inventory_hostname }}"
```

Once we know port 22 is reachable, we know the droplet is up and ready for configuration.

We're now *almost* ready to provision and configure our entire infrastructure on DigitalOcean, but first we need to create one last playbook to tie everything together. Create provision.yml in the project root with the following contents:

```
1  ---
2  - include: provisioners/digitalocean.yml
3  - include: configure.yml
```

That's it! Now, assuming you set the environment variable DO_API_TOKEN, you can run $ ansible-playbook provision.yml to provision and configure the infrastructure on DigitalOcean.

The entire process should take about 15 minutes; once it's complete, you should see something like this:

```
PLAY RECAP *********************************************************
107.170.27.137      : ok=19   changed=13   unreachable=0   failed=0
107.170.3.23        : ok=13   changed=8    unreachable=0   failed=0
107.170.51.216      : ok=40   changed=18   unreachable=0   failed=0
107.170.54.218      : ok=27   changed=16   unreachable=0   failed=0
162.243.20.29       : ok=24   changed=15   unreachable=0   failed=0
192.241.181.197     : ok=40   changed=18   unreachable=0   failed=0
localhost           : ok=2    changed=1    unreachable=0   failed=0
```

Visit the IP address of the varnish server, and you will be greeted with a status page similar to the one generated by the Vagrant-based infrastructure:

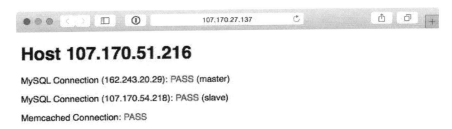

**Highly Available Infrastructure on DigitalOcean.**

Because everything in this playbook is idempotent, running $ `ansible-playbook provision.yml` again should report no changes, and this will help you verify that everything is running correctly.

Ansible will also rebuild and reconfigure any droplets that might be missing from your infrastructure. If you're daring and would like to test this feature, just log into your DigitalOcean account, delete one of the droplets just created by this playbook (perhaps one of the two app servers), and then run the playbook again.

Now that we've tested our infrastructure on DigitalOcean, we can destroy the droplets just as easily as we can create them. To do this, change the `state` parameter in `provisioners/digitalocean.yml` to default to `'absent'` and run $ `ansible-playbook provision.yml` once more.

Next up, we'll build the infrastructure a third time—on Amazon's infrastructure.

## Provisioner Configuration: Amazon Web Services (EC2)

For Amazon Web Services, provisioning is slightly different. Amazon has a broader ecosystem of services surrounding EC2 instances, so for our particular example we will need to configure security groups prior to provisioning instances.

To begin, create `aws.yml` inside the `provisioners` directory and begin the playbook the same way as for DigitalOcean:

```
1   ---
2   - hosts: localhost
3     connection: local
4     gather_facts: false
```

EC2 instances use security groups as an AWS-level firewall (which operates outside the individual instance's OS). We will need to define a list of `security_groups` alongside our EC2 `instances`. First, the `instances`:

```
6     vars:
7       instances:
8         - name: a4d.lamp.varnish
9           group: "lamp-varnish"
10          security_group: ["default", "a4d_lamp_http"]
11        - name: a4d.lamp.www.1
12          group: "lamp-www"
13          security_group: ["default", "a4d_lamp_http"]
14        - name: a4d.lamp.www.2
15          group: "lamp-www"
16          security_group: ["default", "a4d_lamp_http"]
17        - name: a4d.lamp.db.1
18          group: "lamp-db"
19          security_group: ["default", "a4d_lamp_db"]
20        - name: a4d.lamp.db.2
21          group: "lamp-db"
22          security_group: ["default", "a4d_lamp_db"]
23        - name: a4d.lamp.memcached
24          group: "lamp-memcached"
25          security_group: ["default", "a4d_lamp_memcached"]
```

Inside the `instances` variable, each instance is an object with three keys:

- `name`: The name of the instance, which we'll use to tag the instance and ensure only one instance is created per name.
- `group`: The Ansible inventory group in which the instance should belong.

- `security_group`: A list of security groups into which the instance will be placed. The `default` security group is added to your AWS account upon creation, and has one rule to allow outgoing traffic on any port to any IP address.

 If you use AWS exclusively, it would be best to autoscaling groups and change the design of this infrastructure a bit. For this example, we just need to ensure that the six instances we explicitly define are created, so we're using particular `names` and an `exact_count` to enforce the 1:1 relationship.

With our instances defined, we'll next define a `security_groups` variable containing all the required security group configuration for each server:

```
27    security_groups:
28      - name: a4d_lamp_http
29        rules:
30          - proto: tcp
31            from_port: 80
32            to_port: 80
33            cidr_ip: 0.0.0.0/0
34          - proto: tcp
35            from_port: 22
36            to_port: 22
37            cidr_ip: 0.0.0.0/0
38        rules_egress: []
39
40      - name: a4d_lamp_db
41        rules:
42          - proto: tcp
43            from_port: 3306
44            to_port: 3306
45            cidr_ip: 0.0.0.0/0
46          - proto: tcp
```

```
47              from_port: 22
48              to_port: 22
49              cidr_ip: 0.0.0.0/0
50          rules_egress: []
51
52        - name: a4d_lamp_memcached
53          rules:
54            - proto: tcp
55              from_port: 11211
56              to_port: 11211
57              cidr_ip: 0.0.0.0/0
58            - proto: tcp
59              from_port: 22
60              to_port: 22
61              cidr_ip: 0.0.0.0/0
62          rules_egress: []
```

Each security group has a name (which was used to identify the security group in the instances list), rules (a list of firewall rules—like protocol, ports, and IP ranges—to limit *incoming* traffic), and rules_egress (a list of firewall rules to limit *outgoing* traffic).

We need three security groups: a4d_lamp_http to open port 80, a4d_lamp_db to open port 3306, and a4d_lamp_memcached to open port 11211.

Now that we have all the data we need to set up security groups and instances, our first task is to create or verify the existence of the security groups:

```
64    tasks:
65      - name: Configure EC2 Security Groups.
66        ec2_group:
67          name: "{{ item.name }}"
68          description: Example EC2 security group for A4D.
69          region: "{{ item.region | default('us-west-2') }}" # Oregon
70          state: present
71          rules: "{{ item.rules }}"
72          rules_egress: "{{ item.rules_egress }}"
73        with_items: security_groups
```

The ec2_group requires a name, region, and rules for each security group. Security groups will be created if they don't exist, modified to match the supplied values if they do exist, or verified if they both exist and match the given values.

With the security groups configured, we can provision the defined EC2 instances by looping through instances with the ec2 module:

```
75      - name: Provision EC2 instances.
76        ec2:
77          key_name: "{{ item.ssh_key | default('jeff_mba_home') }}"
78          instance_tags:
79            inventory_group: "{{ item.group | default('') }}"
80            inventory_host: "{{ item.name | default('') }}"
81          group: "{{ item.security_group | default('') }}"
82          instance_type: "{{ item.type | default('t2.micro')}}" # Free
83          image: "{{ item.image | default('ami-11125e21') }}" # RHEL6
84          region: "{{ item.region | default('us-west-2') }}" # Oregon
85          wait: yes
86          wait_timeout: 500
87          exact_count: 1
88          count_tag:
89            inventory_group: "{{ item.group | default('') }}"
90            inventory_host: "{{ item.name | default('') }}"
91        register: created_instances
92        with_items: instances
```

This example is slightly more complex than the DigitalOcean example, and a few parts warrant a deeper look:

- EC2 allows SSH keys to be defined by name—in my case, I have a key `jeff_-mba_home` in my AWS account. You should set the `key_name` default to a key that you have in your account.
- Instance tags are tags that AWS will attach to your instance, for categorization purposes. By giving a list of keys and values, I can then use that list later in the `count_tag` parameter.
- `t2.micro` was used as the default instance type, since it falls within EC2's free tier usage. If you just set up an account and keep all AWS resource usage within free tier limits, you won't be billed anything.
- `exact_count` and `count_tag` work together to ensure AWS provisions only one of each of the instances we defined. The `count_tag` tells the `ec2` module to match the given group + host and then `exact_count` tells the module to only provision 1 instance. If you wanted to *remove* all your instances, you could set `exact_count` to 0 and run the playbook again.

Each provisioned instance will have its metadata added to the registered `created_-instances` variable, which we will use to build Ansible inventory groups for the server configuration playbooks.

```
94     - name: Add EC2 instances to inventory groups.
95       add_host:
96         name: "{{ item.1.tagged_instances.0.public_ip }}"
97         groups: "aws,{{ item.1.item.group }},{{ item.1.item.name }}"
98         # You can dynamically add inventory variables per-host.
99         ansible_ssh_user: ec2-user
100        mysql_replication_role: >
101          {{ 'master' if (item.1.item.name == 'a4d.lamp.db.1')
102          else 'slave' }}
103        mysql_server_id: "{{ item.0 }}"
104      when: item.1.instances is defined
105      with_indexed_items: created_instances.results
```

This `add_host` example is slightly simpler than the one for DigitalOcean, because AWS attaches metadata to EC2 instances which we can re-use when building groups or hostnames (e.g. `item.1.item.group`). We don't have to use list indexes to fetch group names from the original `instances` variable.

We still use `with_indexed_items` so we can use the index to generate a unique ID per server for use in building the MySQL master-slave replication.

The final steps in provisioning the EC2 instances are to ensure we can connect to them, and to set `selinux` into permissive mode so the configuration we supply will work correctly.

```
107   # Run some general configuration on all AWS hosts.
108   - hosts: aws
109     gather_facts: false
110
111     tasks:
112       - name: Wait for port 22 to become available.
113         local_action: "wait_for port=22 host={{ inventory_hostname }}"
114
115       - name: Set selinux into 'permissive' mode.
116         selinux: policy=targeted state=permissive
117         become: yes
```

Since we defined `ansible_ssh_user` as `ec2-user` in the dynamically-generated inventory above, we need to ensure the `selinux` task runs explicitly with `sudo` by adding `become: yes`.

Now, modify the `provision.yml` file in the root of the project folder and change the provisioners include to look like the following:

```
1   ---
2   - include: provisioners/aws.yml
3   - include: configure.yml
```

Assuming the environment variables `AWS_ACCESS_KEY_ID` and `AWS_SECRET_ACCESS_-KEY` are set in your current terminal session, you can run `$ ansible-playbook provision.yml` to provision and configure the infrastructure on AWS.

The entire process should take about 15 minutes, and once it's complete, you should see something like this:

```
PLAY RECAP ***************************************************************
54.148.100.44       : ok=24   changed=16   unreachable=0   failed=0
54.148.120.23       : ok=40   changed=19   unreachable=0   failed=0
54.148.41.134       : ok=40   changed=19   unreachable=0   failed=0
54.148.56.137       : ok=13   changed=9    unreachable=0   failed=0
54.69.160.32        : ok=27   changed=17   unreachable=0   failed=0
54.69.86.187        : ok=19   changed=14   unreachable=0   failed=0
localhost           : ok=3    changed=1    unreachable=0   failed=0
```

Visit the IP address of the Varnish server, and you will be greeted with a status page similar to the one generated by the Vagrant and DigitalOcean-based infrastructure:

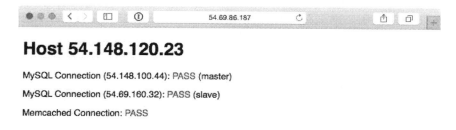

**Highly Available Infrastructure on AWS EC2.**

As with the earlier examples, running `ansible-playbook provision.yml` again should produce no changes, because everything in this playbook is idempotent. If one of your instances was somehow terminated, running the playbook again would recreate and reconfigure the instance in a few minutes.

To terminate all the provisioned instances, you can change the `exact_count` in the ec2 task to 0, and run $ `ansible-playbook provision.yml` again.

## Summary

In the above example, an entire highly-available PHP application infrastructure was defined in a series of short Ansible playbooks, and then provisioning configuration was created to build the infrastructure on either local VMs, DigitalOcean droplets, or AWS EC2 instances.

Once you start working on building infrastructure this way—by abstracting individual servers, then abstracting cloud provisioning—you'll start to see some of Ansible's true power of being more than just a configuration management tool. Imagine being able to create your own multi-datacenter, multi-provider infrastructure with Ansible and some basic configuration.

Amazon, DigitalOcean, Rackspace and other hosting providers have their own tooling and unique infrastructure merits. However, building infrastructure in a provider-agnostic fashion provides the agility and flexibility that allow you to treat hosting providers as commodities, and gives you the freedom to build more reliable and more performant application infrastructure.

Even if you plan on running everything within one hosting provider's network (or in a private cloud, or even on a few bare metal servers), Ansible provides deep stack-specific integration so you can do whatever you need to do and manage the provider's services within your playbooks.

 You can find the entire contents of this example in the Ansible for DevOps GitHub repository[91], in the `lamp-infrastructure` directory.

# ELK Logging with Ansible

Though application, database, and backup servers may be some of the most mission-critical components of a well-rounded infrastructure, one area that is equally important is a decent logging system.

In the old days when one or two servers could handle an entire website or application, you could work with built-in logfiles and rsyslog to troubleshoot issues or check trends in performance, errors, or overall traffic. With a typical modern infrastructure—like the example above, with six separate servers—it pays dividends to find a better solution for application, server, and firewall/authentication logging. Plain text files, logrotate, and grep don't cut it anymore.

---

[91]https://github.com/geerlingguy/ansible-for-devops

Among various modern logging and reporting toolsets, the 'ELK' stack (Elasticsearch, Logstash, and Kibana) has come to the fore as one of the best-performing and easiest-to-configure open source centralized logging solutions.

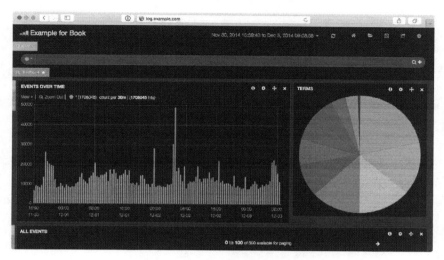

**An example Kibana logging dashboard.**

In our example, we'll configure a single ELK server to handle aggregation, searching, and graphical display of logged data from a variety of other servers, and give some common configuration examples to send common system logs, webserver logs, etc.

## ELK Playbook

Just like our previous example, we're going to let a few roles from Ansible Galaxy do the heavy lifting of actually installing and configuring Elasticsearch, Logstash, and Kibana. If you're interested in reading through the roles that do this work, feel free to peruse them after they've been downloaded.

In this example, I'm going to highlight the important parts rather than walk through each role and variable in detail. Then I'll show how you can use this base server to aggregate logs, then how to point your other servers' log files to it using Logstash Forwarder.

Here's our main playbook, saved as `provisioning/elk/playbook.yml`:

```
1   - hosts: logs
2     gather_facts: yes
3
4     vars_files:
5       - vars/main.yml
6
7     pre_tasks:
8       - name: Update apt cache if needed.
9         apt: update_cache=yes cache_valid_time=86400
10
11    roles:
12      - geerlingguy.java
13      - geerlingguy.nginx
14      - geerlingguy.elasticsearch
15      - geerlingguy.elasticsearch-curator
16      - geerlingguy.kibana
17      - geerlingguy.logstash
18      - geerlingguy.logstash-forwarder
```

This assumes you have a `logs` group in your inventory with at least one server listed. The playbook includes a vars file located in `provisioning/elk/vars/main.yml`, so create that file, and then put the following inside:

```
1   ---
2   java_packages:
3     - openjdk-7-jdk
4
5   nginx_user: www-data
6   nginx_worker_connections: 1024
7   nginx_remove_default_vhost: true
8
9   kibana_server_name: logs
10  kibana_username: kibana
11  kibana_password: password
12
```

```
13   logstash_monitor_local_syslog: false
14   logstash_forwarder_files:
15     - paths:
16         - /var/log/auth.log
17       fields:
18         type: syslog
```

You'll want to use something other than 'password' for `kibana_password`. Other options are straightforward, with the exception of the two `logstash_*` variables.

The first variable tells the `geerlingguy.logstash` role to ignore the local syslog file, because in this case, we're only interested in logging authorization attempts through the local `auth.log`.

The second variable gives the `geerlingguy.logstash-forwarder` role a list of files to monitor, along with metadata to tell logstash what kind of file is being monitored. In this case, we are only worried about the `auth.log` file, and we know it's a syslog-style file. (Logstash needs to know what kind of file you're monitoring so it can parse the logged messages correctly).

If you want to get this ELK server up and running quickly, you can create a local VM using Vagrant like you have in most other examples in the book. Create a `Vagrantfile` in the same directory as the `provisioning` folder, with the following contents:

```
1   # -*- mode: ruby -*-
2   # vi: set ft=ruby :
3
4   VAGRANTFILE_API_VERSION = "2"
5
6   Vagrant.configure(VAGRANTFILE_API_VERSION) do |config|
7     config.vm.box = "geerlingguy/ubuntu1204"
8
9     config.vm.provider :virtualbox do |v|
10      v.customize ["modifyvm", :id, "--natdnshostresolver1", "on"]
11      v.customize ["modifyvm", :id, "--memory", 1024]
12      v.customize ["modifyvm", :id, "--cpus", 2]
```

```
13        v.customize ["modifyvm", :id, "--ioapic", "on"]
14      end
15
16    # ELK server.
17    config.vm.define "logs" do |logs|
18      logs.vm.hostname = "logs"
19      logs.vm.network :private_network, ip: "192.168.9.90"
20
21      logs.vm.provision :ansible do |ansible|
22        ansible.playbook = "provisioning/elk/playbook.yml"
23        ansible.inventory_path = "provisioning/elk/inventory"
24        ansible.sudo = true
25      end
26    end
27
28  end
```

This Vagrant configuration expects an inventory file at provisioning/elk/inventory, so quickly create one with the following contents:

```
1  logs ansible_ssh_host=192.168.9.90 ansible_ssh_port=22
```

Now, run vagrant up. The build should take about five minutes, and upon completion, if you add a line like logs 192.168.9.90 to your /etc/hosts file, you can visit http://logs/ in your browser and see Kibana's default homepage:

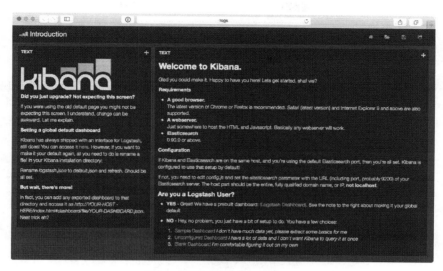

**Kibana's default homepage.**

Kibana helpfully links to an example dashboard for Logstash (under the "Are you a Logstash User?" section), and if you select it, you should see a live dashboard that shows logged activity for the past day:

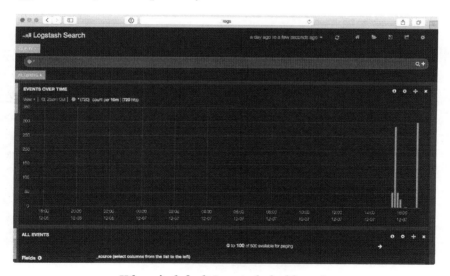

**Kibana's default Logstash dashboard.**

In this example, we won't dive too deep into customizing Kibana's dashboard customization, since there are many guides to using Kibana available freely, including Kibana's official guide[92]. For our purposes, we'll use the default dashboard.

 This example uses Kibana 3.x, but a stable release of Kibana 4.x is on the horizon (as of early 2015). Some of the screenshots may show a different interface than the latest release, but this book will likely be updated with newer screenshots and updated guides once the 4.x release comes out.

## Forwarding Logs from Other Servers

It's great that we have the ELK stack running. Elasticsearch will store and make available log data with one search index per day, Logstash will listen for log entries, Logstash Forwarder will send entries in /var/log/auth.log to Logstash, and Kibana will organize the logged data in useful visualizations.

Configuring additional servers to direct their logs to our new Logstash server is fairly simple using Logstash Forwarder. The basic steps we'll follow are:

1. Set up another server in the Vagrantfile.
2. Set up an Ansible playbook to install and configure Logstash Forwarder alongside the application running on the server.
3. Boot the server and watch as the logs are forwarded to the main ELK server.

Let's begin by creating a new Nginx web server. (It's useful to monitor webserver access logs for a variety of reasons, especially to watch for traffic spikes and increases in non-200 responses for certain resources.) Add the following server definition inside the Vagrantfile, just after the end of the ELK server definition:

---

[92]http://www.elasticsearch.org/guide/en/kibana/current/index.html

```
28    # Web server.
29    config.vm.define "webs" do |webs|
30      webs.vm.hostname = "webs"
31      webs.vm.network :private_network, ip: "192.168.9.91"
32
33      webs.vm.provision :ansible do |ansible|
34        ansible.playbook = "provisioning/web/playbook.yml"
35        ansible.inventory_path = "provisioning/web/inventory"
36        ansible.sudo = true
37      end
38    end
```

We'll next set up the simple playbook to install and configure both Nginx and Logstash Forwarder, at `provisioning/web/playbook.yml`:

```
1   - hosts: webs
2     gather_facts: yes
3
4     vars_files:
5       - vars/main.yml
6
7     pre_tasks:
8       - name: Update apt cache if needed.
9         apt: update_cache=yes cache_valid_time=86400
10
11    roles:
12      - geerlingguy.nginx
13      - geerlingguy.logstash-forwarder
14
15    tasks:
16      - name: Set up virtual host for testing.
17        copy:
18          src: files/example.conf
19          dest: /etc/nginx/conf.d/example.conf
20          owner: root
```

```
21          group: root
22          mode: 0644
23       notify: restart nginx
```

This playbook installs the geerlingguy.nginx and geerlingguy.logstash-forwarder roles, and in the tasks, there is an additional task to configure one virtualhost in a Nginx configuration directory, via the file example.conf. Create that file now at the path provisioning/web/files/example.conf, and define one Nginx virtualhost for our testing:

```
1  server {
2    listen 80 default_server;
3
4    root /usr/share/nginx/www;
5    index index.html index.htm;
6
7    access_log /var/log/nginx/access.log combined;
8    error_log /var/log/nginx/error.log debug;
9  }
```

Since this is the only server definition, and it's set as the default_server on port 80, all requests will be directed to it. We routed the access_log to /var/log/nginx/access.log, and told Nginx to write log entries using the combined format, which is how our Logstash server will expect nginx access logs to be formatted.

Next, set up the required variables to tell the nginx and logstash-forwarder roles how to configure their respective services. Inside provisioning/web/vars/main.yml:

```
1   ---
2   nginx_user: www-data
3   nginx_worker_connections: 1024
4   nginx_remove_default_vhost: true
5
6   logstash_forwarder_logstash_server: 192.168.9.90
7   logstash_forwarder_logstash_server_port: 5000
8
9   logstash_forwarder_files:
10    - paths:
11        - /var/log/secure
12      fields:
13        type: syslog
14    - paths:
15        - /var/log/nginx/access.log
16      fields:
17        type: nginx
```

The nginx variables remove the default virtualhost entry and ensure Nginx will run optimally on our Ubuntu server. The logstash_forwarder variables tell the logstash-forwarder role what logs to forward to our central log server:

- logstash_forwarder_logstash_server and _port: Defines the server IP or domain and port to which logs should be transported.
- logstash_forwarder_files: Defines a list of paths and fields, which identify a file or list of files to be transported to the log server, along with a type for the files. In this case, the authentication log (/var/log/secure) is a syslog-formatted log file, and /var/log/nginx/access.log is of type nginx (which will be parsed correctly on the Logstash server since it's in the combined log format popularized by Apache).

Note that this demonstration configuration does not use a custom certificate to authenticate logging connections. You should normally configure your own secure certificate and give the logstash-forwarder role the path to the certificate using the `logstash_forwarder_ssl_certificate_-file` variable. If you use the example provided with the project, you could expose your logging infrastructure to the outside, and you'll get a `***SECURITY RISK***` warning in the logs every time the Logstash role is run.

To allow Vagrant to pass the proper connection details to Ansible, create `provisioning/web/inventory` with the `webs` host details:

```
1   webs ansible_ssh_host=192.168.9.91 ansible_ssh_port=22
```

Run `vagrant up` again. Vagrant should verify that the first server (`logs`) is running, then create and run the Ansible provisioner on the newly-defined `webs` Nginx server.

You can load `http://192.168.9.91/` or `http://webs/` in your browser, and you should see a `Welcome to nginx!` message on the page. You can refresh the page a few times, then switch back over to `http://logs/` to view some new log entries on the ELK server:

**Entries populating the Logstash Search Kibana dashboard.**

 If you refresh the page a few times, and no entries show up in the Kibana Logstash dashboard, it could be that Nginx is buffering the log entries. In this case, keep refreshing a while (so you generate a few dozen or hundred entries), and Nginx will eventually write the entries to disk (thus allowing Logstash Forwarder to convey the logs to the Logstash server). Read more about Nginx log buffering in the Nginx's ngx_http_log_module documentation[93].

A few requests being logged through logstash forwarder isn't all that exciting. Let's use the popular ab tool available most anywhere to put some load on the web server. On a modest MacBook Air, running the command below resulted in Nginx serving around 1,200 requests per second.

```
ab -n 20000 -c 50 http://webs/
```

During the course of the load test, I set Kibana to show only the past 5 minutes of

---

[93]http://nginx.org/en/docs/http/ngx_http_log_module.html

log data (automatically refreshed every 5 seconds) and I could monitor the requests on the ELK server just a few seconds after they were served by Nginx:

**Monitoring a deluge of Nginx requests in near-realtime.**

Logstash Forwarder uses a highly-efficient TCP-like protocol, Lumberjack, to transmit log entries securely between servers. With the right tuning and scaling, you can efficiently process and display thousands of requests per second across your infrastructure! For most, even the simple example demonstrated above would adequately cover an entire infrastructure's logging and log analysis needs.

## Summary

Log aggregation and analysis are two fields that see constant improvements and innovation. There are many SaaS products and proprietary solutions that can assist with logging, but few match the flexibility, security, and TCO of Elasticsearch, Logstash and Kibana.

Ansible is the simplest way to configure an ELK server and direct all your infrastructure's pertinent log data to the server.

# GlusterFS Distributed File System Configuration with Ansible

Modern infrastructure often involves some amount of horizontal scaling; instead of having one giant server with one storage volume, one database, one application instance, etc., most apps use two, four, ten, or dozens of servers.

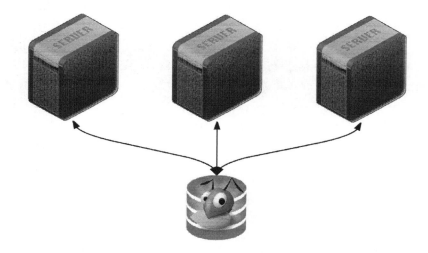

**GlusterFS is a distributed filesystem for servers.**

Many applications can be scaled horizontally with ease. But what happens when you need shared resources, like files, application code, or other transient data, to be shared on all the servers? And how do you have this data scale out with your infrastructure, in a fast but reliable way? There are many different approaches to synchronizing or distributing files across servers:

- Set up rsync either on cron or via inotify to synchronize smaller sets of files on a regular basis.
- Store everything in a code repository (e.g. Git, SVN, etc.) and deploy files to each server using Ansible.
- Have one large volume on a file server and mount it via NFS or some other file sharing protocol.

- Have one master SAN that's mounted on each of the servers.
- Use a distributed file system, like Gluster, Lustre, Fraunhofer, or Ceph.

Some options are easier to set up than others, and all have benefits—and draw-backs. Rsync, git, or NFS offer simple initial setup, and low impact on filesystem performance (in many scenarios). But if you need more flexibility and scalability, less network overhead, and greater fault tolerance, you will have to consider something that requires more configuration (e.g. a distributed file system) and/or more hardware (e.g. a SAN).

GlusterFS is licensed under the AGPL license, has good documentation, and a fairly active support community (especially in the #gluster IRC channel). But to someone new to distributed file systems, it can be daunting to get set it up the first time.

## Configuring Gluster - Basic Overview

To get Gluster working on a basic two-server setup (so you can have one folder synchronized and replicated across the two servers—allowing one server to go down completely, and the other to still have access to the files), you need to do the following:

1. Install Gluster server and client on each server, and start the server daemon.
2. (On both servers) Create a 'brick' directory (where Gluster will store files for a given volume).
3. (On both servers) Create a directory to be used as a mount point (a directory where you'll have Gluster mount the shared volume).
4. (On both servers) Use `gluster peer probe` to have Gluster connect to the other server.
5. (On one server) Use `gluster volume create` to create a new Gluster volume.
6. (On one server) Use `gluster volume start` to start the new Gluster volume.
7. (On both servers) Mount the gluster volume (adding a record to `/etc/fstab` to make the mount permanent).

Additionally, you need to make sure you have the following ports open on both servers (so Gluster can communicate): TCP ports 111, 24007-24011, 49152-49153, and UDP port 111. For each extra server in your Gluster cluster, you need to add an additional TCP port in the 49xxx range.

# Configuring Gluster with Ansible

For demonstration purposes, we'll set up a simple two-server infrastructure using Vagrant, and create a shared volume between the two, with two replicas (meaning all files will be replicated on each server). As your infrastructure grows, you can set other options for data consistency and transport according to your needs.

To build the two-server infrastructure locally, create a folder gluster containing the following Vagrantfile:

```ruby
1   # -*- mode: ruby -*-
2   # vi: set ft=ruby :
3
4   Vagrant.configure("2") do |config|
5     # Base VM OS configuration.
6     config.vm.box = "geerlingguy/ubuntu1404"
7     config.vm.synced_folder '.', '/vagrant', disabled: true
8     config.ssh.insert_key = false
9
10    config.vm.provider :virtualbox do |v|
11      v.memory = 256
12      v.cpus = 1
13    end
14
15    # Define two VMs with static private IP addresses.
16    boxes = [
17      { :name => "gluster1", :ip => "192.168.29.2" },
18      { :name => "gluster2", :ip => "192.168.29.3" }
19    ]
20
21    # Provision each of the VMs.
22    boxes.each do |opts|
23      config.vm.define opts[:name] do |config|
24        config.vm.hostname = opts[:name]
25        config.vm.network :private_network, ip: opts[:ip]
26
```

```
27      # Provision both VMs using Ansible after the last VM is booted.
28      if opts[:name] == "gluster2"
29        config.vm.provision "ansible" do |ansible|
30          ansible.playbook = "playbooks/provision.yml"
31          ansible.inventory_path = "inventory"
32          ansible.limit = "all"
33        end
34      end
35    end
36  end
37
38 end
```

This configuration creates two servers, gluster1 and gluster2, and will run a playbook at playbooks/provision.yml on the servers defined in an inventory file in the same directory as the Vagrantfile.

Create the inventory file to help Ansible connect to the two servers:

```
1  [gluster]
2  192.168.29.2
3  192.168.29.3
4
5  [gluster:vars]
6  ansible_ssh_user=vagrant
7  ansible_ssh_private_key_file=~/.vagrant.d/insecure_private_key
```

Now, create a playbook named provision.yml inside a playbooks directory:

```
 1   ---
 2   - hosts: gluster
 3     become: yes
 4
 5     vars_files:
 6       - vars.yml
 7
 8     roles:
 9       - geerlingguy.firewall
10       - geerlingguy.glusterfs
11
12     tasks:
13       - name: Ensure Gluster brick and mount directories exist.
14         file: "path={{ item }} state=directory mode=0775"
15         with_items:
16           - "{{ gluster_brick_dir }}"
17           - "{{ gluster_mount_dir }}"
18
19       - name: Configure Gluster volume.
20         gluster_volume:
21           state: present
22           name: "{{ gluster_brick_name }}"
23           brick: "{{ gluster_brick_dir }}"
24           replicas: 2
25           cluster: "{{ groups.gluster | join(',') }}"
26           host: "{{ inventory_hostname }}"
27           force: yes
28         run_once: true
29
30       - name: Ensure Gluster volume is mounted.
31         mount:
32           name: "{{ gluster_mount_dir }}"
33           src: "{{ inventory_hostname }}:/{{ gluster_brick_name }}"
34           fstype: glusterfs
35           opts: "defaults,_netdev"
```

`state: mounted`

This playbook uses two roles to set up a firewall and install the required packages for GlusterFS to work. You can manually install both of the required roles with the command `ansible-galaxy install geerlingguy.firewall geerlingguy.glusterfs`, or add them to a `requirements.yml` file and install with `ansible-galaxy install -r requirements.yml`.

Gluster requires a 'brick' directory to use as a virtual filesystem, and our servers also need a directory where the filesystem can be mounted, so the first `file` task ensures both directories exist (`gluster_brick_dir` and `gluster_mount_dir`). Since we need to use these directory paths more than once, we use variables which will be defined later, in `vars.yml`.

Ansible's `gluster_volume` module (added in Ansible 1.9) does all the hard work of probing peer servers, setting up the brick as a Gluster filesystem, and configuring the brick for replication. Some of the most important configuration parameters for the `gluster_volume` module include:

- `state`: Setting this to `present` makes sure the brick is present. It will also start the volume when it is first created by default, though this behavior can be overridden by the `start_on_create` option.
- `name` and `brick` give the Gluster brick a name and location on the server, respectively. In this example, the brick will be located on the boot volume, so we also have to add `force: yes`, or Gluster will complain about not having the brick on a separate volume.
- `replicas` tells Gluster how many replicas to ensure exist; this number can vary depending on how many servers you have in the brick's `cluster`, and how tolerance you have for server outages. We won't get much into tuning GlusterFS for performance and resiliency, but most situations warrant a value of 2 or 3.
- `cluster` defines all the hosts which will contain the distributed filesystem. In this case, all the `gluster` servers in our Ansible inventory should be included, so we use a Jinja2 `join` filter to join all the addresses into a list.
- `host` sets the host for peer probing explicitly. If you don't set this, you can sometimes get errors on brick creation, depending on your network configuration.

We only need to run the `gluster_volume` module once for all the servers, so we add `run_once: true`.

The last task in the playbook uses Ansible's `mount` module to ensure the Gluster volume is mounted on each of the servers, in the `gluster_mount_dir`.

After the playbook is created, we need to define all the variables used in the playbook. Create a `vars.yml` file inside the `playbooks` directory, with the following variables:

```
1    ---
2    # Firewall configuration.
3    firewall_allowed_tcp_ports:
4      - 22
5      # For Gluster.
6      - 111
7      # Port-mapper for Gluster 3.4+.
8      # - 2049
9      # Gluster Daemon.
10     - 24007
11     # 24009+ for Gluster <= 3.3; 49152+ for Gluster 3.4+.
12     - 24009
13     - 24010
14     # Gluster inline NFS server.
15     - 38465
16     - 38466
17   firewall_allowed_udp_ports:
18     - 111
19
20   # Gluster configuration.
21   gluster_mount_dir: /mnt/gluster
22   gluster_brick_dir: /srv/gluster/brick
23   gluster_brick_name: gluster
```

This variables file should be pretty self-explanatory; all the ports required for Gluster are opened in the firewall, and the three Gluster-related variables we use in the playbook are defined.

Now that we have everything set up, the folder structure should look like this:

```
gluster/
  playbooks/
    provision.yml
    main.yml
  inventory
  Vagrantfile
```

Change directory into the gluster directory, and run vagrant up. After a few minutes, provisioning should have completed successfully. To ensure Gluster is working properly, you can run the following two commands, which should give information about Gluster's peer connections and the configured gluster volume:

```
$ ansible gluster -i inventory -a "gluster peer status" -s
192.168.29.2 | success | rc=0 >>
Number of Peers: 1

Hostname: 192.168.29.3
Port: 24007
Uuid: 1340bcf1-1ae6-4e55-9716-2642268792a4
State: Peer in Cluster (Connected)

192.168.29.3 | success | rc=0 >>
Number of Peers: 1

Hostname: 192.168.29.2
Port: 24007
Uuid: 63d4a5c8-6b27-4747-8cc1-16af466e4e10
State: Peer in Cluster (Connected)
```

```
$ ansible gluster -i inventory -a "gluster volume info" -s
192.168.29.3 | success | rc=0 >>

Volume Name: gluster
Type: Replicate
Volume ID: b75e9e45-d39b-478b-a642-ccd16b7d89d8
Status: Started
Number of Bricks: 1 x 2 = 2
Transport-type: tcp
Bricks:
Brick1: 192.168.29.2:/srv/gluster/brick
Brick2: 192.168.29.3:/srv/gluster/brick

192.168.29.2 | success | rc=0 >>

Volume Name: gluster
Type: Replicate
Volume ID: b75e9e45-d39b-478b-a642-ccd16b7d89d8
Status: Started
Number of Bricks: 1 x 2 = 2
Transport-type: tcp
Bricks:
Brick1: 192.168.29.2:/srv/gluster/brick
Brick2: 192.168.29.3:/srv/gluster/brick
```

You can also do the following to confirm that files are being replicated/distributed correctly:

1. Log into the first server: `vagrant ssh gluster1`
2. Create a file in the mounted gluster volume: `sudo touch /mnt/gluster/test`
3. Log out of the first server: `exit`
4. Log into the second server: `vagrant ssh gluster2`
5. List the contents of the gluster directory: `ls /mnt/gluster`

You should see the `test` file you created in step 2; this means Gluster is working correctly!

## Summary

Deploying distributed file systems like Gluster can seem challenging, but Ansible simplifies the process, and more importantly, does so idempotently; each time you run the playbook again, it will ensure everything stays configured as you've set it.

This example Gluster configuration can be found in its entirety on GitHub, in the Gluster example[94] in the Ansible Vagrant Examples project.

# Mac Provisioning with Ansible and Homebrew

The next example will be specific to the Mac, but the principle behind it applies universally. How many times have you wanted to hit the 'reset' button on your day-to-day workstation or personal computer? How much time to you spend automating configuration and testing of applications and infrastructure at your day job, and how little do you spend automating your *own* local environment?

Over the past few years, as I've gone through four Macs (one personal, three employer-provided), I decided to start fresh on each new Mac (rather than transfer all my cruft from my old Mac to my new Mac through Apple's Migration Assistant). I had a problem, though; I had to spend at least 4-6 hours on each Mac, downloading, installing, and configuring everything. And I had another problem—since I actively used at least two separate Macs, I had to manually install and configure new software on both Macs whenever I wanted to try a new tool.

To restore order to this madness, I wrapped up all the configuration I could into a set of dotfiles[95] and used git to synchronize the dotfiles to all my workstations.

However, even with the assistance of Homebrew[96], an excellent package manager for OS X, there was still a lot of manual labor involved in installing and configuring my favorite apps and command line tools.

---

[94]https://github.com/geerlingguy/ansible-vagrant-examples/tree/master/gluster
[95]https://github.com/geerlingguy/dotfiles
[96]http://brew.sh/

## Running Ansible playbooks locally

We saw examples of running playbooks with `connection: local` earlier while provisioning virtual machines in the cloud through our local workstation. But in fact, you can perform *any* Ansible task using a local connection. This is how we will configure our local workstation, using Ansible.

I usually begin building a playbook by adding the basic scaffolding first, then filling in details as I go. You can follow along by creating the playbook `main.yml` with:

```
1   ---
2   - hosts: localhost
3     user: jgeerling
4     connection: local
5
6     vars_files:
7       - vars/main.yml
8
9     roles: []
10
11    tasks: []
```

We'll store any variables we need in the included `vars/main.yml` file. The `user` is set to my local user account (in this case, `jgeerling`), so file permissions are set for my account, and tasks are run under my own account in order to minimize surprises.

> If certain tasks need to be run with sudo privileges, you can add `become: yes` to the task, and either run the playbook with `--ask-sudo-pass` (in which case, Ansible will prompt you for your sudo password before running the playbook) or run the playbook normally, and wait for Ansible to prompt you for your sudo password.

## Automating Homebrew package and app management

Since I use Homebrew (billed as "the missing package manager for OS X") for most of my application installation and configuration, I created the role `geerling-`

guy.homebrew, which first installs Homebrew and then installs all the applications and packages I configure in a few simple variables.

The next step, then, is to add the Homebrew role and configure the required variables. Inside main.yml, update the roles section:

```
 9    roles:
10      - geerlingguy.homebrew
```

Then add the following into vars/main.yml:

```
 1    ---
 2    homebrew_installed_packages:
 3      - ansible
 4      - sqlite
 5      - mysql
 6      - php56
 7      - python
 8      - ssh-copy-id
 9      - cowsay
10      - pv
11      - drush
12      - wget
13      - brew-cask
14
15    homebrew_taps:
16      - caskroom/cask
17      - homebrew/binary
18      - homebrew/dupes
19      - homebrew/php
20      - homebrew/versions
21
22    homebrew_cask_appdir: /Applications
23    homebrew_cask_apps:
24      - google-chrome
25      - firefox
```

```
26      - sequel-pro
27      - sublime-text
28      - vagrant
29      - vagrant-manager
30      - virtualbox
```

Homebrew has a few tricks up its sleeve, like being able to manage general packages like PHP, MySQL, Python, Pipe Viewer, etc. natively (using commands like `brew install [package]` and `brew uninstall package`), and can also install and manage general application installation for many Mac apps, like Chrome, Firefox, VLC, etc. using `brew cask`.

To anyone who's set up a new Mac the old-fashioned way—download 15 .dmg files, mount them, drag the applications to the Applications folder, eject them, delete the .dmg files—Homebrew's simplicity and speed are a true godsend. This Ansible playbook has so far automated that process completely, so you don't even have to run the Homebrew commands manually! The `geerlingguy.homebrew` role uses Ansible's built-in `homebrew` module to manage package installation, along with some custom tasks to manage cask applications.

## Configuring Mac OS X through dotfiles

Just like there's a `homebrew` role on Ansible Galaxy, made for configuring and installing packages via Homebrew, there's a `dotfiles` role you can use to download and configure your local dotfiles.

 Dotfiles are named as such because they are files in your home directory that begin with a .. Many programs and shell environments read local configuration from dotfiles, so dotfiles are a simple, efficient, and easily-synchronized method of customizing your development environment for maximum efficiency.

In this example, we'll use the author's dotfiles, but you can tell the role to use whatever set of dotfiles you want.

Add another role to the `roles` list:

```
 9     roles:
10       - geerlingguy.homebrew
11       - geerlingguy.dotfiles
```

Then, add the following three variables to your vars/main.yml file:

```
2   dotfiles_repo: https://github.com/geerlingguy/dotfiles.git
3   dotfiles_repo_local_destination: ~/repositories/dotfiles
4   dotfiles_files:
5     - .bash_profile
6     - .gitignore
7     - .inputrc
8     - .osx
9     - .vimrc
```

The first variable gives the git repository URL for the dotfiles to be cloned. The second gives a local path for the repository to be stored, and the final variable tells the role which dotfiles it should use from the specified repository.

The dotfiles role clones the specified dotfiles repository locally, then symlinks every one of the dotfiles specified in dotfiles_files into your home folder (removing any existing dotfiles of the same name).

If you want to run the .osx dotfile, which adjusts many system and application settings, add in a new task under the tasks section in the main playbook:

```
1   tasks:
2     - name: Run .osx dotfiles.
3       shell: ~/.osx --no-restart
4       changed_when: false
```

In this case, the .osx dotfile allows a --no-restart flag to be passed to prevent the script from restarting certain apps and services including Terminal—which is good, since you'd likely be running the playbook from within Terminal.

At this point, you already have the majority of your local environment set up. Copying additional settings and tweaking things further is an exercise in adjusting your dotfiles or including another playbook that copies or links preference files into the right places.

I'm constantly tweaking my own development workstation, and for the most part, all my configuration is wrapped up in my Mac Development Ansible Playbook[97], available on GitHub. I'd encourage you to fork that project, as well as my dotfiles, if you'd like to get started automating the build of your own development workstation. Even if you don't use a Mac, most of the structure is similar; just substitute a different package manager, and start automating!

## Summary

Ansible is the best way to automate infrastructure provisioning and configuration. Ansible can also be used to configure your own workstation, saving you the time and frustration it takes to do so yourself. Unfortunately, you can't yet provision yourself a new top-of-the-line workstation with Ansible!

You can find the full playbook I'm currently using to configure my Macs on GitHub: Mac Development Ansible Playbook[98].

# Docker-based Infrastructure with Ansible

Docker is a highly optimized platform for building and running containers on local machines and servers in a highly efficient manner. You can think of Docker containers as sort-of lightweight virtual machines. This book won't go into the details of how Docker and Linux containers work, but will provide an introduction to how Ansible can integrate with Docker to build, manage, and deploy containers.

 Prior to running example Docker commands or building and managing containers using Ansible, you'll need to make sure Docker is installed either on your workstation or a VM or server where you'll be testing everything. Please see the installation guide for Docker[99] for help installing Docker on whatever platform you're using.

---

[97]https://github.com/geerlingguy/mac-dev-playbook
[98]https://github.com/geerlingguy/mac-dev-playbook
[99]https://docs.docker.com/installation/

# A brief introduction to Docker containers

Starting with an extremely simple example, let's build a Docker image from a Dockerfile. In this case, we want to show how Dockerfiles work and how we can use Ansible to build the image in the same way as if we were to use the command line with `docker build`.

Let's start with a really simple Dockerfile:

```
1   # Build an example Docker container image.
2   FROM busybox
3   MAINTAINER Jeff Geerling <geerlingguy@mac.com>
4
5   # Run a command when the container starts.
6   CMD ["/bin/true"]
```

This Docker container doesn't do much, but that's okay; we just want to build it and verify that it's present and working—first with Docker, then with Ansible.

Save the above file as `Dockerfile` inside a new directory, and then on the command line, run the following command to build the container:

```
$ docker build -t test .
```

After a few seconds, the Docker image should be built, and if you list all local images with `docker image`, you should see your new test image (along with the busybox image, which was used as a base):

```
$ docker images
REPOSITORY    TAG      IMAGE ID       CREATED             VIRTUAL SIZE
test          latest   50d6e6479bc7   About a minute ago  2.433 MB
busybox       latest   4986bf8c1536   2 weeks ago         2.433 MB
```

If you want to run the container image you just created, enter the following:

```
$ docker run --name=test test
```

This creates a Docker container with the name test, and starts the container. Since the only thing our container does is calls /bin/true, the container will run the command, then exit. You can see the current status of all your containers (whether or not they're actively running) with the docker ps -a command:

```
$ docker ps -a
CONTAINER ID   IMAGE         [...]   CREATED        STATUS
bae0972c26d4   test:latest   [...]   3 seconds ago  Exited (0) 2s ago
```

You can control the container using either the container ID (in this case, bae0972c26d4) or the name (test); start with docker start [container], stop with docker stop [container], delete/remove with docker rm [container].

If you delete the container (docker rm test) and the image you built (docker rmi test), you can experiment with the Dockerfile by changing it and rebuilding the image with docker build, then running the resulting image with docker run. For example, if you change the command from /bin/true to /bin/false, then run build and run the container, docker ps -a will show that the container exited with the status code 1 instead of 0.

For our purposes, this is a simple enough introduction to how Docker works. To summarize:

- Dockerfiles contain the instructions Docker uses to build containers.
- docker build builds Dockerfiles and generates container images.
- docker images lists all images present on the system.
- docker run runs created images.
- docker ps -a lists all containers, both running and stopped.

When developing Dockerfiles to containerize your own applications, you will likely want to get familiar with the Docker CLI and how the process works from a manual perspective. But when building the final images and running them on your servers, Ansible can help ease the process.

## Using Ansible to build and manage containers

Ansible has a built-in Docker module[100] that integrates nicely with Docker for container management. We're going to use it to automate the building and running of the container (managed by the Dockerfile) we just created.

Move the Dockerfile you had into a subdirectory, and create a new Ansible playbook (call it main.yml) in the project root directory. The directory layout should look like:

```
docker/
  main.yml
  test/
    Dockerfile
```

Inside the new playbook, add the following:

```
1   ---
2   - hosts: localhost
3     connection: local
4
5     tasks:
6       - name: Build Docker image from Dockerfiles.
7         docker_image:
8           name: test
9           path: test
10          state: build
```

The playbook uses the docker_image module to build an image. Provide a name for the image, the path to the Dockerfile (in this case, inside the test directory), and tell Ansible via the state parameter whether the image should be present, absent, or built (via build).

 Ansible's Docker integration may require you to install an extra Docker python library on the system running the Ansible playbook. For example, on ArchLinux, if you get the error "failed to import Python module", you will need to install the python2-docker-py package.

---

[100]http://docs.ansible.com/docker_module.html

The `docker_image` module is listed as being deprecated as of early 2015. The module's functionality will soon be moved into the main `docker` module, but until that time, this playbook should work as-is.

Run the playbook ($ `ansible-playbook main.yml`), and then list all the Docker images ($ `docker images`). If all was successful, you should see a fresh `test` image in the list.

Run `docker ps -a` again, though, and you'll see that the new `test` image was never run and is absent from the output. Let's remedy that by adding another task to our Ansible playbook:

```
12  - name: Run the test container.
13    docker:
14      image: test:latest
15      name: test
16      state: running
```

If you run the playbook again, Ansible will run the Docker container. Check the list of containers with `docker ps -a`, and you'll note that the `test` container is again present.

You can remove the container and the image via ansible by changing the `state` parameter to `absent` for both tasks.

 This playbook assumes you have both Docker and Ansible installed on whatever host you're using to test Docker containers. If this is not the case, you may need to modify the example so the Ansible playbook is targeting the correct `hosts` and using the right connection settings. Additionally, if the user account under which you run the playbook can't run `docker` commands, you may need to use `become` with this playbook.

 The code example above can be found in the Ansible for DevOps GitHub repository[101].

---

[101]https://github.com/geerlingguy/ansible-for-devops/tree/master/docker

# Building a Flask app with Ansible and Docker

Let's build a more useful Docker-powered environment, with a container that runs our application (built with Flask, a lightweight Python web framework), and a container that runs a database (MySQL), along with a data container. We need a separate data container to persist the MySQL database, because data changed inside the MySQL container is lost every time the container stops.

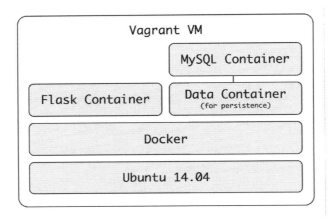

**Docker stack for Flask App**

We'll create a VM using Vagrant to run our Docker containers so the same Docker configuration can be tested on on any machine capable of running Ansible and Vagrant. Create a docker folder, and inside it, the following Vagrantfile:

```
1   # -*- mode: ruby -*-
2   # vi: set ft=ruby :
3
4   VAGRANTFILE_API_VERSION = "2"
5
6   Vagrant.configure(VAGRANTFILE_API_VERSION) do |config|
7     config.vm.box = "geerlingguy/ubuntu1404"
8     config.vm.network :private_network, ip: "192.168.33.39"
9     config.ssh.insert_key = false
10
```

```
11    config.vm.provider :virtualbox do |v|
12      v.customize ["modifyvm", :id, "--name", "docker.dev"]
13      v.customize ["modifyvm", :id, "--natdnshostresolver1", "on"]
14      v.customize ["modifyvm", :id, "--memory", 1024]
15      v.customize ["modifyvm", :id, "--cpus", 2]
16      v.customize ["modifyvm", :id, "--ioapic", "on"]
17    end
18
19    # Enable provisioning with Ansible.
20    config.vm.provision "ansible" do |ansible|
21      ansible.playbook = "provisioning/main.yml"
22    end
23
24  end
```

We'll use Ubuntu 14.04 for this example, and we've specified an Ansible playbook (`provisioning/main.yml`) to set everything up. Inside `provisioning/main.yml`, we need to first install and configure Docker (which we'll do using the Ansible Galaxy role `angstwad.docker_ubuntu`), then run some additional setup tasks, and finally build and start the required Docker containers:

```
1   ---
2   - hosts: all
3     become: yes
4
5     roles:
6       - role: angstwad.docker_ubuntu
7
8     tasks:
9       - include: setup.yml
10      - include: docker.yml
```

We're using `sudo` for everything because Docker either requires root privileges, or requires the current user account to be in the `docker` group. It's simplest for our purposes to set everything up with `sudo` by setting `become: yes`.

Angstwad's `docker_ubuntu` role requires no additional settings or configuration, so we can move on to `setup.yml` (in the same `provisioning` directory alongside `main.yml`):

```
1   ---
2   - name: Install Pip.
3     apt: name=python-pip state=present
4     become: yes
5
6   - name: Install Docker Python library.
7     pip: name=docker-py state=present
8     become: yes
```

Ansible needs the `docker-py` library in order to control Docker via Python, so we install `pip`, then use it to install `docker-py`.

Next is the meat of the playbook: `docker.yml` (also in the `provisioning` directory). The first task is to build Docker images for our data, application, and database containers:

```
1    ---
2    - name: Build Docker images from Dockerfiles.
3      docker_image:
4        name: "{{ item.name }}"
5        tag: "{{ item.tag }}"
6        path: "/vagrant/provisioning/{{ item.directory }}"
7        state: build
8      with_items:
9        - { name: data, tag: "data", directory: data }
10       - { name: www, tag: "flask", directory: www }
11       - { name: db, tag: mysql, directory: db }
```

Don't worry that we haven't yet created the actual Dockerfiles required to create the Docker images; we'll do that after we finish structuring everything with Ansible.

Like our earlier usage of `docker_image`, we supply a `name`, `path`, and `state` for each image. In this example, we're also adding a `tag`, which behaves like a git tag, allowing future Docker commands to use the images we created at a specific version. We'll be building three containers, data, www, and db, and we're pointing Docker to the path /vagrant/provisioning/[directory], where [directory] contains the Dockerfile and any other helpful files to be used to build the Docker image.

After building the images, we will need to start each of them (or at least make sure a container is *present*, in the case of the data container—since you can use data volumes from non-running containers). We'll do that in three separate docker tasks:

```
13    # Data containers don't need to be running to be utilized.
14    - name: Run a Data container.
15      docker:
16        image: data:data
17        name: data
18        state: present
19
20    - name: Run a Flask container.
21      docker:
22        image: www:flask
23        name: www
24        state: running
25        command: python /opt/www/index.py
26        ports: "80:80"
27
28    - name: Run a MySQL container.
29      docker:
30        image: db:mysql
31        name: db
32        state: running
33        volumes_from: data
34        command: /opt/start-mysql.sh
35        ports: "3306:3306"
```

Each of these containers' configuration is a little more involved than the previous. In the case of the first container, it's just present; Ansible will ensure a data container is present.

For the Flask container, we need to make sure our app is not only running, but *continues* to run. So, unlike our earlier usage of /bin/true to run a container briefly and exit, in this case we will provide an explicit command to run:

```
command: python /opt/www/index.py
```

Calling the script directly will launch the app in the foreground and log everything to stdout, making it easy to inspect what's going on with docker logs [container] if needed.

Additionally, we want to map the container's port 80 to the host's port 80, so external users can load pages over HTTP. This is done using the ports option, passing data just as you would using Docker's --publish syntax.

The Flask container will have a static web application running on it, and has no need for extra non-transient file storage, but the MySQL container will mount a data volume from the data container, so it has a place to store data that won't vanish when the container dies and is restarted.

Thus, for the db container, we have two special options: the volumes_from option, which mounts volumes from the specified container (in this case, the data container), and the command, which calls a shell script to start MySQL. We'll get to why we're running a shell script and not launching a MySQL daemon directly in a bit.

Now that we have the playbook structured to build our simple Docker-based infrastructure, we'll build out each of the three Dockerfiles and related configuration to support the data, www, and db containers.

At this point, we should have a directory structure like:

```
docker/
  provisioning/
    data/
    db/
    www/
    docker.yml
    main.yml
    setup.yml
  Vagrantfile
```

 It's best to use lightweight base images without any extra frills instead of heavyweight 'VM-like' images. Additionally, lightweight server environments where containers are built and run, like CoreOS, don't need the baggage of a standard Linux distribution. If you need Ansible available for configuration and container management in such an environment, you also need to have Python and other dependencies installed. Check out these two resources in particular for tips and tricks with managing and configuring containers with Ansible on CoreOS servers: Managing CoreOS with Ansible[102] and Provisioning CoreOS with Ansible[103].

## Data storage container

For the data storage container, we don't need much; we just need to create a directory and set it as an exposed mount point using VOLUME:

---

[102]https://coreos.com/blog/managing-coreos-with-ansible/

[103]http://www.tazj.in/en/1410951452

```
1   # Build a simple MySQL data volume Docker container.
2   FROM busybox
3   MAINTAINER Jeff Geerling <geerlingguy@mac.com>
4
5   # Create data volume for MySQL.
6   RUN mkdir -p /var/lib/mysql
7   VOLUME /var/lib/mysql
```

We create a directory (line 6), and expose the directory as a volume (line 7) which can be mounted by the host or other containers. Save the above into a new file, `docker/provisioning/data/Dockerfile`.

 This container builds on top of the official `busybox` base image. Busybox is an extremely simple distribution that is Linux-like but does not contain every option or application generally found in popular distributions like Debian, Ubuntu, or RHEL. Since we only need to create and share a directory, we don't need any additional 'baggage' inside the container. In the Docker world, it's best to use the most minimal base images possible, and to only install and run the bare necessities inside each container to support the container's app.

## Flask container

Flask[104] is a lightweight Python web framework "based on Werkzeug, Jinja 2 and good intentions". It's a great web framework for small, fast, and robust websites and apps, or even a simple API. For our purposes, we need to build a Flask app that connects to a MySQL database and displays the status of the connection on a simple web page (very much like our PHP example, in the earlier Highly-Available Infrastructure example).

Here's the code for the Flask app (save it as `docker/provisioning/www/index.py.j2`):

---

[104]http://flask.pocoo.org/

```
1    # Infrastructure test page.
2    from flask import Flask
3    from flask import Markup
4    from flask import render_template
5    from flask.ext.sqlalchemy import SQLAlchemy
6
7    app = Flask(__name__)
8
9    # Configure MySQL connection.
10   db = SQLAlchemy()
11   db_uri = 'mysql://admin:admin@{{ host_ip_address }}/\
12   information_schema'
13   app.config['SQLALCHEMY_DATABASE_URI'] = db_uri
14   db.init_app(app)
15
16   @app.route("/")
17   def test():
18       mysql_result = False
19       try:
20           if db.session.query("1").from_statement("SELECT 1").all():
21               mysql_result = True
22       except:
23           pass
24
25       if mysql_result:
26           result = Markup('<span style="color: green;">PASS</span>')
27       else:
28           result = Markup('<span style="color: red;">FAIL</span>')
29
30       # Return the page with the result.
31       return render_template('index.html', result=result)
32
33   if __name__ == "__main__":
34       app.run(host="0.0.0.0", port=80)
```

This simple app defines one route (/), listens on every interface on port 80, and shows

a MySQL connection status page rendered by the template index.html. There's
nothing particularly complicated in this application, but there is one Jinja2 varible ({{
host_ip_address }}) which an Ansible playbook will replace during deployment,
and the app has a few dependencies (like flask-sqlalchemy) which will need to be
installed via the Dockerfile.

Since we are using a Jinja2 template to render the page, let's create that template
in docker/provisioning/www/templates/index.html (Flask automatically picks up
any templates inside a templates directory):

```
1   <!DOCTYPE html>
2   <html>
3   <head>
4     <title>Flask + MySQL Docker Example</title>
5     <style>* { font-family: Helvetica, Arial, sans-serif }</style>
6   </head>
7   <body>
8     <h1>Flask + MySQL Docker Example</h1>
9     <p>MySQL Connection: {{ result }}</p>
10  </body>
11  </html>
```

In this case, the .html template contains a Jinja2 variable ({{ result }}), and Flask
will fill in that variable with the status of the MySQL connection.

Now that we have the app defined, we need to build the container to run the app.
Here is a Dockerfile that will install all the required dependencies, then copy a simple
Ansible playbook and the app itself into place so we can do the more complicated
configuration (like copying a template with variable replacement) through Ansible:

```
1   # A simple Flask app container.
2   FROM ansible/ubuntu14.04-ansible
3   MAINTAINER Jeff Geerling <geerlingguy@mac.com>
4
5   # Install Flask app dependencies.
6   RUN apt-get install -y libmysqlclient-dev python-dev
7   RUN pip install flask flask-sqlalchemy mysql-python
8
9   # Install playbook and run it.
10  COPY playbook.yml /etc/ansible/playbook.yml
11  COPY index.py.j2 /etc/ansible/index.py.j2
12  COPY templates /etc/ansible/templates
13  RUN mkdir -m 755 /opt/www
14  RUN ansible-playbook /etc/ansible/playbook.yml --connection=local
15
16  EXPOSE 80
```

Instead of installing apt and pip packages using Ansible, we'll install them using RUN commands in the Dockerfile. This allows those commands to be cached by Docker. Generally, more complicated package installation and configuration is easier and more maintainable inside Ansible, but in the case of simple package installation, having Docker cache the steps so future docker build commands take seconds instead of minutes is worth the verbosity of the Dockerfile.

At the end of the Dockerfile, we run a playbook (which should be located in the same directory as the Dockerfile) and expose port 80 so the app can be accessed via HTTP by the outside world. Next we'll create the app deployment playbook.

Purists might cringe at the sight of an Ansible playbook inside a Dockerfile, and for good reason! Commands like the `ansible-playbook` command cover up configuration that might normally be done (and cached)
within Docker. Additionally, using the `ansible/ubuntu14.04-ansible`
base image (which includes Ansible) requires an initial download that's
50+ MB larger than a comparable debian or ubuntu image without Ansible. However, for brevity and ease of maintenance, we're using Ansible
to manage all the app configuration inside the container (otherwise we'd
need to run a bunch of verbose and incomprehensible shell commands to
replace Ansible's `template` functionality).

In order for the Flask app to function properly, we need to get the `host_ip_address`,
then replace the variable in the `index.py.j2` template. Create the Flask deployment
playbook at `docker/provisioning/www/playbook.yml`:

```
1   ---
2   - hosts: localhost
3     become: yes
4
5     tasks:
6       - name: Get host IP address.
7         shell: "/sbin/ip route|awk '/default/ { print $3 }'"
8         register: host_ip
9         changed_when: false
10
11      - name: Set host_ip_address variable.
12        set_fact:
13          host_ip_address: "{{ host_ip.stdout }}"
14
15      - name: Copy Flask app into place.
16        template:
17          src: /etc/ansible/index.py.j2
18          dest: /opt/www/index.py
19          mode: 0755
20
21      - name: Copy Flask templates into place.
```

```
22        copy:
23          src: /etc/ansible/templates
24          dest: /opt/www
25          mode: 0755
```

The shell command that registers the host_ip is a simple way to retrieve the IP while still letting Docker do it's own virtual network management.

The last two tasks copy the flask app and templates directory into place.

The docker/provisioning/www directory should now contain the following:

```
www/
  templates/
    index.html
  Dockerfile
  index.py.j2
  playbook.yml
```

## MySQL container

We've configured MySQL a few times throughout this book, so little time will be spent discussing how MySQL is set up. We'll instead dive into how MySQL is configured to work inside a Docker container, with a persistent data volume from the previously-configured data container.

First, we'll create a really simple Ansible playbook to install and configure MySQL using the geerlingguy.mysql role:

```
1   ---
2   - hosts: localhost
3     become: yes
4
5     vars:
6       mysql_users:
7         - name: admin
8           host: "%"
9           password: admin
10          priv: "*.*:ALL"
11
12    roles:
13      - geerlingguy.mysql
```

This playbook sets up one MySQL user using the mysql_users variable and runs the geerlingguy.mysql role. Save it as docker/provisioning/db/playbook.yml.

Next, we need to account for the fact that there are two conditions under which MySQL will be started:

1. When Docker builds the container initially (using docker build through Ansible's docker_image module).
2. When we launch the container and pass in the data volume (using docker run through Ansible's docker module).

In the latter case, the data volume's /var/lib/mysql directory will supplant the container's own directory, but it will be empty! Therefore, instead of just launching the MySQL daemon like we launched the Flask app in the www container, we need to build a small shell script that will run on container start to detect whether MySQL has already been setup inside /var/lib/mysql, and if it hasn't, to reconfigure MySQL so the data is there.

Here's a simple script to do just that, using the playbook we just created to do most of the heavy lifting. Save this as docker/provisioning/db/start-mysql.sh:

```
 1  #!/bin/bash
 2
 3  # If connecting to a new data volume, we need to reconfigure MySQL.
 4  if [[ ! -d /var/lib/mysql/mysql ]]; then
 5      rm -f ~/.my.cnf
 6      mysql_install_db
 7      ansible-playbook /etc/ansible/playbook.yml --connection=local
 8      mysqladmin shutdown
 9  fi
10
11  exec /usr/bin/mysqld_safe
```

This bash script checks if there's already a mysql directory inside MySQL's default data directory, and if not (as is the case when we run the container with the data volume), it will remove any existing .my.cnf connection file, run mysql_install_db to initialize MySQL, then run the playbook, and shut down MySQL.

Once that's all done (or if the persistent data volume has already been set up previously), MySQL is started with the mysqld_safe startup script which, according to the MySQL documentation[105], is "the recommended way to start a mysqld server on Unix".

Next comes the Dockerfile, where we'll make sure the playbook.yml playbook and start-mysql.sh script are put in the right places, and expose the MySQL port so other containers can connect to MySQL.

```
 1  # A simple MySQL container.
 2  FROM ansible/ubuntu14.04-ansible
 3  MAINTAINER Jeff Geerling <geerlingguy@mac.com>
 4
 5  # Install required Ansible roles.
 6  RUN ansible-galaxy install geerlingguy.mysql
 7
 8  # Copy startup script.
 9  COPY start-mysql.sh /opt/start-mysql.sh
```

---

[105]http://dev.mysql.com/doc/refman/5.6/en/mysqld-safe.html

```
10    RUN chmod +x /opt/start-mysql.sh
11
12    # Install playbook and run it.
13    COPY playbook.yml /etc/ansible/playbook.yml
14    RUN ansible-playbook /etc/ansible/playbook.yml --connection=local
15
16    EXPOSE 3306
```

Just as with the Flask app container, we're using a base image with Ubuntu 14.04 and Ansible. This time, since we're doing a bit more configuration via the playbook, we also need to install the `geerlingguy.mysql` role via Ansible Galaxy.

The `start-mysql.sh` script needs to be located in the `docker.yml` file we set up much earlier, where we're calling it with `command: /opt/start-mysql.sh`, so we copy it in place, then give +x permissions so Docker can execute the file.

Finally, the Ansible playbook that configures MySQL is copied into place, then run, and port 3306 is exposed.

The `docker/provisioning/db` directory should now contain the following:

```
db/
  Dockerfile
  playbook.yml
  start-mysql.sh
```

## Ship it!

Now that everything's in place, you should be able to cd into the main `docker` directory, and run `vagrant up`. After 10 minutes or so, Vagrant should show that Ansible provisioning was successful, and if you visit `http://192.168.33.39/` in your browser, you should see something like the following:

**Flask + MySQL Docker Example**

MySQL Connection: PASS

**Docker orchestration success!**

If you see "MySQL Connection: PASS", congratulations, everything worked! If it shows 'FAIL', you might need to give the MySQL a little extra time to finish it's reconfiguration, since it has to rebuild the database on first launch. If the page doesn't show up at all, you might want to compare your code with the Docker LAMP example[106] on GitHub.

## Summary

The entire Docker LAMP example[107] is available on GitHub, if you'd like to clone it and try it locally.

The Docker examples shown here barely scratch the surface of what makes Docker a fascinating and useful application deployment tool. Docker is still in its infancy, so there are dozens of ways to manage the building of Dockerfiles, the deployment of images, and the running and linking of containers. Ansible is a solid contender for managing Docker containers (*and* the infrastruction on which they run), and can even be used within a Dockerfile to simplify complex container configurations.

```
 _____
/ Any sufficiently advanced technology is \
| indistinguishable from magic.           |
\ (Arthur C. Clarke)                      /
 ----------------------------------------
        \   ^__^
         \  (oo)_____
            (__)\       )\/\
                ||----w |
                ||     ||
```

---

[106]https://github.com/geerlingguy/ansible-vagrant-examples/tree/master/docker
[107]https://github.com/geerlingguy/ansible-vagrant-examples/tree/master/docker

# Chapter 9 - Deployments with Ansible

Deploying application code to servers is one of the hardest, but most rewarding, tasks of any development team. Most shops using traditional deployment techniques (manual steps, shell scripts, and prayers) dread deployments, especially for complex, monolithic apps.

Deployments are less daunting when you adopt modern deployment processes and use the right amount of automation. In the best case, deployments become so boring and routine they barely register as a blip on your team's radar.

Consider Etsy, a company whose engineers are deploying code to production up to 40 times per day[108], with no manual intervention from the operations team. The operations team is free to work on more creative endeavors, and the developers see their code go live in near-real-time!

Etsy's production deployment schedule is enabled by a strong DevOps-oriented culture (with robust code repository management, continuous integration, well-tested code, feature flags, etc.). While it may not be immediately possible to start deploying *your* application to production 20 times a day, you can move a long way towards effortless deployments by automating deployments with Ansible.

## Deployment strategies

There are dozens of ways to deploy code to servers. For the most basic applications, you may only need to switch to a new tag in a code repository on the server and restarting a service.

For more complex applications, you might do a full Blue-Green deployment, where you build an entire new infrastructure alongside your current production infrastructure, run tests on the new infrastructure, then automatically cut over to the new

---

[108]http://www.slideshare.net/mikebrittain/principles-and-practices-in-continuous-deployment-at-etsy

instances. This may be overkill for many applications (especially if <100% uptime is acceptable), but it is becoming more and more common—and Ansible automates the entire process.

In this chapter, we will be covering the following deployment strategies:

1. Single-server deployments.
2. Zero-downtime multi-server deployments.
3. Capistrano-style and blue-green deployments.

These are three of the most common deployment techniques, and they cover many common use cases. There are other ways to strengthen your deployment processes, often involving application-level and organizational change, but those deployment aspects are out of the scope of this book.

# Simple single-server deployments

The vast majority of small applications and websites are easily run on a single virtual machine or dedicated server. Using Ansible to provision and manage the configuration on the server is a no-brainer. Even though you only have to manage *one* server, it's better to encapsulate all the setup so you don't end up with a *snowflake server.*

In this instance, we are managing a Ruby on Rails site that allows users to perform CRUD operations on articles (database records with a title and body).

The code repository for this app is located on GitHub in the demo-rails-app repository[109].

Begin by creating a new Vagrant VM for local testing using the following Vagrantfile:

---

[109]https://github.com/geerlingguy/demo-rails-app

```
1   # -*- mode: ruby -*-
2   # vi: set ft=ruby :
3
4   Vagrant.configure(2) do |config|
5     config.vm.box = "geerlingguy/ubuntu1404"
6
7     config.vm.provider "virtualbox" do |v|
8       v.name = "rails-demo"
9       v.memory = 1024
10      v.cpus = 2
11    end
12
13    config.vm.hostname = "rails-demo"
14    config.vm.network :private_network, ip: "192.168.33.7"
15
16    config.vm.provision "ansible" do |ansible|
17      ansible.playbook = "playbooks/main.yml"
18      ansible.sudo = true
19    end
20
21  end
```

In this case, we have a VM at the IP address 192.168.33.7. When provisioned, it will run the Ansible playbook defined in playbooks/main.yml on the VM.

## Provisioning a Ruby on Rails server

To prepare for our application deployment, we need to do the following:

1. Install git (our application is version controlled in a git repository).
2. Install Node.js (asset compilation requires its Javascript runtime).
3. Install Ruby (our application requires version 2.2.0 or later).
4. Install Passenger with Nginx (we need a fast web server to run our rails application).

5.  Install any other dependencies, and prepare the server for deployment.

Let's create a new playbook just for the provisioning tasks (we'll worry about deployment later), in a new file, playbooks/provision.yml:

```
1   ---
2   - hosts: all
3     become: yes
4
5     vars_files:
6       - vars.yml
7
8     roles:
9       - geerlingguy.git
10      - geerlingguy.nodejs
11      - geerlingguy.ruby
12      - geerlingguy.passenger
13
14    tasks:
15      - name: Install app dependencies.
16        apt: "name={{ item }} state=present"
17        with_items:
18          - libsqlite3-dev
19          - libreadline-dev
20
21      - name: Ensure app directory exists and is writeable.
22        file:
23          path: "{{ app_directory }}"
24          state: directory
25          owner: "{{ app_user }}"
26          group: "{{ app_user }}"
27          mode: 0755
```

This is a straightforward playbook. We'll need to define a few variables to make sure the geerlingguy.ruby role installs the correct version of Ruby (at least 2.2.0), and the geerlingguy.passenger role is configured to serve our app correctly.

There are also a few other variables we will need, like `app_directory` and `app_user`, so let's create the variables file now, at `playbooks/vars.yml`:

```
1  # Variables for our app.
2  app_directory: /opt/demo-rails-app
3  app_user: www-data
4
5  # Variables for Passenger and Nginx.
6  passenger_server_name: 0.0.0.0
7  passenger_app_root: /opt/demo-rails-app/public
8  passenger_app_env: production
9  passenger_ruby: /usr/local/bin/ruby
10
11 # Variables for Ruby installation.
12 ruby_install_from_source: true
13 ruby_download_url: http://cache.ruby-lang.org/pub/ruby/2.2/\
14 ruby-2.2.0.tar.gz
15 ruby_version: 2.2.0
```

The passenger variables tell Passenger to run a server available on every network interface, and to launch our app (which will be located in `/opt/demo-rails-app/public`) with `production` settings (the app's environment), using the `ruby` binary we have installed in `/usr/local/bin/ruby`.

The Ruby variables tell the `ruby` role to install Ruby 2.2.0 from source, since the packages available through Ubuntu's standard apt repositories only contain older versions.

The playbook specified in our Vagrantfile, `playbooks/main.yml`, doesn't yet exist. Let's create the playbook and include the above `provisioning.yml` playbook so our server will be provisioned successfully. We'll separate out the deployment steps into another playbook and include that separately. Inside `playbooks/main.yml`:

```
1  ---
2  - include: provision.yml
```

## Deploying a Rails app to the server

All the dependencies for our app's deployment were configured in `provision.yml`, so we're ready to build a playbook to perform all the deployment tasks.

Add a line to the `main.yml` file to include a new `deploy.yml` playbook:

```
1   ---
2   - include: provision.yml
3   - include: deploy.yml
```

Now we're ready to create the `deploy.yml` playbook, which will do the following:

1. Use git to check out the latest production release of the Rails app.
2. Copy over a `secrets.yml` template with secure app data required for running the app.
3. Make sure all the gems required for the app are installed (via Bundler).
4. Create the database (if it doesn't already exist).
5. Run `rake` tasks to make sure the database schema is up-to-date and all assets (like JS and CSS) are compiled.
6. Make sure the app files' ownership is set correctly so Passenger and Nginx serve them without error.
7. If any changes or updates were made, restart Passenger and Nginx.

Most of these tasks will use Ansible's modules, but for a few, we'll just wrap the normal deployment-related commands in `shell` since there aren't pre-existing modules to take care of them for us:

```
1    ---
2    - hosts: all
3      become: yes
4
5      vars_files:
6        - vars.yml
7
8      roles:
9        - geerlingguy.passenger
10
11     tasks:
12       - name: Ensure demo application is at correct release.
13         git:
14           repo: https://github.com/geerlingguy/demo-rails-app.git
15           version: "{{ app_version }}"
16           dest: "{{ app_directory }}"
17           accept_hostkey: true
18           force: yes
19         register: app_updated
20         notify: restart nginx
21
22       - name: Ensure secrets file is present.
23         template:
24           src: templates/secrets.yml.j2
25           dest: "{{ app_directory }}/config/secrets.yml"
26           owner: "{{ app_user }}"
27           group: "{{ app_user }}"
28           mode: 0664
29         notify: restart nginx
30
31       - name: Install required dependencies with bundler.
32         shell: "bundle install --path vendor/bundle \
33    chdir={{ app_directory }}"
34         when: app_updated.changed == true
35         notify: restart nginx
```

```
36
37      - name: Check if database exists.
38        stat: "path={{ app_directory }}/db/{{ app_environment.\
39 RAILS_ENV }}.sqlite3"
40        register: app_db_exists
41
42      - name: Create database.
43        shell: "bundle exec rake db:create chdir={{ app_directory }}"
44        when: app_db_exists.stat.exists == false
45        notify: restart nginx
46
47      - name: Perform deployment-related rake tasks.
48        shell: "{{ item }} chdir={{ app_directory }}"
49        with_items:
50          - bundle exec rake db:migrate
51          - bundle exec rake assets:precompile
52        environment: app_environment
53        when: app_updated.changed == true
54        notify: restart nginx
55
56      - name: Ensure demo application has correct user for files.
57        file:
58          path: "{{ app_directory }}"
59          state: directory
60          owner: "{{ app_user }}"
61          group: "{{ app_user }}"
62          recurse: yes
63        notify: restart nginx
```

The first thing you'll notice (besides the fact we've included the vars.yml file
again, since we need those variables in this playbook as well) is we've added
the geerlingguy.passenger role in this playbook. Since we'll be using one of the
handlers defined in that role (restart nginx), we need to include the role explicitly.
We could've added a separate handler specific to this playbook, but it's more
maintainable to reuse handlers from roles if necessary.

Let's walk through the tasks, one-by-one:

1. (Lines 12-20) We put all the application files in place by checking out the git repository at the version `app_version` into the directory `app_directory`. We set `accept_hostkey` to true so this task doesn't hang the first time we deploy the app (since we haven't yet accepted the Git server's hostkey).
2. (Lines 22-29) We copy a `secrets.yml` file to the application's configuration directory. There are different ways to deploy app secrets, but this is the easiest, and allows us to store the app secrets in an Ansible Vault-protected vars file if we so desire.
3. (Lines 31-34) If the `app_updated` variable shows a change occurred as part of the first `git` task, we'll run a bundler command to ensure all the latest bundled dependencies are installed in the `vendor/bundle` directory.
4. (Lines 36-43) Create the application database with `rake db:create` if it doesn't already exist. Since this application uses a SQLite database, it's a matter of checking if the .sqlite3 file exists, and if not, running the `db:create` task.
5. (Lines 45-52) If the `app_updated` variable shows a change occurred as part of the first `git` task, we'll also run a couple `rake` tasks to make sure the database schema is up to date, and all assets (like scripts and stylesheets) are compiled.
6. (Lines 54-61) Make sure all app files have the correct permissions for Passenger/Nginx to serve them correctly.

Because many of the tasks result in filesystem changes that could change the behavior of the application, they all notify the `restart nginx` handler provided by the `geerlingguy.passenger` role, so Passenger reloads the configuration and restarts the app.

There are a few new variables we need to add to `vars.yml`, and we also need to add the `secrets.yml.j2` template mentioned in the task that copies it into place.

First, we'll create the secrets file, inside `playbooks/templates/secrets.yml.j2`:

```
1  development:
2    secret_key_base: {{ app_secrets.dev }}
3
4  test:
5    secret_key_base: {{ app_secrets.test }}
6
7  production:
8    secret_key_base: {{ app_secrets.prod }}
```

We'll be using a dictionary variable for app_secrets, so let's add it and all the other new variables to playbooks/vars.yml:

```
1  ---
2  # Variables for our app.
3  app_version: 1.2.2
4  app_directory: /opt/demo-rails-app
5  app_user: www-data
6  app_secrets:
7    dev: fe562ec1e21eecc5af4d83f6a157a7
8    test: 4408f36dd290766d2f368fdfcedf4d
9    prod: 9bf801da1a24c9a103ea86a1438caa
10 app_environment:
11   RAILS_ENV: production
12
13 # Variables for Passenger and Nginx.
14 passenger_server_name: 0.0.0.0
15 passenger_app_root: /opt/demo-rails-app/public
16 passenger_app_env: production
17 passenger_ruby: /usr/local/bin/ruby
18
19 # Variables for Ruby installation.
20 ruby_install_from_source: true
21 ruby_download_url: http://cache.ruby-lang.org/pub/ruby/2.2/\
22 ruby-2.2.0.tar.gz
23 ruby_version: 2.2.0
```

Note the addition of the following variables to support our `deploy.yml` playbook:

- `app_version`: This is the git tag or branch tip to be deployed to the server.
- `app_secrets`: A dictionary of Rails app secrets, which are used to verify the integrity of signed app cookies. You can generate new, unique strings for these variables using `rake secret`.
- `app_environment`: Environment settings required for certain commands (like `bundle exec` and `rake`) to run with the correct Rails application environment.

## Provisioning and Deploying the Rails App

Since we now have our `provision.yml` and `deploy.yml` playbooks completed, and both are `included` in the `main.yml` playbook Vagrant will run, it's time to bring up the new VM using Vagrant, and see if our application works!

The structure of your project folder should look like this:

```
deployments/
  playbooks/
    templates/
      secrets.yml.j2
    deploy.yml
    main.yml
    provision.yml
    vars.yml
  Vagrantfile
```

Before running the playbook, we need to make sure all the role dependencies are present. If you were building everything from scratch, you might have a `roles` directory with all the roles inside, but in this case, since we're using roles from Ansible Galaxy, it's best to not include the role files directly with our playbook, but instead, add a `requirements.yml` file to the project and install the roles automatically with Galaxy.

Inside `requirements.yml`:

```
1    ---
2    - src: geerlingguy.git
3    - src: geerlingguy.ruby
4    - src: geerlingguy.nodejs
5    - src: geerlingguy.passenger
```

In the same directory as the requirements file, run the command $ `ansible-galaxy install -r requirements.yml`, and after a minute, all the required roles will be downloaded to your default Ansible roles directory, if they're not already present.

Change directory back to the main directory containing the `Vagrantfile`, and run `vagrant up`. Assuming everything runs correctly, you should see the playbook complete successfully after a few minutes:

```
TASK: [Ensure demo application has correct user for files.] *********
changed: [default]

NOTIFIED: [geerlingguy.passenger | restart nginx] ******************
changed: [default]

PLAY RECAP ********************************************************
default                    : ok=46    changed=28    unreachable=0    failed=0
```

Now, jump over to a web browser and load `http://192.168.33.7/`. You should see something like the following:

**Demonstration Rails app running successfully.**

Try creating, updating, and deleting a few articles to make sure the database and all app functionality is working correctly:

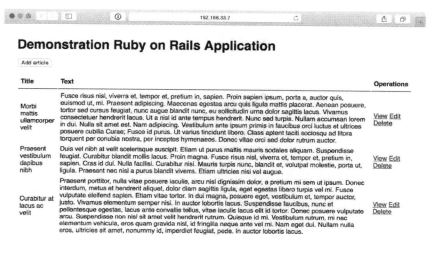

**A Rails app to perform CRUD operations on Articles.**

The app seems to function perfectly, but it could use some improvements. After more development work, we have a new version of to deploy. We could update the `app_version` variable in `vars.yml` and run `vagrant provision` to run the entire provisioning and deployment playbook again, but to save time using our flexible playbook layout (with separate provisioning and deployment playbooks), we can run the `deploy.yml` playbook separately.

## Deploying application updates

First, to test deployment without provisioning, we need to create an inventory file to tell Ansible how to connect directly to the Vagrant-managed VM.

Create the file `playbooks/inventory-ansible` with the following contents:

```
1  [rails]
2  192.168.33.7
3
4  [rails:vars]
5  ansible_ssh_user=vagrant
6  ansible_ssh_private_key_file=~/.vagrant.d/insecure_private_key
```

 If you were creating this playbook for a server or VM running outside of Vagrant's control, you'd probably have already created an inventory file or added the server to your global inventory, but when we're working with Vagrant, it's often convenient to use Vagrant's own dynamically-managed inventory. Running playbooks outside of Vagrant's up/provision functionality requires us to create a separate inventory file.

Test the ability to run the deploy.yml playbook by running the following command inside the playbooks directory:

```
$ ansible-playbook deploy.yml -i inventory-ansible
```

Hopefully the playbook completed its run successfully. It may have reported a change in the "Ensure demo application has correct user for files" task, and if so, it will have restarted Passenger. Run it again, and ansible should report no changes:

```
PLAY RECAP *********************************************************
192.168.33.7              : ok=16   changed=0   unreachable=0    failed=0
```

Hopefully you've noticed running the deploy.yml playbook standalone is much faster than running the provision and deploy playbooks together (deployment only takes 16 tasks, while both playbooks add up to 70+ tasks!). In the future, we can deploy application updates using only the deploy.yml playbook and changing the app_version either in vars.yml or by specifying the version on the command line in the ansible-playbook command.

It's generally preferred to change variables in vars files that are versioned with your playbooks, rather than specify them through inventory files, environment variables, or on the command line. This way the entire state of your infrastructure is encapsulated in your playbook files, which ideally should be version controlled and managed similarly to the application they deploy. Plus, who wants to enter any more information on the command line than is absolutely required?

Our application is a fairly generic web application with updates to application code (which require a webserver reload), styles (which need recompiling), and possibly the database schema (which needs `rake migrate` tasks to be run). Any time `app_version` is changed inside `playbooks/vars.yml`, the deploy playbook will automatically run all the required tasks to get our app running with the latest code.

Update `app_version` to `1.3.0`, and then run the following command again:

```
$ ansible-playbook deploy.yml -i inventory-ansible
```

After a minute or so, the deployment should complete. Once complete, you'll see the much improved new version of the Demonstration Ruby on Rails Application:

**Rails app - version 1.3.0 with a responsive UI.**

Application update deployments involve incrementing the `app_version` to the latest git tag, then running the `deploy.yml` playbook again. The `main.yml` playbook can be run to ensure the entire server stack is in the correct state, but it's faster to just deploy the app updates.

# Zero-downtime multi-server deployments

If you need to run an application on multiple servers for horizontal scalability or redundancy, deployments can be cumbersome, resulting in downtime and complicated deployment processes—but not when you use Ansible!

Server Check.in[110] is a server and website monitoring service with a microservices-based architecture; there is a website, an API application, and a server checking application.

The server checking application needs to run on a variety of servers hosted around the world by different providers to provide redundancy and reliability. Server Check.in

---

[110]https://servercheck.in/

uses Ansible to manage *rolling deployments* for this application, so new code is deployed across all the servers in minutes while maintaining 100% uptime!

We'll emulate part of Server Check.in's infrastructure (the check server application) by deploying and updating a small Node.js application to a set of virtual machines. The code repository for this app is located on GitHub in the demo-nodejs-api repository[111]. Here's a diagram of the infrastructure we'll be building:

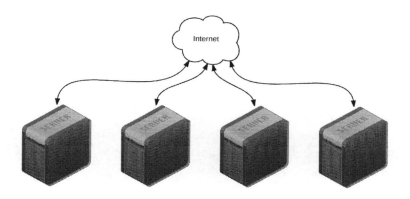

**Four servers connected to the Internet.**

To begin, create four lightweight Vagrant VMs using the following Vagrantfile:

```ruby
1   # -*- mode: ruby -*-
2   # vi: set ft=ruby :
3
4   Vagrant.configure("2") do |config|
5     # Base VM OS configuration.
6     config.vm.box = "geerlingguy/ubuntu1404"
7     config.vm.synced_folder '.', '/vagrant', disabled: true
8     config.ssh.insert_key = false
9
10    config.vm.provider :virtualbox do |v|
11      v.memory = 256
```

---

[111]https://github.com/geerlingguy/demo-nodejs-api

```
12      v.cpus = 1
13      v.linked_clone = true
14    end
15
16    # Define four VMs with static private IP addresses.
17    boxes = [
18      { :name => "nodejs1", :ip => "192.168.3.2" },
19      { :name => "nodejs2", :ip => "192.168.3.3" },
20      { :name => "nodejs3", :ip => "192.168.3.4" },
21      { :name => "nodejs4", :ip => "192.168.3.5" }
22    ]
23
24    # Provision each of the VMs.
25    boxes.each do |opts|
26      config.vm.define opts[:name] do |config|
27        config.vm.hostname = opts[:name]
28        config.vm.network :private_network, ip: opts[:ip]
29
30        # Provision all the VMs using Ansible after last VM is up.
31        if opts[:name] == "nodejs4"
32          config.vm.provision "ansible" do |ansible|
33            ansible.playbook = "playbooks/main.yml"
34            ansible.inventory_path = "inventory"
35            ansible.limit = "all"
36          end
37        end
38      end
39    end
40
41  end
```

The above `Vagrantfile` defines four VMs with 256MB of RAM and a unique hostname and IP address (defined by the `boxes` variable). Our Node.js app doesn't require much in the way of processing power or memory.

In the `provision` section of the playbook, we told Vagrant to provision the all the

VMs with Ansible, using the inventory file `inventory`, and the playbook `playbooks/main.yml`. Create these two files in the same folder as your Vagrantfile:

```
deployments-rolling/
  playbooks/
    main.yml
  inventory
  Vagrantfile
```

Inside the `inventory` file, we just need to define a list of all the Node.js API app VMs by IP address:

```
1   [nodejs-api]
2   192.168.3.2
3   192.168.3.3
4   192.168.3.4
5   192.168.3.5
6
7   [nodejs-api:vars]
8   ansible_ssh_user=vagrant
9   ansible_ssh_private_key_file=~/.vagrant.d/insecure_private_key
```

Inside the `main.yml` playbook, we'll call out two separate playbooks—one for the initial provisioning (installing Node.js and making sure the server is configured correctly), and another for deployment (ensuring our Node.js API app is present and running):

```
1   ---
2   - include: provision.yml
3   - include: deploy.yml
```

Go ahead and create the `provision.yml` and `deploy.yml` playbooks, starting with `provision.yml`:

```
1   ---
2   - hosts: nodejs-api
3     become: yes
4
5     vars:
6       nodejs_forever: true
7       firewall_allowed_tcp_ports:
8         - "22"
9         - "8080"
10
11    roles:
12      - geerlingguy.firewall
13      - geerlingguy.nodejs
```

This playbook runs on all the servers defined in our inventory file, and runs two roles on the servers: geerlingguy.firewall (which installs and configures a firewall, in this case opening ports 22 for SSH and 8080 for our app) and geerlingguy.nodejs (which installs Node.js, NPM, and forever, which we'll use to run our app as a daemon).

Since we're using two roles from Ansible Galaxy, it's best practice to also include those roles in a requirements file so CI tools and others using this playbook can install all the required roles.

Create a requirements.yml file in the root folder and add the following:

```
1   ---
2   - src: geerlingguy.firewall
3   - src: geerlingguy.nodejs
```

Whenever someone wants to run the playbook, the command ansible-galaxy install -r requirements.yml will install all the required roles.

At this point, your project directory should be structured like the following:

```
deployments-rolling/
  playbooks/
    deploy.yml
    main.yml
    provision.yml
  inventory
  requirements.yml
  Vagrantfile
```

Before we run `vagrant up` and see our infrastructure in action, we need to build out the `deploy.yml` playbook, which will ensure our app is present and running correctly on all the servers.

Inside `deploy.yml`, add the following:

```
1  ---
2  - hosts: nodejs-api
3    gather_facts: no
4    become: yes
5
6    vars_files:
7      - vars.yml
```

Use `become`, and set `gather_facts` to `no` to save a little time during deployments, since our app doesn't require any of the gathered system facts to run.

Since we have a few variables to define, and we'd like to track them separately for easier file revision history, we'll define the variables in a `vars.yml` file in the same directory as the `deploy.yml` playbook:

```
1  ---
2  app_repository: https://github.com/geerlingguy/demo-nodejs-api.git
3  app_version: "1.0.0"
4  app_directory: /opt/demo-nodejs-api
```

Once you've saved the `vars.yml` file, continue building out `deploy.yml`, starting with a task to clone the app's repository (which we just defined in `vars.yml`):

```
 9    tasks:
10      - name: Ensure Node.js API app is present.
11        git:
12          repo: "{{ app_repository }}"
13          version: "{{ app_version }}"
14          dest: "{{ app_directory }}"
15          accept_hostkey: true
16        register: app_updated
17        notify: restart forever apps
```

Using variables for the git module's repo and version affords flexibility; app version changes might happen frequently, and it's easier to manage them in a separate vars.yml file.

We also want to notify a restart forever apps handler whenever the codebase is changed. We'll define the restart forever apps handler later in the playbook.

```
18      - name: Stop all running instances of the app.
19        command: "forever stopall"
20        when: app_updated.changed
21
22      - name: Ensure Node.js API app dependencies are present.
23        npm: "path={{ app_directory }}"
24        when: app_updated.changed
25
26      - name: Run Node.js API app tests.
27        command: "npm test chdir={{ app_directory }}"
28        when: app_updated.changed
```

Once the app is present on the server, we need to use npm to install dependencies (using Ansible's npm module), then run the app's test suite using npm test. To save time, we only stop the application, update dependencies, and run tests if the application has changed (using the app_updated variable we registered when checking out the application code).

Running the tests for the app during every deployment ensures the app is present and in a functioning state. Having a thorough unit and integration test suite running on every deployment is prerequisite to a frequent or continuously-integrated project! Running the tests during deployments also enables zero-downtime deployments, as we'll see later.

```
25      - name: Get list of all running Node.js apps.
26        command: forever list
27        register: forever_list
28        changed_when: false
29
30      - name: Ensure Node.js API app is started.
31        command: "forever start {{ app_directory }}/app.js"
32        when: "forever_list.stdout.find('app.js') == -1"
```

Once the app is present and running correctly, we need to make sure it's started. There's a command to get the list of all running apps (using forever), then a command to start the app if it's not already running.

```
34      - name: Add cron entry to start Node.js API app on reboot.
35        cron:
36          name: "Start Node.js API app"
37          special_time: reboot
38          job: "forever start {{ app_directory }}/app.js"
```

The final task adds a cron job to make sure the app is started after the server reboots. Since we're managing the deamonization of our app using forever instead of the OS's init system, it's best to make sure the app starts on system boot using a reboot cron job.

Remember when we added the line notify: restart forever apps to the task that ensured the app was present on the server? It's time to define this handler, which runs the command forever restartall (which does exactly what it says):

```
40    handlers:
41      - name: restart forever apps
42        command: "forever restartall"
```

At this point, the Ansible playbooks and Vagrant configuration should be complete. The playbook will clone the demo-nodejs-api project, run its tests to make sure everything's working correctly, then start the app using forever and make sure it's started whenever the the server reboots.

Run the command below to test all the new servers and make sure the app is running correctly:

```
$ for i in {2..5}; \
    do curl -w "\n" "http://192.168.3.$i:8080/hello/john"; \
  done
```

If all the servers are online, you should see the text "hello john" repeated four times (once for each server):

```
"hello john"
"hello john"
"hello john"
"hello john"
```

Run vagrant provision to run the entire provisioning and deployment process again, or just run ansible-playbook -i inventory playbooks/deploy.yml to run the deployment playbook again. In either case, you should see no changes, and Ansible should verify everything is ok.

You now have a fleet of Node.js API servers similar to Server Check.in's server checking infrastructure—except it doesn't do much yet! Luckily, the project has seen some new feature development since the initial 1.0.0 version you just deployed. We now need a way to get the new version deployed to and running on all the servers while maintaining 100% uptime for the API as a whole.

# Ensuring zero downtime with `serial` and integration tests

Now, after a little extra time in development, we have new features to deploy in a `1.0.1` version. You could run the exact same `ansible-playbook` command as above, adding in `--extra-vars "app_version=1.0.1"`, but best practice is to update the variable in your included variables file, since that change is tracked in version control and used for automated deployments.

Change the `app_version` in `playbooks/vars.yml` to `1.0.1`, and run the deployment playbook again:

```
ansible-playbook -i inventory playbooks/deploy.yml
```

Uh oh—after we deployed the new version, our tests started failing! Since we deployed to all four servers asynchronously, all four application servers are offline, and our boss and customers are going to be very angry.

In this case, rolling back is simple: revert to `1.0.0` and redeploy. Doing this now fixes the problem *this* time, but if part of the application update changed a database schema you could be in a world of hurt!

Ansible has two particular settings to protect you when you deploy to many servers while maintaining your infrastructure's overall integrity during a failed deployment.

Open the deployment playbook (`playbooks/deploy.yml`) and modify the initial settings to match the following:

```
1   ---
2   - hosts: nodejs-api
3     gather_facts: no
4     become: yes
5     serial: 2
```

Note the addition of `serial: 2`. This tells Ansible to run the entire playbook on two servers at a time. If you update `app_version` to `1.0.1` again, and run the playbook, you should see it run on two of the four servers, and once it hits the test failure, the playbook execution will stop—leaving your other two servers up (and saving you a few hours on a conference bridge explaining the outage).

You could again revert back to 1.0.0, but in the time you were deploying the failed version, developers finished a new version that got all tests passing again, 1.0.2. Go ahead and update app_version and run the playbook again.

```
PLAY RECAP ***********************************************************
192.168.3.2            : ok=8    changed=5    unreachable=0    failed=0
192.168.3.3            : ok=8    changed=5    unreachable=0    failed=0
192.168.3.4            : ok=8    changed=5    unreachable=0    failed=0
192.168.3.5            : ok=8    changed=5    unreachable=0    failed=0
```

*Whew!* Everything is back online and operational, and all tests are passing with the latest version of the application.

   Tests should rarely fail only on production. But there are many times where networking issues or even latency in third party services causes a random failure or two. Whenever you move beyond one server (usually to provide both redundancy and cacpacity), you will run into these transient issues. It's best to account for them in your automated deployment process by tuning serial and similar settings well.

Ansible exposes two different settings for controlling rolling deployment failure scenarios:

1. serial: Can be an integer (e.g. 3) or a percentage (e.g. 30%). Used to control how many hosts Ansible will manage at once.
2. max_fail_percentage: An integer between 1-100. Used to tell Ansible what percentage of hosts can fail a task before the play will be aborted.

If you have some headroom in your infrastructure, set these values higher. If you have only as much infrastructure running as your application needs, and having more than one or two servers offline would put your infrastructure into a bad state, you should be more conservative with these settings—and maybe provision a little more capacity!

# Deploying to app servers behind a load balancer

In the case of Server Check.in, there are two separate API layers that manage the complexity of ensuring all server checks happen, regardless of whether certain servers are up or down. The 'load balancing' occurs on the application layer instead of as a separate infrastructure layer (this is extremely helpful when dealing with global latency and network reliability variation).

For many applications, especially those with app servers close together (e.g. in the same data center) the infrastructure layer follows a more traditional layout, with a load balancer to handle the API request distribution:

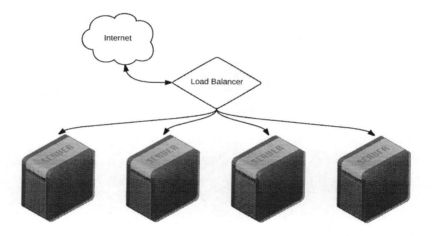

**Four servers behind a load balancer.**

For a demonstration of zero-downtime deployment with a load balancer, let's build a local infrastructure with one HAProxy load balancer and two Apache webservers.

First, create a new project folder `deployments-balancer`, and within it, create the following Vagrantfile:

```ruby
1   # -*- mode: ruby -*-
2   # vi: set ft=ruby :
3
4   Vagrant.configure("2") do |config|
5     # Base VM OS configuration.
6     config.vm.box = "geerlingguy/ubuntu1404"
7     config.vm.synced_folder '.', '/vagrant', disabled: true
8     config.ssh.insert_key = false
9
10    config.vm.provider :virtualbox do |v|
11      v.memory = 256
12      v.cpus = 1
13      v.linked_clone = true
14    end
15
16    # Define four VMs with static private IP addresses.
17    boxes = [
18      { :name => "bal1", :ip => "192.168.4.2" },
19      { :name => "app1", :ip => "192.168.4.3" },
20      { :name => "app2", :ip => "192.168.4.4" }
21    ]
22
23    # Provision each of the VMs.
24    boxes.each do |opts|
25      config.vm.define opts[:name] do |config|
26        config.vm.hostname = opts[:name]
27        config.vm.network :private_network, ip: opts[:ip]
28
29        # Provision all the VMs using Ansible after last VM is up.
30        if opts[:name] == "app2"
31          config.vm.provision "ansible" do |ansible|
32            ansible.playbook = "playbooks/provision.yml"
33            ansible.inventory_path = "inventory"
34            ansible.limit = "all"
35          end
```

```
36          end
37        end
38      end
39
40  end
```

This Vagrantfile will create three servers running Ubuntu 14.04: bal1 (the balancer), and app1 and app2 (the application servers). We referenced an Ansible playbook at playbooks/provision.yml (to install the required software on the servers), as well as a custom inventory file at inventory. First, create the inventory file (inventory, in the same directory as the Vagrantfile), with the appropriate groupings and connection variables:

```
1   [balancer]
2   192.168.4.2
3
4   [app]
5   192.168.4.3
6   192.168.4.4
7
8   [deployments:children]
9   balancer
10  app
11
12  [deployments:vars]
13  ansible_ssh_user=vagrant
14  ansible_ssh_private_key_file=~/.vagrant.d/insecure_private_key
```

With this inventory, we can operate on just the balancer, just the app servers, or all the servers together (in the deployments group). Next, create a playbook (at playbooks/provision.yml) to provision the servers:

```
1    ---
2    - hosts: balancer
3      become: yes
4
5      vars:
6        firewall_allowed_tcp_ports:
7          - "22"
8          - "80"
9        haproxy_backend_servers:
10         - name: 192.168.4.3
11           address: 192.168.4.3:80
12         - name: 192.168.4.4
13           address: 192.168.4.4:80
14
15     roles:
16       - geerlingguy.firewall
17       - geerlingguy.haproxy
18
19   - hosts: app
20     become: yes
21
22     vars:
23       firewall_allowed_tcp_ports:
24         - "22"
25         - "80"
26
27     roles:
28       - geerlingguy.firewall
29       - geerlingguy.apache
```

These two plays set up a firewall on both servers, and configure HAProxy on the load balancer, and Apache (with its default configuration) on the app servers. The only required configuration to get this infrastructure working is haproxy_backend_servers. We let the geerlingguy.firewall, geerlingguy.haproxy, and geerlingguy.apache roles do all the hard work for us.

Now, to make sure we have all these roles installed, create a requirements file to install the roles from Ansible Galaxy. Create `requirements.yml` in the same directory as the Vagrantfile, with the following contents:

```
1   ---
2   - src: geerlingguy.firewall
3   - src: geerlingguy.haproxy
4   - src: geerlingguy.apache
```

To install the required roles, run `sudo ansible-galaxy install -r requirements.yml`.

At this point, if you want to bring up your local load-balanced infrastructure, run `vagrant up` in the `deployments-balancer` directory, and wait a few minutes. Once everything is up and running, visit `http://192.168.4.2/`, and you should see the default Ubuntu Apache2 landing page:

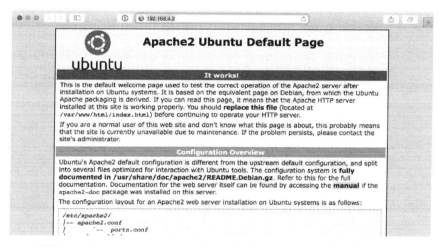

**HAProxy is serving requests through the Apache backend servers.**

Verify round-robin load balancing is working by running the following command:

```
1  $ for i in {1..5}; do curl -Is http://192.168.4.2/ | grep Cookie; \
2  done
3  Set-Cookie: SERVERID=192.168.4.4; path=/
4  Set-Cookie: SERVERID=192.168.4.3; path=/
5  Set-Cookie: SERVERID=192.168.4.4; path=/
6  Set-Cookie: SERVERID=192.168.4.3; path=/
7  Set-Cookie: SERVERID=192.168.4.4; path=/
```

You should see the load balancer distributing requests between the two backend app servers.

When you deploy new code to the application servers, you need to guarantee the load balancer always has an app server from which requests can be served, so you want to use serial to do the deployment on each server (or groups of servers) in sequence. To make sure the servers are properly removed from HAProxy, then added again post-deploy, use pre_tasks and post_tasks.

Create another playbook alongside provision.yml called deploy.yml, with the following contents:

```
1  ---
2  - hosts: app
3    become: yes
4    serial: 1
5
6    pre_tasks:
7      - name: Disable the backend server in HAProxy.
8        haproxy:
9          state: disabled
10         host: '{{ inventory_hostname }}'
11         socket: /var/lib/haproxy/stats
12         backend: habackend
13       delegate_to: "{{ item }}"
14       with_items: groups.balancer
15
16   tasks:
```

```
17        - debug: msg="Deployment would be done here."
18
19      post_tasks:
20        - name: Wait for backend to come back up.
21          wait_for:
22            host: '{{ inventory_hostname }}'
23            port: 80
24            state: started
25            timeout: 60
26
27        - name: Enable the backend server in HAProxy.
28          haproxy:
29            state: enabled
30            host: '{{ inventory_hostname }}'
31            socket: /var/lib/haproxy/stats
32            backend: habackend
33          delegate_to: "{{ item }}"
34          with_items: groups.balancer
```

This playbook doesn't do much in terms of actual deployment, but it does illustrate how to do a zero-downtime rolling update over two or more application servers:

1. In pre_tasks, the haproxy module disables the current app server (using the inventory_hostname variable) on all the load balancers in the balancer group, using with_items. The HAProxy task is delegated to each of the balancer servers (in our case, only one), since the task affects the load balancer, not the current app host.
2. In the post_tasks, we first wait_for port 80 to be available, and once it is, the haproxy module re-enables the current app server on all the load balancers.

Run the playbook on the local infrastructure with the following command:

```
1  $ ansible-playbook -i inventory playbooks/deploy.yml
```

It should only take a few seconds to run, and once it's finished, all the servers should be back in the mix for the load balancer. If you want to quickly confirm the deployment playbook is working as it should, add a task which always fails, immediately following the debug task:

```
15  [...]
16  tasks:
17    - debug: msg="Deployment would be done here."
18    - command: /bin/false
19
20  post_tasks:
21  [...]
```

If you run the deployment playbook again, wait for it to fail, then run the curl command again, you'll notice all the requests are being directed to the second app server:

```
1  $ for i in {1..5}; do curl -Is http://192.168.4.2/ | grep Cookie; do\
2  ne
3  Set-Cookie: SERVERID=192.168.4.4; path=/
4  Set-Cookie: SERVERID=192.168.4.4; path=/
5  Set-Cookie: SERVERID=192.168.4.4; path=/
6  Set-Cookie: SERVERID=192.168.4.4; path=/
7  Set-Cookie: SERVERID=192.168.4.4; path=/
```

Fix the deployment by removing the /bin/false command. Run the playbook one more time to restore the infrastructure to a fully functional state.

This demonstration may seem basic, but the pre_tasks and post_tasks in the playbook are identical to what many large-scale production infrastructure deployments use!

# Capistrano-style and blue-green deployments

Many developers who deal with Ruby applications are familiar with Capistrano[112], a task automation and application deployment application built with Ruby. Capis-

---

[112]http://capistranorb.com/

trano's basic style of deployment is to create dated release directories, then symlink the current release into a stable application directory, along with resources that are continuous among releases (like logs and uploaded files).

Capistrano does a lot more than that basic deployment model, but many people want to replicate a simple application deployment workflow (which also makes rollbacks easy, since you just revert the symlink to the previous release directory!). This is easy to do with Ansible, and rather than walk you through the entire process in this book, I'll point you to a few great resources and an Ansible Galaxy role that coordinates Capistrano-style deployments with ease:

- Rebuilding Capistrano-like deployment with Ansible[113]
- project_deploy role on Ansible Galaxy[114]
- Thoughts on deploying with Ansible[115] (background for the above role)
- Ansible project-deploy[116] (presentation about the above role)

Extending things a little further, many organizations use **blue-green** deployments. The basic concept involves bringing up a parallel production infrastructure, then switching over to it. The cutover may take only a few milliseconds and no active production infrastructure is ever offline during the deployment process.

A few different technologies and concepts, like container-based infrasturcture and microservices (which are faster to deploy), and better cloud autoscaling and load balancing options, have made blue-green deployments much easier than in the past.

This book won't go through a detailed example of this style of deployment, as the process is similar to other examples provided, the only difference being an additional task of switching a load balancer from the old to the new infrastructure once it's up and running. Ansible's blog has an excellent overview of AWS-based blue-green deployments: Immutable Systems and Ansible[117], and there are built-in modules to

---

[113]http://blog.versioneye.com/2014/09/24/rebuilding-capistrano-like-deployment-with-ansible/

[114]https://galaxy.ansible.com/list#/roles/732

[115]http://www.future500.nl/articles/2014/07/thoughts-on-deploying-with-ansible/

[116]http://www.slideshare.net/ramondelafuente/ansible-projectdeploy

[117]http://www.ansible.com/blog/immutable-systems

manage almost any type of load balancer you could use, including F5's BIG-IP[118], HAProxy[119], Citrix NetScaler[120], and Amazon ELB[121].

# Additional Deployment Features

There are a few other Ansible modules and options which are helpful in the context of deployments:

run_once[122] and delegate_to are extremely helpful in scenarios like updating a database schema or clearing an application's cache, where you need a particular task to only run one time, on a particular server:

```
- command: /opt/app/upgrade-database-schema
  run_once: true
  delegate_to: app1.example.com
```

Using run_once with delegate_to is similar to the pattern of using when: inventory_hostname == groups.groupname[0], but is a little more precise in describing what you're trying to achieve—running a command once on a specific host.

Another important aspect of a successful deployment is communication. If you're running playbooks as part of a CI/CD process, or in some other automated fashion, use one of the many built-in Ansible notification modules to share the deployment's progress via chat, email, or even text-to-speech on your Mac with the osx_say module! Ansible includes easy-to-use notification modules for:

- Campfire
- HipChat
- IRC
- Jabber

---

[118]http://docs.ansible.com/list_of_network_modules.html#f5

[119]http://docs.ansible.com/haproxy_module.html

[120]http://docs.ansible.com/netscaler_module.html

[121]http://docs.ansible.com/ec2_elb_module.html

[122]http://docs.ansible.com/playbooks_delegation.html#run-once

- Email
- Slack
- Twilio
- Amazon SNS
- etc.

Many playbooks include notifications in both the `pre_tasks` and `post_tasks` sections, notifying admins in a chat channel when a deployment begins or ends. For example:

```
post_tasks:
  - name: Tell everyone on IRC the deployment is complete.
    irc:
      channel: my-org
      server: irc.example.com
      msg: "Deployment complete!"
    delegate_to: 127.0.0.1
```

For a great primer on Ansible notifications, see Ansible Inc's blog post: Listen to your Servers Talk[123].

# Summary

Automating deployments with Ansible enables your development team to have their code on production servers more reliably and quickly, and it enables your operations team to spend less time on repetitive tasks, and more time improving your infrastructure.

This chapter outlined only a few of the most popular deployment techniques, but Ansible is flexible enough to handle almost any situation out of the box.

---

[123]http://www.ansible.com/blog/listen-to-your-servers-talk

```
 _____
/ One machine can do the work of fifty \
| ordinary men. No machine can do the   |
| work of one extraordinary man.        |
\ (Elbert Hubbard)                      /
 ------------------------------------
        \    ^__^
         \   (oo)_____
            (__)\        )\/\
                ||----w  |
                ||       ||
```

# Chapter 10 - Server Security and Ansible

The first configuration to be performed on any new server—especially any server with any exposure (direct or indirect) to the public Internet)—is security configuration.

There are nine basic measures to ensure servers are secure from unauthorized access or intercepted communications:

1. Use secure and encrypted communication.
2. Disable root login and use sudo.
3. Remove unused software, open only required ports.
4. Use the principle of least privilege.
5. Update the OS and installed software.
6. Use a properly-configured firewall.
7. Make sure log files are populated and rotated.
8. Monitor logins and block suspect IP addresses.
9. Use SELinux (Security-Enhanced Linux).

Your infrastructure is as weak as the weakest server; in many high-profile security breaches, one poorly-secured server acts as a gateway into the rest of the network. Don't let your servers be *those* servers! Good security also helps you achieve the holy grail of system administration—100% uptime.

In this chapter, you'll learn about Linux security and how Ansible helps secure your servers, following the basic topics above.

# A brief history of SSH and remote access

In the beginning, computers were the size of large conference rooms. A punch card reader would merrily accept pieces of paper with instructions the computer would run, and then a printer would etch the results into another piece of paper. Thousands of mechanical parts worked harmoniously (when they *did* work) to compute relatively simple commands.

As time progressed, computers became somewhat smaller, and interactive terminals became more user-friendly, but they were still wired directly into the computer being used. Mainframes came to the fore in the 1960s, originally used via typewriter and teletype interfaces, then via keyboards and small text displays. As networked computing became more mainstream in the 1970s and 1980s, remote terminal access was used to interact with the large central computers.

The first remote terminal interfaces assumed a high level of trust between the central computer and all those on the network, because the small, centralized networks used were physically isolated from one another.

## Telnet

In the late 1960s, the Telnet protocol was defined and started being used over TCP networks (normally on port 23) for remote control over larger private networks, and eventually the public Internet.

Telnet's underlying technology (a text-based protocol to transfer data between different systems) was the basis for many foundational communications protocols in use today, including HTTP, FTP, and POP3. However, plain text streams are not secure, and even with the addition of TLS and SASL, Telnet was never very secure by default. With the advent of SSH (which we'll get to in a bit), the protocol has declined in popularity for most remote administration purposes.

Telnet still has uses like configuring devices over local serial connections, or checking if a particular service is operating correctly on a remote server (like an HTTP server on port 80, mysql on port 3306, or munin on port 4949), but it is not installed by default on modern Linux distributions.

Plain text communications over a network are only as secure as the network's weakest link. In the early days of computer networking, networks were usually isolated to a specific company or educational institution, so transmitting things like passwords or secrets in plain text using the TCP protocol wasn't such a bad idea. Every part of the network (cabling, switches, and routers) was contained inside a secured physical perimeter. When connections started moving to the public Internet, this changed.

TCP packets can be intercepted over the Internet, at any point between the client and server, and these packets can easily be read if not encrypted. Therefore, plain text protocols are highly insecure, and should never be used to transmit sensitive information or system control data. Even on highly secure networks with properly-configured firewalls, it's a bad idea to use insecure communication methods like plain text rlogin and telnet connections for authentication and remote control.

Try running `traceroute google.com` in your terminal. Look at each of the hops between you and Google's CDN. Do you know who controls each of the devices between your computer and Google? Do you trust these operators with all of your personal or corporate secrets? Probably not. Each of these connection points—and each network device and cable connecting them—is a weak point exposing you to a man-in-the-middle attack. Strong encryption is needed between your computer and the destination if you want to ensure data security.

## rlogin, rsh and rcp

`rlogin` was introduced in BSD 4.2 in 1983, and has been distributed with many UNIX-like systems alongside Telnet until recently. rlogin was used widely during the 80s and much of the 90s.

Just like Telnet, a user could log into the remote system with a password, but rlogin additionally allowed automatic (passwordless) logins for users on trusted remote computers. rlogin also worked better than telnet for remote administration, as it worked correctly with certain characters and commands where telnet required extra translation.

However, like Telnet, rlogin still used plain text communications over TCP port 513 by default. rlogin also didn't have many safeguards against clients spoofing their true identities. Some of rlogin's intrinsic flaws were highlighted in a 1998 report by Carnegie Mellon, rlogin: The Untold Story[124].

rsh ("remote shell") is a command line program used alongside rlogin to execute individual shell commands remotely, and rcp ("remote copy") is used for remote file copies. rsh and rcp inherited the same security problems as rlogin, since they use the same connection method (over different ports).

## SSH

Secure Shell was created in 1995 by Finland native Tatu Ylönen, in response to a password-sniffing attack[125] at his university. Seeing the flaws in plain text communication for secure information, Tatu created Secure Shell/SSH with a strong emphasis on encryption and security.

His version of SSH was developed for a few years as freeware with liberal licensing, but as his SSH Communications Security Corporation[126] began limiting the license and commercializing SSH, alternative forks began to gain in popularity. The most popular fork, OSSH, by Swedish programmer Bjoern Groenvall, was chosen as a starting point by some developers from the OpenBSD project.

OpenBSD was (and still is!) a highly secure, free version of BSD UNIX, and the project's developers needed a secure remote communication protocol, so a few project members worked to clean up and improve OSSH[127] so it could be included in OpenBSD's 2.6 release in December 1999. From there, it was quickly ported and adopted for all major versions of Linux, and is now ubiquitous in the world of POSIX-compliant operating systems.

How does SSH work, and what makes it better than telnet or rlogin? It starts with the basic connection. SSH connection encryption works similarly to SSL for secure HTTP connections, but its authentication layer adds more security:

1. When you enter ssh user@example.host to connect to the example.host server as user, your client and the host exchange keys.

---

[124]http://resources.sei.cmu.edu/asset_files/TechnicalReport/1998_005_001_16670.pdf

[125]http://en.wikipedia.org/wiki/Secure_Shell#Version_1.x

[126]http://www.ssh.com/

[127]http://www.openbsd.org/openssh/history.html

2. If you're connecting to a host the first time, or if the host's key has changed since last time you connected (this happens often when connecting via DNS rather than directly by IP), SSH will prompt you for your approval of the host key.

3. If you have a private key in your ~/.ssh folder matching one of the keys in ~/.ssh/authorized_keys on the remote system, the connection continues to step 4. Otherwise, if password authentication is allowed, SSH prompts you for your password. There are other authentication methods as well, such as Kerberos, but they are less common and not covered in this book.

4. The transferred key is used to create a session key used for the remainder of the connection, encrypting all communication with a cipher such as AES, 3DES, Blowfish or RC4 ('arcfour').

5. The connection remains encrypted and persists until you exit out of the remote connection (in the case of an interactive session), or until the operation being performed (an scp or sftp file transfer, for example) is complete.

SSH uses encrypted keys to identify the client and host (which adds a layer of security over telnet and rlogin's defaults), and then sets up a per-session encrypted channel for further communication. This same connection method is used for interactive ssh sessions, as well as for services like:

- scp (secure copy), SSH's counterpart to rlogin's rcp.
- sftp (secure FTP), SSH's client/server file transfer protocol.
- SSH port forwarding (so you can run services securely over remote servers).
- SSH X11 forwarding (so you can use X windows securely).

(A full list of features is available on OpenBSD's site: OpenSSH Features[128]).

The full suite of SSH packages also includes helpful utilities like ssh-keygen, which generates public/private key pairs suitable for use when connecting via SSH. You can also install the utility ssh-copy-id, which speeds up the process of manually adding your identity file to a remote server.

SSH is fairly secure by default—certainly more so than telnet or rlogin's default configuration—but for even greater security, there are a few extra settings you should

---

[128]http://www.openbsd.org/openssh/features.html

use (all of these settings are configured in /etc/ssh/sshd_config, and require a restart of the sshd service to take effect):

1. **Disable password-based SSH authentication**. Even though passwords are not sent in the clear, disabling password-based authentication makes it impossible for brute-force password attacks to even be *attempted*, even if you have the additional (and recommended) layer of something like Fail2Ban running. Set PasswordAuthentication no in the configuration.

2. **Disable root account remote login**. You shouldn't log in as the root user regardless (use sudo instead), but to reinforce this good habit, disable remote root user account login by setting PermitRootLogin no in the configuration. If you need to perform actions as root, either use sudo (preferred), or if it's absolutely necessary to work interactively as root, login with a normal account, then su to the root account.

3. **Explicitly allow/deny SSH for users**. Enable or disable SSH access for particular users on your system with AllowUsers and DenyUsers. To allow only 'John' to log in, the rule would be AllowUsers John. To allow any user *except* John to log in, the rule would be DenyUsers John.

4. **Use a non-standard port**. Change the default SSH port from 22 to something more obscure, like 2849, and prevent thousands of 'script kiddie' attacks that look for servers responding on port 22. While security through obscurity is no substitute for actually securing SSH overall, it provides a slight extra layer of protection. To change the port, set Port [new-port-number] in the configuration.

We'll cover how to configure some of these particular options in SSH in the next section.

## The evolution of SSH and the future of remote access

It has been over a decade since OpenSSH became the *de facto* standard of remote access protocols, and since then Internet connectivity has changed dramatically. For reliable, low-latency LAN and Internet connections, SSH is still the king due to its simplicity, speed, and security. But in high-latency environments (think 3G or

4G mobile network connections, or satellite uplinks), using SSH is often a painful experience.

In some circumstances, just *establishing a connection* takes time. Additionally, once connected, the delay inherent in SSH's TCP interface (where every packet must reach its destination and be acknowledged before further input will be accepted) means entering commands or viewing progress over a high-latency connection is an exercise in frustration.

Mosh[129], "the mobile shell", a new alternative to SSH, uses SSH to establish an initial connection, then synchronizes the following local session with a remote session on the server via UDP.

Using UDP instead of TCP requires Mosh to do a little extra behind-the-scenes work to synchronize the local and remote sessions (instead of sending all local keystrokes over the wire serially via TCP, then waiting for stdout and stderr to be returned, like SSH).

Mosh also promises better UTF-8 support than SSH, and is well supported by all the major POSIX-like operating systems (it even runs inside Google Chrome!).

It will be interesting to see where the future leads with regard to remote terminal access, but one thing is for sure: Ansible will continue to support the most secure, fast, and reliable connection methods to help you build and manage your infrastructure!

# Use secure and encrypted communication

We spent a lot of time discussing SSH's heritage and the way it works because it is, in many ways, the foundation of a secure infrastructure—in almost every circumstance, you will allow SSH remote access for your servers, so it's important you know how it works, and how to configure it to ensure you always administer the server securely, over an encrypted connection.

Let's look at the security settings configured in /etc/ssh/sshd_config (mentioned earlier), and how to control them with Ansible.

---

[129]https://www.usenix.org/system/files/conference/atc12/atc12-final32.pdf

For our secure server, we want to disable password-based SSH authentication (make sure you can already log in via your SSH key before you do this!), disable remote root login, and change the port over which SSH operates. Let's do it!

```
1   - hosts: example
2     tasks:
3       - name: Update SSH configuration to be more secure.
4         lineinfile:
5           dest: /etc/ssh/sshd_config
6           regexp: "{{ item.regexp }}"
7           line: "{{ item.line }}"
8           state: present
9         with_items:
10          - regexp: "^PasswordAuthentication"
11            line: "PasswordAuthentication no"
12          - regexp: "^PermitRootLogin"
13            line: "PermitRootLogin no"
14          - regexp: "^Port"
15            line: "Port 2849"
16        notify: restart ssh
17
18    handlers:
19      - name: restart ssh
20        service: name=ssh state=restarted
```

In this extremely simple playbook, we set three options in SSH configuration (PasswordAuthentication no, PermitRootLogin no, and Port 2849) using Ansible's lineinfile module, then use a handler we define in the handlers section to restart the ssh service.

 If you change certain SSH settings, like the port for SSH, you need to make sure Ansible's inventory is updated. You can explicitly define the SSH port for a host with the option ansible_ssh_port, and the local path to a private key file (identity file) with ansible_ssh_private_key_file, though Ansible uses keys defined by your ssh-agent setup, so typically a manual definition of the key file is not required.

# Disable root login and use sudo

We've already disabled root login with Ansible's lineinfile module in the previous section, but we'll cover a general Linux best practice here: don't use the root account if you don't absolutely need to use it.

Linux's sudo allows you (or other users) to run certain commands with root privileges (by default—you can also run commands as another user), ensuring you can perform actions needing elevated privileges without requiring you to be logged in as root (or another user).

Using sudo also forces you to be more explicit when performing certain actions with security implications, which is always a good thing. You don't want to accidentally delete a necessary file, or turn off a required service, which is easy to do if you're root.

In Ansible, it's preferred you log into the remote server with a normal or admin-level system account, and use the sudo parameter with a value of yes with any play or playbook include requiring elevated privileges. For example, if restarting Apache requires elevated privileges, you would write the play like so:

```
- name: Restart Apache.
  service: name=httpd state=restarted
  become: yes
```

Add become_user: [username] to a task to specify a specific user account to use with sudo (this will only apply if become is already set on the task or in the playbook).

You can also use Ansible to control sudo's configuration, defining who should have access to what commands and whether the user should be required to enter a password, among other things.

As an example, set up the user johndoe with permission to use any command as root via sudo by adding a line in the /etc/sudoers file with Ansible's lineinfile module:

```
- name: Add sudo group rights for deployment user.
  lineinfile:
    dest: /etc/sudoers
    regexp: '^%johndoe'
    line: 'johndoe ALL=(ALL) NOPASSWD: ALL'
    state: present
```

If you're ever editing the sudoers file by hand, you should use visudo, which validates your changes and makes sure you don't break sudo when you save the changes. When using Ansible with lineinfile, you have to use caution when making changes, and make sure your syntax is correct.

Another way of changing the sudoers file, and ensuring the integrity of the file, is to create a sudoers file locally, and copy it using Ansible's copy module, with a validation command, like so:

```
- name: Copy validated sudoers file into place.
  copy:
    src: sudoers
    dest: /etc/sudoers
    validate: 'visudo -cf %s'
```

The %s is a placeholder for the file's path, and will be filled in by Ansible before the sudoers file is copied into its final destination. The same parameter can be passed into Ansible's template module, if you need to copy a filled-in template to the server instead of a static file.

The sudoers file syntax is very powerful and flexible, but also a bit obtuse. Read the entire Sudoers Manual[130] for all the details, or check out the sample sudoers file[131] for some practical examples.

---

[130]http://www.sudo.ws/sudoers.man.html

[131]http://www.sudo.ws/sudo/sample.sudoers

# Remove unused software, open only required ports

Before the widespread use of configuration management tools for servers, when snowflake servers were the norm, servers would become bloated with extra software no longer in active use, open ports for old and unnecessary services, and old configuration settings opening up potential attack vectors.

If you're not actively using a piece of software, or there's an obsolete cron task, get rid of it. If you're using Ansible for your entire infrastructure, this shouldn't be an issue, since you could just bring up new servers to replace old ones when you have major configuration and/or package changes. But if not, consider adding in a 'cleanup' role or at least a task to remove packages that shouldn't be installed, like:

```
1  - name: Remove unused packages.
2    apt: name={{ item }} state=absent purge=yes
3    with_items:
4      - apache2
5      - nano
6      - mailutils
```

With modules like yum, apt, file, and mysql_db, a state=absent parameter means Ansible will remove whatever packages, files or databases you want, and will check to make sure this is still the case during future runs of your playbook.

Opening only required ports helps reduce the surface area for attack, requiring only a few firewall rules. This will be covered fully in the "Use a properly-configured firewall" section, but as an example, don't leave port 25 open on your server unless your server will be used as an SMTP relay server. Further, make sure the services you have listening on your open ports are configured to only allow access from trusted clients.

# Use the principle of least privilege

Users, applications, and processes should only be able to access information (files) and resources (memory, network ports, etc) necessary for their operation.

Many of the other basic security measures in this chapter are tangentially related to the principle of least privilege, but user account configuration and file permissions are two main areas directly related to the principle.

## User account configuration

New user accounts, by default, have fairly limited permissions on a Linux server. They usually have a home folder, over which they have complete control, but any other folder or file on the system is only available for reading, writing, or execution if the folder has group permissions set.

Usually, users gain access to other files and services through two methods:

1. Adding the user to another group with wider access privileges.
2. Allowing the user to use the `sudo` command to execute commands and access files as `root` or another user.

For the former method, please read the next section on file permissions to learn how to limit access. For the latter, please make sure you understand the use of sudoers as explained earlier in this chapter.

## File permissions

Every Ansible module that deals with files has file ownership and permission parameters available, including `owner`, `group`, and `mode`. Almost every time you handle files (using `copy`, `template`, `file`, etc.), you should explicitly define the correct permissions and ownership. For example, for a configuration file (in our example, the GitLab configuration file) that should *only* be readable or writeable by the root user, set the following:

```
1    - name: Configure the GitLab global configuration file.
2      file:
3        path: /etc/gitlab/gitlab.rb
4        owner: root
5        group: root
6        mode: 0600
```

 File permissions may seem a bit obtuse, and sometimes, they may cause headaches. But in reality, using octal numbers to represent file permissions is a helpful way to encapsulate a lot of configuration in three numbers. The main thing to remember is the following: for each of the file's *user*, *group*, and for *everyone* (each of the three digits), use the following digits to represent permission levels:

```
7: rwx (read/write/execute)
6: rw- (read/write)
5: r-x (read/execute)
4: r-- (read)
3: -wx (write/execute)
2: -w- (write)
1: --x (execute)
0: --- (no permissions)
```

Basically, 4 = read, 2 = write and 1 = execute. Therefore read (4) and write (2) is 6 in the octal representation, and read (4) and execute (1) is 5.

Less experienced admins are overly permissive, setting files and directories to 777 to fix issues they have with their applications. To allow one user (for example, your webserver user, httpd or nginx) access to a directory or some files, you should consider setting the directory's or files' *group* to the user's group instead of giving permissions to *every user on the system*!

For example, if you have a directory of web application files, the *user* (or in Ansible's terminology, "owner") might be your personal user account, or a deployment or service account on the server. Set the *group* for the files to a group the webserver user is in, and the webserver should now be able to access the files (assuming you have the same permissions set for the user and group, like 664).

# Update the OS and installed software

Every year, hundreds of security updates are released for the packages running on your servers, some of them fixing critical bugs. If you don't keep your server software up to date, you will be extremely vulnerable, especially when large exposures like Heartbleed[132] are uncovered.

At a minimum, you should schedule regular patch maintenance and package upgrade windows, and make sure you test the upgrades and patches on non-critical servers to make sure your applications work *before* applying the same on your production infrastructure.

With Ansible, since you already have your entire infrastructure described via Ansible inventories, you should be able to use a command like the following to upgrade all installed packages on a RHEL system:

```
$ ansible webservers -m yum -a "name=* state=latest"
```

On a Debian-based system, the syntax is similar:

```
$ ansible webservers -m apt -a "upgrade=dist update_cache=yes"
```

The above commands will upgrade *everything* installed on your server. Sometimes, you only want to install security-related updates, or exclude certain packages. In those cases, you need to configure yum or apt to tell them what to do (edit /etc/yum.conf for yum on RHEL-based systems, or use apt-mark hold [package-name] to keep a certain package at its current version on Debian-based systems).

---

[132]http://heartbleed.com/

# Automating updates

Fully automated daily or weekly package and system upgrades provide even greater security. Not every environment or corporation can accommodate frequent automated upgrades (especially if your application has been known to break due to past package updates, or relies on custom builds or specific package versions), but if you do it for your servers, it will increase the depth of your infrastructure's security.

 As mentioned in an earlier sidebar, GPG package signature checking is enabled by default for all package-related functionality. It's best to leave GPG checks in place, and import keys from trusted sources when necessary, *especially* when using automatic updates, if you want to prevent potentially insecure packages from being installed on your servers!

## Automating updates for RHEL systems

RHEL 6 and later (and modern versions of Fedora, and RHEL derivatives like CentOS) uses a cron-based package, `yum-cron`, for automatic updates. For basic, set-and-forget usage, install `yum-cron` and make sure it's started and set to run on system boot:

```
1  - name: Install yum-cron.
2    yum: name=yum-cron state=present
3
4  - name: Ensure yum-cron is running and enabled on boot.
5    service: name=yum-cron state=started enabled=yes
```

Further configuration (such as packages to exclude from automatic updates) is done in the `yum.conf` file, at `/etc/yum.conf`.

## Automating updates for Debian-based systems

Debian and its derivatives typically use the `unattended-upgrades` package to configure automatic updates. Like `yum-cron`, it is easy to install, and its configuration is placed in a variety of files within `/etc/apt/apt.conf.d/`:

```
 1  - name: Install unattended upgrades package.
 2    apt: name=unattended-upgrades state=present
 3
 4  - name: Copy unattended-upgrades configuration files in place.
 5    template:
 6      src: "../templates/{{ item }}.j2"
 7      dest: "/etc/apt/apt.conf.d/{{ item }}"
 8      owner: root
 9      group: root
10      mode: 0644
11    with_items:
12      - 10periodic
13      - 50unattended-upgrades
```

The template files copied in the second task should look something like the following:

```
 1  # File: /etc/apt/apt.conf.d/10periodic
 2  APT::Periodic::Update-Package-Lists "1";
 3  APT::Periodic::Download-Upgradeable-Packages "1";
 4  APT::Periodic::AutocleanInterval "7";
 5  APT::Periodic::Unattended-Upgrade "1";
```

This file provides configuration for the apt script that runs as part of the unattended upgrades package, and tells apt whether to enable unattended upgrades.

```
 1  # File: /etc/apt/apt.conf.d/50unattended-upgrades
 2  Unattended-Upgrade::Automatic-Reboot "false";
 3
 4  Unattended-Upgrade::Allowed-Origins {
 5          "Ubuntu lucid-security";
 6  //      "Ubuntu lucid-updates";
 7  };
```

This file provides further configuration for unattended upgrades, like whether to automatically restart the server for package and kernel upgrades requiring a reboot, or what apt sources should be checked for updated packages.

Make sure you get notifications or check in on your servers period-ically so you know when they'll need a manual reboot if you have `Automatic-Reboot` set to `false`!

# Use a properly-configured firewall

If you were building a secure bank vault, you wouldn't want to have a many doors and windows leading into the vault. You'd instead build reinforced concrete walls, and have one or two strong metal doors.

Similarly, should close any port not explicitly required to remain open on all your servers—whether in a DMZ in your network or open the the entire Internet. There are dozens of different ways to manage firewalls nowadays, from `iptables` and helpful tools like `ufw` and `firewalld` that help make iptables configuration easier, to AWS security groups and other external firewall services.

Ansible includes built-in support for configuring server firewalls with `ufw` (common on newer Debian and Ubuntu distributions) and `firewalld` (common on newer Fedora, RHEL, and CentOS distributions).

## Configuring a firewall with `ufw` on Debian or Ubuntu

Below is an entire firewall configuration to lock down most everything on a Debian or Ubuntu server, allowing traffic only through ports 22 (SSH), 80 (HTTP), and 123 (NTP):

```
1   - name: Configure open ports with ufw.
2     ufw:
3       rule: "{{ item.rule }}"
4       port: "{{ item.port }}"
5       proto: "{{ item.proto }}"
6     with_items:
7       - { rule: 'allow', port: 22, proto: 'tcp' }
8       - { rule: 'allow', port: 80, proto: 'tcp' }
9       - { rule: 'allow', port: 123, proto: 'udp' }
10
11  - name: Configure default incoming/outgoing rules with ufw.
12    ufw:
13      direction: "{{ item.direction }}"
14      policy: "{{ item.policy }}"
15      state: enabled
16    with_items:
17      - { direction: outgoing, policy: allow }
18      - { direction: incoming, policy: deny }
```

If you run a playbook with the above rules, the log into the machine (or use the `ansible` command) and run `sudo ufw status verbose`, you should see the configuration has been updated to the following:

```
$ sudo ufw status verbose
Status: active
Logging: on (low)
Default: deny (incoming), allow (outgoing), disabled (routed)
New profiles: skip

To                        Action      From
--                        ------      ----
22/tcp                    ALLOW IN    Anywhere
80/tcp                    ALLOW IN    Anywhere
123/udp                   ALLOW IN    Anywhere
22/tcp (v6)               ALLOW IN    Anywhere (v6)
```

```
80/tcp (v6)              ALLOW IN    Anywhere (v6)
123/udp (v6)             ALLOW IN    Anywhere (v6)
```

## Configuring a firewall with `firewalld` on RHEL, Fedora, or CentOS

The same firewall configuration can be done via `firewalld` for RHEL-based systems with similar ease:

```
1   - name: Configure open ports with firewalld.
2     firewalld:
3       state: "{{ item.state }}"
4       port: "{{ item.port }}"
5       zone: external
6       immediate: yes
7       permanent: yes
8     with_items:
9       - { state: 'enabled', port: '22/tcp' }
10      - { state: 'enabled', port: '80/tcp' }
11      - { state: 'enabled', port: '123/udp' }
```

 The `immediate` parameter was added in Ansible 1.9, and is required to make the rules effective immediately when the `permanent` parameter is set to yes. If you are running an older version of Ansible, you will need to restart to see your changes, or set `permanent` to no.

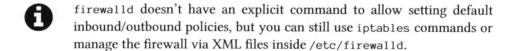 `firewalld` doesn't have an explicit command to allow setting default inbound/outbound policies, but you can still use `iptables` commands or manage the firewall via XML files inside `/etc/firewalld`.

If you run `sudo firewall-cmd --zone=external --list-all`, you should see the open ports:

```
$ sudo firewall-cmd --zone=external --list-all
external
  interfaces:
  sources:
  services: ssh
  ports: 123/udp 80/tcp 22/tcp
  masquerade: yes
  forward-ports:
  icmp-blocks:
  rich rules:
```

Some still prefer configuring firewalls with `iptables` (which is sometimes obtuse, but is almost infinitely malleable). This approach is used in the `geerlingguy.firewall` role on Ansible Galaxy, which translates variables like `firewall_allowed_tcp_ports` and `firewall_forwarded_tcp_ports` into `iptables` rules, and provides a `firewall` service for loading firewall rules.

It doesn't really matter what method you use to control access to your server, but the *principle of least privilege* applies here, as in most security-related discussions: only allow access on ports absolutely necessary for the functionality of your server, and restrict the use of those ports to only the hosts or subnets needing access to the services listening on the ports.

 When you're building up a firewall, make sure you don't accidentally lock down ports or IP addresses that will lock you out of the server entirely, otherwise you'll have to connect to the server through a local terminal connection and start over!

# Make sure log files are populated and rotated

Checking server logs is one of the most effective ways to not only see what attacks have taken place on a server, but also to see trends over time and predict high-traffic periods, potential attack vectors, and potential catastrophe.

But logs are completely worthless if they aren't being populated with effective data, aren't being monitored in any way, or are *the cause* of an outage! Many root cause analyses conclude, "the server's disk was full because log file *x* took up all the free space".

**I have my eyes on you, 218.78.214.9...**

```
 1  sshd[19731]: input_userauth_request: invalid user db2admin
 2  sshd[19731]: Received disconnect from 218.78.214.9: 11: Bye Bye
 3  sshd[19732]: Invalid user jenkins from 218.78.214.9
 4  sshd[19733]: input_userauth_request: invalid user jenkins
 5  sshd[19733]: Received disconnect from 218.78.214.9: 11: Bye Bye
 6  sshd[19734]: Invalid user jenkins from 218.78.214.9
 7  sshd[19735]: input_userauth_request: invalid user jenkins
 8  sshd[19735]: Received disconnect from 218.78.214.9: 11: Bye Bye
 9  sshd[19736]: Invalid user minecraft from 218.78.214.9
10  sshd[19737]: input_userauth_request: invalid user minecraft
11  sshd[19737]: Received disconnect from 218.78.214.9: 11: Bye Bye
```

Only you will know what logs are the most important to monitor on your servers, but some of the most common ones are database slow query logs, webserver access and error logs, authorization logs, and cron logs. Use tools like the ELK stack (demonstrated in a cookbook in Chapter 8), Munin, Nagios, or even a hosted service to make sure logs are populated and monitored.

Additionally, you should always make sure log files are rotated and archived (according to your infrastructure's needs) using a tool like logrotate, and you should have monitoring enabled on log file sizes so you have an early warning when a particular log file or directory grows a bit too large. There are a number of logrotate roles on Ansible Galaxy (e.g. Nick Hammond's logrotate role[133]) that make rotation configuration easy.

---

[133]https://galaxy.ansible.com/list#/roles/1117

# Monitor logins and block suspect IP addresses

If you've ever set up a new server on the public internet and enabled SSH on port 22 with password-based login enabled, you know how quickly the deluge of script-based logins begins. Many honeypot servers detect hundreds or thousands of such attempts per hour.

If you allow password-based login (for SSH, for your web app, or for anything else), you need to implement some form of monitoring and rate limiting. At a most basic level, you should install a tool like Fail2Ban[134], which monitors log files and bans IP addresses when it detects too many unsuccessful login attempts in a given period of time.

Here's a set of tasks you could add to your playbook to install Fail2Ban and make sure it's started on either Debian or RHEL-based distributions:

```
1   - name: Install fail2ban (RedHat).
2     yum: name=fail2ban state=present enablerepo=epel
3     when: ansible_os_family == 'RedHat'
4
5   - name: Install fail2ban (Debian).
6     apt: name=fail2ban state=present
7     when: ansible_os_family == 'Debian'
8
9   - name: Ensure fail2ban is running and enabled on boot.
10      service: name=fail2ban state=started enabled=yes
```

Fail2Ban configuration is managed in a series of .conf files inside /etc/fail2ban, and most configuration can be done by overriding defaults in a local override file, /etc/fail2ban/jail.local. See the Fail2Ban manual[135] for more information.

---

[134]http://www.fail2ban.org/wiki/index.php/Main_Page

[135]http://www.fail2ban.org/wiki/index.php/MANUAL_0_8

# Use SELinux (Security-Enhanced Linux) or AppArmor

SELinux and AppArmor are two different tools which allow you to construct security sandboxes for memory and filesystem access, so, for example, one application can't easily access another application's resources. It's a little like user and group file permissions, but allowing far finer detail—with far more complexity.

You'd be forgiven if you disabled SELinux or AppArmor in the past; both require extra work to set up and configure for your particular servers, especially if you're using less popular distribution packages (extremely popular packages like Apache and MySQL are extremely well supported out-of-the-box on most distributions).

However, both of these tools are excellent ways to add *defense in depth* to your infrastructure. You should already have decent configurations for firewalls, file permissions, users and groups, OS updates, etc. But if you're running a web-facing application—especially one running on a server with any other applications—it's great to have the extra protection SELinux or AppArmor provides from applications accessing things they shouldn't.

SELinux is usually installed and enabled by default on Fedora, RHEL and CentOS systems, is available and supported on most other Linux platforms, and is widely supported through Ansible modules, so we'll cover SELinux in a bit more depth.

To enable SELinux in `targeted` mode (which is the most secure mode without being almost impossible to work with), make sure the Python SELinux library is installed, then use Ansible's `selinux` module:

```
- name: Install Python SELinux library.
  yum: name=libselinux-python state=present

- Ensure SELinux is enabled in `targeted` mode.
  selinux: policy=targeted state=enforcing
```

Ansible also has a `seboolean` module that allows setting SELinux booleans. A very common setting for web servers involves setting the `httpd_can_network_connect` boolean:

```
- name: Ensure httpd can connect to the network.
  seboolean: name=httpd_can_network_connect state=yes persistent=yes
```

The Ansible `file` module also integrates well with SELinux, allowing the four security context fields for a file or directory to be set, one per parameter:

1. `selevel`
2. `serole`
3. `setype`
4. `seuser`

Building custom SELinux policies for more complex scenarios is out of the scope of this chapter, but you should be able to use tools like `setroubleshoot`, `setroubleshoot-server`, `getsebool`, and `aureport` to see what is being blocked, what booleans are available (and/or enabled currently), and even get helpful notifications when SELinux denies access to an application. Read Getting started with SELinux[136] for an excellent and concise introduction.

Next time you're tempted to disable SELinux instead of fixing the underlying problem, spend a little time investigating the correct boolean settings to configuring your system correctly for SELinux.

## Summary and further reading

This chapter contains a broad overview of some Linux security best practices, and how Ansible helps you conform to them. There is a wealth of good information on the Internet to help you secure your servers, including articles and publications like the following:

- Linode Library: Linux Security Basics[137]
- My First Five Minutes on a Server[138]

---

[136]https://major.io/2012/01/25/getting-started-with-selinux/

[137]https://library.linode.com/security/basics

[138]http://plusbryan.com/my-first-5-minutes-on-a-server-or-essential-security-for-linux-servers

- 20 Linux Server Hardening Security Tips[139]
- Unix and Linux System Administration Handbook[140]

Much of the security configuration in this chapter is encapsulated in a role on Ansible Galaxy, for use on your own servers: security role by geerlingguy[141].

```
 _____
/ Bad planning on your part does not    \
| constitute an emergency on my part.   |
\ (Proverb)                             /
 ---------------------------------------
           \     ^__^
            \   (oo)_____
               (__)\       )\/\
                   ||----w |
                   ||     ||
```

---

[139]http://www.cyberciti.biz/tips/linux-security.html
[140]http://www.admin.com/
[141]https://galaxy.ansible.com/list#/roles/1030

# Chapter 11 - Automating Your Automation - Ansible Tower and CI/CD

At this point, you should be able to convert almost any bit of your infrastructure's configuration into Ansible playbooks, roles, and inventories. And before deploying any infrastructure changes, you should test the changes in a non-production environment (just like you would with application releases). Manually running a playbook that configures your entire infrastructure, then making sure it does what you expect, is a good start towards order and stability.

Since all your infrastructure is defined in code, you can start automating all the aspects of infrastructure deployment, and even run unit, functional, and integration tests on your infrastructure, just like you do for your applications.

This section will cover different levels of infrastructure automation and testing, and highlight tools and techniques you can use to automate and streamline infrastructure operations.

## Ansible Tower

All the examples in this book use Ansible's CLI to run playbooks and report back the results. For smaller teams, especially when everyone on the team is well-versed in how to use Ansible, YAML syntax, and security best practices, using the CLI is a sustainable approach.

But for many organizations, basic CLI use is inadequate:

- The business needs detailed reporting of infrastructure deployments and failures, especially for audit purposes.

- Team-based infrastructure management requires varying levels of involvement in playbook management, inventory management, and key and password access.
- A thorough visual overview of the current and historical playbook runs and server health helps identify potential issues before they affect the bottom line.
- Playbook scheduling ensures infrastructure remains in a known state.

Ansible Tower checks off these items—and many more—and provides a great mechanism for team-based Ansible usage. The product is currently free for teams managing ten or fewer servers (it's basically an 'unlimited trial' mode), and has flexible pricing for teams managing dozens to thousands of servers.

While this book includes a brief overview of Tower, it is highly recommended you read through Ansible, Inc's extensive Tower User Guide[142], which includes details this book won't be covering such as LDAP integration and multiple-team playbook management workflows.

## Getting and Installing Ansible Tower

Ansible has a very thorough Ansible Tower User Guide[143], which details the installation and configuration of Ansible Tower. For the purposes of this chapter, since we just want to download and try out Tower locally, we are going to use Ansible's official Vagrant box to quickly build an Ansible Tower VM.

Make sure you have Vagrant[144] and VirtualBox[145] installed, then create a directory (e.g. tower) and do the following within the directory:

---

[142]http://releases.ansible.com/ansible-tower/docs/tower_user_guide-latest.pdf

[143]http://releases.ansible.com/ansible-tower/docs/tower_user_guide-latest.pdf

[144]https://www.vagrantup.com/downloads.html

[145]https://www.virtualbox.org/wiki/Downloads

```
# Create a new Vagrantfile using the Tower base box from Ansible.
$ vagrant init tower http://vms.ansible.com/ansible-tower-2.3.1-\
virtualbox.box

# Build the Tower VM.
$ vagrant up

# Log into the VM (Tower will display connection information).
$ vagrant ssh
```

 The above installation instructions and Vagrant box come from a blog post on Ansible's official blog, Ansible Tower and Vagrant[146].

Visit the URL provided by the login welcome message (e.g. `https://10.42.0.42/`), and after confirming a security exception for the Ansible Tower certificate, login with the credentials from step 3.

At this point, you will need to register a free trial license of Ansible Tower following the instructions on the screen. The free trial allows you to use all of Tower's features for up to 10 servers, and is great for experimenting and seeing how Tower fits into your workflow. After you get the license (it's a block of JSON which you paste into the license field), you should get to Tower's default dashboard page:

---

[146]http://www.ansible.com/blog/ansible-vagrant

**Ansible Tower's Dashboard**

# Using Ansible Tower

Ansible Tower is centered around the idea of organizing *Projects* (which run your playbooks via *Jobs*) and *Inventories* (which describe the servers on which your playbooks should be run) inside of *Organizations*. *Organizations* are then set up with different levels of access based on *Users* and *Credentials* grouped in different *Teams*. It's a little overwhelming at first, but once the initial structure is configured, you'll see the power and flexibility Tower's Project workflow affords.

Let's get started with our first project!

The first step is to make sure you have a test playbook you can run using Ansible Tower. Generally, your playbooks should be stored in a source code repository (e.g. Git or Subversion), with Tower configured to check out the latest version of the playbook from the repository and run it. For this example, however, we will create a playbook in Tower's default `projects` directory located in `/var/lib/awx/projects`:

1. Log into the Tower VM: `vagrant ssh`
2. Switch to the `awx` user: `sudo su - awx`
3. Go to Tower's default `projects` directory: `cd /var/lib/awx/projects`

4. Create a new project directory: `mkdir ansible-for-devops && cd ansible-for-devops`
5. Create a new playbook file, `main.yml`, within the new directory, with the following contents:

```
1  ---
2  - hosts: all
3    gather_facts: no
4    connection: local
5
6    tasks:
7      - name: Check the date on the server.
8        command: date
```

Switch back to your web browser and get everything set up to run the test playbook inside Ansible Tower's web UI:

1. Create a new *Organization*, called 'Ansible for DevOps'.
2. Add a new User to the Organization, named John Doe, with the username `johndoe` and password `johndoe1234`.
3. Create a new *Team*, called 'DevOps Engineers', in the 'Ansible for DevOps' Organization.
4. Under the Team's Credentials section, add in SSH credentials by selecting 'Machine' for the Credential type, and setting 'Name' to `Vagrant`, 'Type' to `Machine`, 'SSH Username' to `vagrant`, and 'SSH Password' to `vagrant`.
5. Under the Team's Projects section, add a new *Project*. Set the 'Name' to `Tower Test`, 'Organization' to `Ansible for DevOps`, 'SCM Type' to `Manual`, and 'Playbook Directory' to `ansible-for-devops` (Tower automatically detects all folders placed inside `/var/lib/awx/projects`, but you could also use an alternate Project Base Path if you want to store projects elsewhere).
6. Under the Inventories section, add an *Inventory*. Set the 'Name' to `Tower Local`, and 'Organization' set to `Ansible for DevOps`. Once the inventory is saved: 1. Add a 'Group' with the Name `localhost`. Click on the group once it's saved. 2. Add a 'Host' with the Host Name `127.0.0.1`.

New *Credentials* have a somewhat dizzying array of options, and offer login and API key support for a variety of services, like SSH, AWS, Rackspace, VMWare vCenter, and SCM systems. If you can login to a system, Tower likely supports the login mechanism!

Now that we have all the structure for running playbooks configured, we need only create a *Job Template* to run the playbook on the localhost and see whether we've succeeded. Click on 'Job Templates', and create a new Job Template with the following configuration:

- **Name:** Tower Test
- **Inventory:** Tower Local
- **Project:** Tower Test
- **Playbook:** main.yml
- **Machine Credential:** Vagrant

Save the Job Template, then click the small Rocketship button to start a job using the template. You'll be redirected to a Job status page, which provides live updates of the job status, and then a summary of the playbook run when complete:

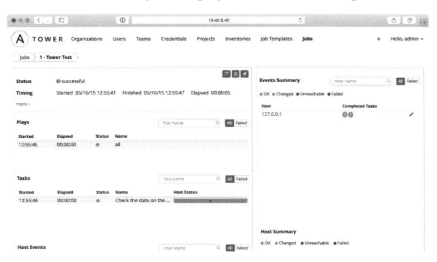

**Tower Test job completed successfully!**

You can view the playbook run's standard output in real-time (or review it after the fact) with the 'View standard out' button. You can also stop a running job, delete a job's record, or relaunch a job with the same parameters using the respective buttons on the job's page.

The job's dashboard page is very useful for giving an overview of how many hosts were successful, how many tasks resulted in changes, and the timing of the different parts of the playbook run.

## Other Tower Features of Note

In our walkthrough above, we used Tower to run a playbook on the local server; setting up Tower to run playbooks on real-world infastructure or other local VMs is just as easy, and the tools Ansible Tower provides are very handy, especially when working in larger team environments.

This book won't walk through the entirety of Ansible Tower's documentation, but a few other features you should try out include:

  • Setting up scheduled Job runs (especially with the 'Check' option instead of 'Run') for CI/CD.
  • Integrating user accounts and Teams with LDAP users and groups for automatic team-based project management.
  • Setting different levels of permissions for Users and Teams so certain users can only edit, run, or view certain jobs within an Organization.
  • Configuring Ansible Vault credentials to easily and automatically use Vault-protected variables in your playbooks.
  • Setting up Provisioning Callbacks so newly-provisioned servers can self-provision via a URL per Job Template.
  • Surveys, which allow users to add extra information based on a 'Survey' of questions per job run.
  • Inventory Scripts, which allow you to build inventory dynamically.
  • Built-in Munin monitoring (to monitor the Tower server), available with the same admin credentials at `https://[tower-hostname]/munin`.

Ansible Tower continues to improve rapidly, and is one of the best ways to run Ansible Playbooks from a central CI/CD-style server with team-based access and extremely detailed live and historical status reporting.

## Tower Alternatives

Ansible Tower is purpose-built for use with Ansible playbooks, but there are many other ways to run playbooks on your servers with a solid workflow. If price is a major concern, and you don't need all the bells and whistles Tower provides, you can use other popular tools like Jenkins[147], Rundeck[148], or Go CI[149].

All these tools provide flexiblity and security for running Ansible Playbooks, and each one requires a different amount of setup and configuration before it will work well for common usage scenarios. One of the most popular and long-standing CI tools is Jenkins, so we'll explore how to configure a similar Playbook run in Jenkins next.

# Jenkins CI

Jenkins is a Java-based open source continuous integration tool. It was forked from the Hudson project in 2011, but has a long history as a robust build tool for most any software project.

Jenkins is easy to install and configure, with the Java SDK as its only requirement. Jenkins runs on any modern OS, but for the purposes of this demonstration, we'll build a local VM using Vagrant, install Jenkins inside the VM using Ansible, then use Jenkins to run an Ansible playbook.

## Build a local Jenkins server with Ansible

Create a new directory for the Jenkins VM named `jenkins`. Inside the directory, create a `Vagrantfile` to describe the machine and the Ansible provisioning to Vagrant, with the following contents:

---

[147]http://jenkins-ci.org/

[148]http://rundeck.org/

[149]http://www.go.cd/

```
1   VAGRANTFILE_API_VERSION = "2"
2
3   Vagrant.configure(VAGRANTFILE_API_VERSION) do |config|
4     config.vm.box = "geerlingguy/centos7"
5     config.vm.hostname = "jenkins.dev"
6     config.vm.network :private_network, ip: "192.168.76.76"
7     config.ssh.insert_key = false
8
9     config.vm.provider :virtualbox do |v|
10      v.memory = 512
11    end
12
13    # Ansible provisioning.
14    config.vm.provision "ansible" do |ansible|
15      ansible.playbook = "provision.yml"
16      ansible.sudo = true
17    end
18  end
```

This Vagrantfile will create a new VM running CentOS 7, with the IP address 192.168.76.76 and the hostname jenkins.dev. Go ahead and add an entry for 192.168.76.76 jenkins.dev to your hosts file, and then create a new provision.yml playbook so Vagrant can run it with Ansible (as described in the config.vm.provision block in the Vagrantfile). Put the following in the provision.yml file:

```
1   ---
2   - hosts: all
3
4     vars:
5       firewall_allowed_tcp_ports:
6         - "22"
7         - "8080"
8       jenkins_plugins:
9         - ansicolor
```

```
10
11    roles:
12      - geerlingguy.firewall
13      - geerlingguy.ansible
14      - geerlingguy.java
15      - geerlingguy.jenkins
```

This playbook uses a set of roles from Ansible Galaxy to install all the required components for our Jenkins CI server. To make sure you have all the required roles installed on your host machine, add a `requirements.yml` file in the `jenkins` folder, containing all the roles being used in the playbook:

```
1    ---
2    - src: geerlingguy.firewall
3    - src: geerlingguy.ansible
4    - src: geerlingguy.java
5    - src: geerlingguy.jenkins
```

The `geerlingguy.ansible` role installs Ansible on the VM, so Jenkins can run Ansible playbooks and ad-hoc commands. The `geerlingguy.java` role is a dependency of `geerlingguy.jenkins`, and the `geerlingguy.firewall` role configures a firewall to limit access on ports besides 22 (for SSH) and 8080 (Jenkins' default port).

Finally, we tell the `geerlingguy.jenkins` role a set of plugins to install through the `jenkins_plugins` variable; in this case, we just want the `ansicolor` plugin, which gives us full color display in Jenkins' console logs (so our Ansible playbook output is easier to read).

 There is an official Ansible plugin for Jenkins[150] which can be used to run Ansible Ad-Hoc tasks and Playbooks, and may help you integrate Ansible and Jenkins more easily.

To build the VM and run the playbook, do the following (inside the `jenkins` folder):

---

[150]https://wiki.jenkins-ci.org/display/JENKINS/Ansible+Plugin

1. Run `ansible-galaxy install -r requirements.yml` to install the required roles.
2. Run `vagrant up` to build the VM and install and configure Jenkins.

After a few minutes, the provisioning should complete, and you should be able to access Jenkins at `http://jenkins.dev:8080/` (if you configured the hostname in your hosts file).

## Create an Ansible playbook on the Jenkins server

It's preferred to keep your playbooks and server configuration in a code repository (e.g. Git or SVN), but for simplicity's sake, this example requires a playbook stored locally on the Jenkins server, similar to the earlier Ansible Tower example.

1. Log into the Jenkins VM: `vagrant ssh`
2. Go to the `/opt` directory: `cd /opt`
3. Create a new project directory: `sudo mkdir ansible-for-devops && cd ansible-for-devops`
4. Create a new playbook file, `main.yml`, within the new directory, with the following contents (use sudo to create the file, e.g. `sudo vi main.yml`):

```
1  ---
2  - hosts: 127.0.0.1
3    gather_facts: no
4    connection: local
5
6    tasks:
7      - name: Check the date on the server.
8        command: date
```

If you want, test the playbook while you're logged in: `ansible-playbook main.yml`.

## Create a Jenkins job to run an Ansible Playbook

With Jenkins running, configure a Jenkins job to run a playbook on the local server with Ansible. Visit `http://jenkins.dev:8080/`, and once the page loads, click the 'New Item' link to create a new 'Freestyle project' with a title 'ansible-local-test'. Click 'OK' and when configuring the job, and set the following configuration:

- Under 'Build Environment', check the 'Color ANSI Console Output' option. This allows Ansible's helpful colored output to pass through the Jenkins console, so it is easier to read during and after the run.
- Under 'Build', click 'Add Build Step', then choose 'Execute shell'. In the 'Command' field, add the following code, which will run the local Ansible playbook:

```
1  # Force Ansible to output jobs with color.
2  export ANSIBLE_FORCE_COLOR=true
3
4  # Run the local test playbook.
5  ansible-playbook /opt/ansible-for-devops/main.yml
```

Click 'Save' to save the 'Ansible Local Test' job, and on the project's page, click the 'Build Now' link to start a build. After a few seconds, you should see a new item in the 'Build History' block. Click on the (hopefully) blue circle to the left of '#1', and it will take you to the console output of the job. It should look something like this:

**Jenkins job completed successfully!**

This is a basic example, but hopefully it's enough to show you how easy it is to get at least some of your baseline CI/CD automation done using a free and open source tool. Most of the more difficult aspects of managing infrastructure through Jenkins surrounds the ability to manage SSH keys, certificates, and other credentials through Jenkins, but there is already plenty of documentation surrounding these things elsewhere online and in Jenkins documentation, so this will be left as an exercise for the reader.

The rest of this chapter focuses on ways to test and debug your playbooks and your infrastructure as a whole, and while many examples use Travis CI or plain command line options, anything you see can be automated with Jenkins jobs!

# Unit, Integration, and Functional Testing

When determining how you should test your infrastructure, you need to understand the different kinds of testing, and then determine the kinds of testing on which you should focus more effort.

*Unit* testing, when applied to applications, is testing of the smallest units of code (usually functions or class methods). In Ansible, unit testing would typically apply to individual playbooks. You could run individual playbooks in an isolated environment, but it's often not worth the effort. What *is* worth your effort is at least checking the playbook syntax, to make sure you didn't just commit a YAML file that will break an entire deployment because of a missing quotation mark, or a whitespace issue!

*Integration* testing, which is definitely more valuable when it comes to Ansible, is the testing of small groupings of individual units of code, to make sure they work correctly together. Breaking your infrastructure definition into many task-specific roles and playbooks allows you to do this; if you've structured your playbooks so they have no or limited dependencies, you could test each role individually in a fresh virtual machine, before you use the role as part of a full infrastructure deployment.

*Functional* testing involves the whole shebang. Basically, you set up a complete infrastructure environment, and then run tests against it to make sure *everything* was successfully installed, deployed, and configured. Ansible's own reporting is helpful in this kind of testing, and there are external tools available to test infrastructure even more deeply.

It is often possible to perform all the testing you need on your own local workstation, using Virtual Machines (as demonstrated in earlier chapters), using tools like VirtualBox or VMWare. And with most cloud services providing robust control APIs and hourly billing, it's inexpensive and just as fast to test directly on cloud instances mirroring your production infrastructure!

We'll begin with the most basic tests using Ansible, along with common debugging techniques, then progress to full-fledged functional testing methods with an automated process.

## Debugging and Asserting

For most playbooks, testing configuration changes and the result of commands being run as you go is all the testing you need. And having tests run *during your playbook runs* using some of Ansible's built-in utility modules means you have immediate assurance the system is in the state you want.

If at all possible, you should try to bake all simple test cases (e.g. comparison and state checks) into your playbooks directly. Ansible has three modules that simplify this process.

## The debug **module**

When actively developing an Ansible playbook, or even for historical logging purposes (e.g. if you're running Ansible playbooks using Tower or another CI system), it's often handy to print values of variables or output of certain commands during the playbook run.

For this purpose, Ansible has a debug module, which prints variables or messages during playbook execution.

As an extremely basic example, here are two of the ways I normally use debug while building a playbook:

```
1  - hosts: 127.0.0.1
2    gather_facts: no
3    connection: local
4
5    tasks:
6      - name: Register the output of the 'uptime' command.
7        command: uptime
8        register: system_uptime
9
10     - name: Print the registered output of the 'uptime' command.
11       debug: var=system_uptime.stdout
12
13     - name: Print a simple message if a command resulted in a change.
14       debug: msg="Command resulted in a change!"
15       when: system_uptime.changed
```

Running this playbook gives the following output:

```
$ ansible-playbook debug.yml

PLAY [127.0.0.1] ****************************************************

TASK: [Register the output of the 'uptime' command.] ***************
changed: [127.0.0.1]

TASK: [Print the registered output of the 'uptime' command.] *******
ok: [127.0.0.1] => {
    "var": {
        "system_uptime.stdout":
            "15:01  up 15:18, 2 users, load averages: 1.23 1.33 1.42"
    }
}

TASK: [Print a simple message if a command resulted in a change.] ***
ok: [127.0.0.1] => {
    "msg": "Command resulted in a change!"
}

PLAY RECAP **********************************************************
127.0.0.1                : ok=3    changed=1    unreachable=0    failed=0
```

Debug messages are helpful when actively debugging a playbook or when you need extra verbosity in the playbook's output, but if you need to perform an explicit test on some variable, or bail out of a playbook for some reason, Ansible provides the fail module, and its more terse cousin, assert.

## The fail and assert modules

Both fail and assert, when triggered, will abort the playbook run, and the only difference is in the simplicity of their usage. To illustrate, let's look at an example:

```
1   - hosts: 127.0.0.1
2     gather_facts: no
3     connection: local
4
5     vars:
6       should_fail_via_fail: true
7       should_fail_via_assert: false
8       should_fail_via_complex_assert: false
9
10    tasks:
11      - name: Fail if conditions warrant a failure.
12        fail: msg="There was an epic failure."
13        when: should_fail_via_fail
14
15      - name: Stop playbook if an assertion isn't validated.
16        assert: that="should_fail_via_assert != true"
17
18      - name: Assertions can have contain conditions.
19        assert:
20          that:
21            - should_fail_via_fail != true
22            - should_fail_via_assert != true
23            - should_fail_via_complex_assert != true
```

Switch the boolean values of `should_fail_via_fail`, `should_fail_via_assert`, and `should_fail_via_complex_assert` to trigger each of the three `fail`/`assert` tasks, to see how they work.

For most test cases, `debug`, `fail`, and `assert` are all you need to ensure your infrastructure is in the correct state during a playbook run.

## Checking syntax and performing dry runs

Two checks you should include in an automated playbook testing workflow are `--syntax-check` (which checks the playbook syntax to find quoting, formatting, or whitespace errors) and `--check` (which will run your entire playbook in `check` mode).

Syntax checking is extremely straightforward, and only requires a few seconds for even larger, more complex playbooks with dozens or hundreds of includes. You should include an `ansible-playbook my-playbook.yml --syntax-check` in your basic CI tests, and it's best practice to run a syntax check in a pre-commit hook when developing playbooks.

Running a playbook in `check` mode is more involved, since Ansible runs the entire playbook on your live infrastructure, but without performing any changes. Instead, Ansible highlights tasks that *would've* resulted in a change to show what will happen when you *actually* run the playbook later.

This is helpful for two purposes:

1. To prevent 'configuration drift', where a server configuration may have drifted away from your coded configuration. This could happen due to human intervention or other factors. But it's good to discover configuration drift without forcefully changing it.
2. To make sure changes you make to a playbook that shouldn't break idempotency *don't*, in fact, break idempotency. For example, if you're changing a configuration file's structure, but with the goal of maintaining the same resulting file, running the playbook with `--check` alerts you when you might accidentally change the live file as a result of the playbook changes. Time to fix your playbook!

When using `--check` mode, certain tasks may need to always run to ensure the playbook completes successfully (e.g. `command` tasks that register variables used in later tasks). The `always_run` option indicates such tasks:

```
- name: A task that runs all the time, even in check mode.
  command: mytask --option1 --option2
  register: my_var
  always_run: true
```

For even more detailed information about what changes would occur, add the `--diff` option, and Ansible will output changes that *would've* been made to your servers line-by-line. This option produces a lot of output if `check` mode makes a lot of changes, so use it conservatively unless you want to scroll through a lot of text!

In addition to Ansible's `--syntax-check` and `--check` modes, you might be interested in also running Ansible Lint[151] on your playbooks. Ansible Lint allows you to check for deprecated syntax or inefficient task structures, and is highly configurable so you can set up the linting to follow the playbook standards you and your team choose.

# Automated testing on GitHub using Travis CI

Automated testing using a continuous integration tool like Travis CI (which is free for public projects and integrated very well with GitHub) allows you to run tests against Ansible playbooks or roles you have hosted on GitHub with every commit.

There are four main things to test when building and maintaining Ansible playbooks or roles:

1. The playbook or role's syntax (are all the .yml files formatted correctly?).
2. Whether the playbook or role will run through all the included tasks without failing.
3. The playbook or role's idempotence (if run again, it should not make any changes!).
4. The playbook or role's success (does the role do what it should be doing?).

Ultimately, the most important aspect is #4, because what's the point of a playbook or role if it doesn't do what you want it to do (e.g. start a web server, configure a database, deploy an app, etc.)?

We're going to assume you're testing a role you have on GitHub, though the example can be applied just as easily for standalone Ansible playbooks.

## Setting up a role for testing

Since you're going to need an Ansible playbook and inventory file to test your role, create both inside a new 'tests' directory in your Ansible role:

---

[151]https://github.com/willthames/ansible-lint

```
1  # Directory structure:
2  my_role/
3    tests/
4      test.yml <-- your test playbook
5      inventory <-- an inventory file to use with the playbook
```

Inside the inventory file, add:

```
1  localhost
```

We just want to tell Ansible to run commands on the local machine (we'll use the −connection=local option when running the test playbook).

Inside test.yml, add:

```
1  ---
2  - hosts: localhost
3    remote_user: root
4    roles:
5      - github-role-project-name
```

Substitude your own role name for github-role-project-name (e.g. ansible-role-django). This is a typical Ansible playbook, and we tell Ansible to run the tasks on localhost, with the root user (otherwise, you could run tasks with travis if you want, and use sudo on certain tasks). You can add vars, vars_files, etc. if you want, but we'll keep things simple, because for many smaller roles, the role is pre-packaged with sane defaults and all the other info it needs to run.

The next step is to add a .travis.yml file to your role so Travis CI will pick it up and use it for testing. Add the file to the root level of your role, and add the following to kick things off:

```
1   ---
2   language: python
3   python: "2.7"
4
5   before_install:
6     # Make sure everything's up to date.
7     - sudo apt-get update -qq
8
9   install:
10    # Install Ansible.
11    - pip install ansible
12
13    # Add ansible.cfg to pick up roles path.
14    - "printf '[defaults]\nroles_path = ../' > ansible.cfg"
15
16  script:
17    # We'll add some commands to test the role here.
```

The only surprising part here is the `printf` line in the `install` section; I've added that line to create a quick and dirty `ansible.cfg` configuration file Ansible will use to set the `roles_path` one directory up from the current working directory. That way, we can include roles like `github-role-project-name`, or if we use `ansible-galaxy` to download dependencies (as another command in the install section), we can use `- galaxy-role-name-here` to include the role in our `test.yml` playbook.

Now that we have the basic structure, it's time to start adding the commands to test our role.

## Testing the role's syntax

This is the easiest test; `ansible-playbook` has a built in command to check a playbook's syntax (including all the included files and roles), and return 0 if there are no problems, or an error code and some output if there were any syntax issues.

```
1  ansible-playbook -i tests/inventory tests/test.yml --syntax-check
```

Add this as a command in the `script` section of `.travis.yml`:

```
1  script:
2    # Check the role/playbook's syntax.
3    - ansible-playbook -i tests/inventory tests/test.yml --syntax-check
```

If there are any syntax errors, Travis will fail the build and output the errors in the log.

## Role success - first run

The next aspect to check is whether the role runs correctly or fails on its first run.

```
1  # Run the role/playbook with ansible-playbook.
2  - "ansible-playbook -i tests/inventory tests/test.yml
3  --connection=local --sudo"
```

This is a basic ansible-playbook command, which runs the playbook test.yml against the local host, using --sudo, and with the inventory file we added to the role's tests directory.

Ansible returns a non-zero exit code if the playbook run fails, so Travis will know whether the command succeeded or failed.

## Role idempotence

Another important test is the idempotence test—does the role change anything if it runs a second time? It should not, since all tasks you perform via Ansible should be idempotent (ensuring a static/unchanging configuration on subsequent runs with the same settings).

```
1  # Run the role/playbook again, checking to make sure it's idempotent.
2  - >
3    ansible-playbook -i tests/inventory tests/test.yml
4    --connection=local --sudo
5    | grep -q 'changed=0.*failed=0'
6    && (echo 'Idempotence test: pass' && exit 0)
7    || (echo 'Idempotence test: fail' && exit 1)
```

This command runs the exact same command as before, but pipes the results through grep, which checks to make sure 'changed' and 'failed' both report 0. If there were no changes or failures, the idempotence test passes (and Travis sees the 0 exit and is happy), but if there were any changes or failures, the test fails (and Travis sees the 1 exit and reports a build failure).

## Role success - final result

The last thing I check is whether the role actually did what it was supposed to do. If it configured a web server, is the server responding on port 80 or 443 without any errors? If it configured a command line application, does the application work when invoked, and do the things it's supposed to do?

```
1  # Request a page via the web server, to make sure it responds.
2  - "curl http://localhost/"
```

In this example, I'm testing a web server by loading 'localhost'; curl will exit with a 0 status (and dump the output of the web server's response) if the server responds with a 200 OK status, or will exit with a non-zero status if the server responds with an error status (like 500) or is unavailable.

Taking this a step further, you could even run a deployed application or service's own automated tests after Ansible is finished with the deployment, thus testing your infrastructure and application in one go—but we're getting ahead of ourselves here... that's a topic for later!

## Some notes about Travis CI

There are a few things you need to know about Travis CI, especially if you're testing Ansible, which will rely heavily on the VM environment inside which it is running:

- **Ubuntu 12.04**: As of this writing, the only OS available via Travis CI is Ubuntu 12.04. Most of my roles work with Ubuntu/Debian/RHEL/CentOS, so it's not an issue for me... but if your roles strictly target a non-Debian-flavored distro, you probably won't get much mileage out of Travis. (There is an open issue[152] to get Travis upgraded to Ubuntu 14.04, at least).
- **Preinstalled packages**: Travis CI comes with a bunch of services installed out of the box, like MySQL, Elasticsearch, Ruby, etc. In the `.travis.yml` `before_install` section, you may need to do some `apt-get remove --purge [package]` commands and/or other cleanup commands to make sure the VM is fresh for your Ansible role's run.
- **Networking/Disk/Memory**: Travis CI continously shifts the VM specs you're using, so don't assume you'll have X amount of RAM, disk space, or network capacity. Add commands like `cat /proc/cpuinfo`, `cat /proc/meminfo`, `free -m`, etc. in the `.travis.yml` `before_install` section if you need to figure out the resources available in your VM.

See much more information about the VM environment on the Travis CI Build Environment page[153].

## Real-world examples

This style of testing is integrated into many of the `geerlingguy.*` roles on Ansible Galaxy; here are a few example roles using Travis CI integration in the way outlined above:

- https://github.com/geerlingguy/ansible-role-apache
- https://github.com/geerlingguy/ansible-role-gitlab

---

[152]https://github.com/travis-ci/travis-ci/issues/2046

[153]http://docs.travis-ci.com/user/ci-environment/

- https://github.com/geerlingguy/ansible-role-mysql

If you would like to run your tests using a slightly more simplified and more self-contained test running environment, you might be interested in the rolespec[154] project, which formalizes and simplifies much of the code in the Travis CI examples shown above. Your tests will be dependent on another library for test runs, but doing this allows you to run the tests more easily in environments other than Travis CI.

## Functional testing using serverspec

Serverspec[155] is a tool to help automate server tests using RSpec tests, which use a Ruby-like DSL to ensure your server configuration matches your expectations. In a sense, it's another way of building well-tested infrastructure.

Serverspec tests can be run locally, via SSH, through Docker's APIs, or through other means, without the need for an agent installed on your servers, so it's a lightweight tool for testing your infrastructure (just like Ansible is a lightweight tool for *managing* your infrastructure).

There's a lot of debate over whether well-written Ansible playbooks themselves (especially along with the dry-run `--check` mode) are adequate for well-tested infrastructure, but many teams are more comfortable maintaining infrastructure tests in Serverspec instead (especially if the team is already familiar with how Serverspec and Rspec works!).

Consider this: a truly idempotent Ansible playbook is already a great testing tool if it uses Ansible's robust core modules and `fail`, `assert`, `wait_for` and other tests to ensure a specific state for your server. If you use Ansible's `user` module to ensure a given user exists and is in a given group, and run the same playbook with `--check` and get `ok` for the same task, isn't that a good enough test your server is configured correctly?

This book will not provide a detailed guide for using Serverspec with your Ansible-managed servers, but here are a few resources in case you'd like to use it:

---

[154]https://github.com/nickjj/rolespec
[155]http://serverspec.org/

- A brief introduction to server testing with Serverspec[156]
- Testing Ansible Roles with Test Kitchen, Serverspec and RSpec[157]
- Testing infrastructure with serverspec[158]

# Summary

Tools to help manage, test, and run playbooks regularly and easily, such as Travis CI, Jenkins, and Ansible Tower, also help deliver certainty when applying changes to your infrastructure using Ansible. In addition the information contained in this chapter, read through the Testing Strategies[159] documentation in Ansible's documentation for a comprehensive overview of infrastructure testing and Ansible.

```
 _____
/ The first rule of any technology used \
| in a business is that automation      |
| applied to an efficient operation will |
| magnify the efficiency. The second is  |
| that automation applied to an          |
| inefficient operation will magnify the |
\ inefficiency. (Bill Gates)            /
 ----------------------------------------
        \   ^__^
         \  (oo)_____
            (__)\       )\/\
                ||----w |
                ||     ||
```

[156]https://www.debian-administration.org/article/703/A_brief_introduction_to_server-testing_with_serverspec

[157]http://www.slideshare.net/MartinEtmajer/testing-ansible-roles-with-test-kitchen-serverspec-and-rspec-48185017

[158]http://vincent.bernat.im/en/blog/2014-serverspec-test-infrastructure.html

[159]http://docs.ansible.com/test_strategies.html

# Afterword

You should be well on your way towards streamlined infrastructure management. Many developers and sysadmins have been helped by this book, and many have even gone further and contributed *back* to the book, in the form of corrections, suggestions, and fruitful discussion!

Thanks to you for purchasing and reading this book, and a special thanks to all those who have given direct feedback:

@LeeVanSteerthem, Jonathan Nakatsui, Joel Shprentz, Hugo Posca, Jon Forrest, Rohit Bhute, George Boobyer (@ibluebag), Jason Baker (@Alchemister5), Jonathan Le (@jonathanhle), Barry McClendon, Nestor Feliciano, @dan_bohea, @lekum, Juan Martinez, @wimvandijck, André, @39digits, @aazon, Ned Schumann, @andypost, @michel_slm, @erimar77, @geoand, Larry B, Tim Gerla, @b_borysenko, Stephen H, @chesterbr, @mrjester888, @gkedge, @opratr, @briants5, @atweb, @devtux_at, @sillygwailo, Anthony R, @arbabnazar, and Leroy H!

# Appendix A - Using Ansible on Windows workstations

Ansible works primarily over the SSH protocol, which is supported natively by most every server, workstation, and operating system on the planet, with one exception— Microsoft's venerable Windows OS.

To use SSH on Windows, you need additional software. But Ansible also requires other utilities and subsystems only present on Linux or other UNIX-like operating systems. This poses a problem for many system administrators who are either forced to use or have chosen to use Windows as their primary OS.

This appendix will guide Windows users through the author's preferred method of using Ansible on a Windows workstation.

 Ansible 1.7 and later can manage Windows hosts (see Ansible's Windows Support[160] documentation), but doesn't run within Windows natively. You still need to follow the instructions here to run the Ansible client on a Windows host.

## Prerequisites

Our goal is to have a virtual machine running Linux running on your computer. The easiest way to do this is to download and install Vagrant and VirtualBox (both 100% free!), and then use Vagrant to install Linux, and PuTTY to connect and use Ansible. Here are the links to download these applications:

1. Vagrant[161]

---

[160]http://docs.ansible.com/intro_windows.html
[161]http://www.vagrantup.com/downloads.html

2. VirtualBox[162]
3. PuTTY[163]

Once you've installed all three applications, you can use either the command prompt (cmd), Windows PowerShell, or a Linux terminal emulator like Cygwin to boot up a basic Linux VM with Vagrant (if you use Cygwin, which is not covered here, you could install its SSH component and use it for SSH, and avoid using PuTTY).

# Set up an Ubuntu Linux Virtual Machine

Open PowerShell (open the Start Menu or go to the Windows home and type in 'PowerShell'), and change directory to a place where you will store some metadata about the virtual machine you're about to boot. I like having a 'VMs' folder in my home directory to contain all my virtual machines:

```
# Change directory to your user directory.
PS > cd C:/Users/[username]
# Make a 'VMs' directory and cd to it.
PS > md -Name VMs
PS > cd VMs
# Make a 'Ubuntu64' directory and cd to it.
PS > md -Name ubuntu-trusty-64
PS > cd ubuntu-trusty-64
```

Now, use vagrant to create the scaffolding for our new virtual machine:

```
PS > vagrant init ubuntu/trusty64
```

Vagrant creates a 'Vagrantfile' describing a basic Ubuntu Trusty (14.04) 64-bit virtual machine in the current directory, and is now ready for you to run vagrant up to download and build the machine. Run vagrant up, and wait for the box to be downloaded and installed:

---

[162]https://www.virtualbox.org/
[163]http://www.chiark.greenend.org.uk/~sgtatham/putty/download.html

```
PS > vagrant up
```

After a few minutes, the box will be downloaded and a new virtual machine set up inside VirtualBox. Vagrant will boot and configure the machine according to the defaults defined in the Vagrantfile. Once the VM is booted and you're back at the command prompt, it's time to log into the VM.

# Log into the Virtual Machine

Use `vagrant ssh-config` to grab the SSH connection details, which you will then enter into PuTTY to connect to the VM.

```
PS > vagrant ssh-config
```

It should show something like:

```
Host default
  Hostname 127.0.0.1
  User vagrant
  Port 2222
  UserKnownHostsFile /dev/null
  StrictHostKeyChecking no
  PasswordAuthentication no
  IdentityFile C:/Users/[username]/.vagrant.d/insecure_private_key
  IdentitiesOnly yes
  LogLevel FATAL
```

The lines we're interested in are the Hostname, User, Port, and IdentityFile.

Launch PuTTY, and enter the connection details:

- **Host Name (or IP address)**: 127.0.0.1
- **Port**: 2222

Click Open to connect, and if you receive a Security Alert concerning the server's host key, click 'Yes' to tell PuTTY to trust the host. You can save the connection details by entering a name in the 'Saved Sessions' field and clicking 'Save' to save the details.

PuTTY will ask for login credentials; we'll use the default login for a Vagrant box (vagrant for both the username and password):

```
login as: vagrant
vagrant@127.0.0.1's password: vagrant
```

You should now be connected to the virtual machine, and see the message of the day:

```
Welcome to Ubuntu 14.04.3 LTS (GNU/Linux 3.13.0-43-generic x86_64)

vagrant@trusty64:~$
```

If you see this prompt, you're logged in, and you can start administering the VM. The next (and final) step is to install Ansible.

 This example uses PuTTY to log into the VM, but other applications like Cygwin[164] or Git for Windows[165] work just as well, and may be easier to use. Since these alternatives have built-in SSH support, you don't need to do any extra connection configuration, or even launch the apps manually; just cd to the same location as the Vagrantfile, and enter vagrant ssh!

# Install Ansible

Before installing Ansible, make sure your package list is up to date by updating apt-get:

---

[164]http://cygwin.com/install.html

[165]http://git-scm.com/download/win

```
$ sudo apt-get update
```

The easiest way to install Ansible is to use pip, a package manager for Python. Python should already be installed on the system, but pip may not be, so let's install it, along with Python's development header files (which are in the python-dev package).

```
$ sudo apt-get install -y python-pip python-dev
```

After the installation is complete, install Ansible:

```
$ sudo pip install ansible
```

After Ansible and all its dependencies are downloaded and installed, make sure Ansible is running and working:

```
$ ansible --version
ansible 2.1.0.0
```

 Upgrading Ansible is also easy with pip: Run sudo pip install --upgrade ansible to get the latest version.

## Summary

You should now have Ansible installed within a virtual machine running on your Windows workstation. You can control the virtual machine with Vagrant (cd to the location of the Vagrantfile), using up to boot or wake the VM, halt to shut down the VM, or suspend to sleep the VM. Log into the VM manually using PuTTY or via vagrant ssh with Cygwin or Git's Windows shell.

Use Ansible from within the virtual machine just as you would on a Linux or Mac workstation directly. If you need to share files between your Windows environment and the VM, Vagrant conveniently maps /vagrant on the VM to the same folder where your Vagrantfile is located. You can also connect between the two via other methods (SSH, SMB, SFTP etc.) if you so desire.

Finally, there are also other ways to 'hack' Ansible into running natively within Windows (without a Linux VM), such as the ansible-babun-bootstrap[166], but I still recommend running everything within a Linux VM as performance will be optimal and the number of environment-related problems you encounter will be greatly reduced!

---

[166]https://github.com/jonathanhle/ansible-babun-bootstrap

# Appendix B - Ansible Best Practices and Conventions

Ansible's flexibility allows for a variety of organization methods and configuration syntaxes. You may have many tasks in one main file, or a few tasks in many files. You might prefer defining variables in group variable files, host variable files, inventories, or elsewhere, or you might try to find ways of avoiding variables in inventories altogether.

There are few *universal* best practices in Ansible, but this appendix contains helpful suggestions for organizing playbooks, writing tasks, using roles, and otherwise build infrastructure with Ansible.

In addition to this appendix (which contains mostly observations from the author's own daily use of Ansible), please read through the official Ansible Best Practices[167] guide, which contains a wealth of hard-earned knowledge.

## Playbook Organization

Playbooks are Ansible's bread and butter, so it's important to organize them in a logical manner for easier debugging and maintenance.

### Write comments and use name liberally

Many tasks you write will be fairly obvious when you write them, but less so six months later when you are making changes. Just like application code, Ansible playbooks should be documented so you spend less time familiarizing yourself with what a particular task is supposed to do, and more time fixing problems or extending your playbooks.

---

[167]http://docs.ansible.com/playbooks_best_practices.html

In YAML, write comments by starting a line with a hash (#). If the comment spans multiple lines, start each line with #.

It's also a good idea to use a name for every task you write, besides the most trivial. If you're using the git module to check out a specific tag, use a name to indicate what repository you're using, why a tag instead of a commit hash, etc. This way, whenever your playbook is run, you'll see the comment you wrote and be assured what's going on.

```
- hosts: all

  tasks:

    # This task takes up to five minutes and is required so we will
    # have access to the images used in our application.
    - name: Copy the entire file repository to the application.
      copy:
        src: [...]
```

This advice assumes your comments actually indicate what's happening in your playbooks! I use full sentences with a period for all comments and names, but it's okay to use a slightly different style. Just be consistent, and remember, *bad comments are worse than no comments at all*.

## Include related variables and tasks

If you find yourself writing a playbook over 50-100 lines and configuring three or four different applications or services, it may help to separate each group of tasks into a separate file, and use include to place them in a playbook.

Additionally, variables are usually better left in their own file and included using vars_files rather than defined inline with a playbook.

```
- hosts: all

  vars_files:
    - vars/main.yml

  handlers:
    - include: handlers/handlers.yml

  tasks:
    - include: tasks/init.yml
    - include: tasks/database.yml
    - include: tasks/app.yml
```

Using a more hierarchical model like this allows you to see what your playbook is doing at a higher level, and also lets you manage each portion of a configuration or deployment separately. I generally split tasks into separate files once I reach 15-20 tasks in a given file.

## Use Roles to bundle logical groupings of configuration

Along the same lines as using included files to better organize your playbooks and separate bits of configuration logically, Ansible roles supercharge your ability to manage infrastructure well.

Using loosely-coupled roles to configure individual components of your servers (like databases, application deployments, the networking stack, monitoring packages, etc.) allows you to write configuration once, and use it on all your servers, regardless of their role.

You'll probably configure something like NTP (Network Time Protocol) on every single server you manage, or at a minimum, set a timezone for the server. Instead of adding two or three tasks to every playbook you manage, set up a role (maybe call it `time` or `ntp`) to do this configuration, and use a few variables to allow different groups of servers to have customized settings.

Additionally, if you learn to build robust and generic roles, you could share them on Ansible Galaxy so others use them and help you make them even better!

## Use role defaults and vars correctly

Set all role default variables likely to be overridden inside `defaults/main.yml`, and set variables likely never to be overridden in `vars/main.yml`.

If you have a variable that needs to be overridden, but you need to include it in a platform-specific vars file (e.g. one vars file for Debian, one for RHEL), then create the variable in `vars/[file].yml` as `__varname`, and use `set_fact` to set the variable at runtime if the variable `varname` is not defined. This way playbooks using your role can still override one of these variables.

For example, if you need to have a variable like `package_config_path` that is defaulted to one value on Debian, and another on RHEL, but may need to be overridden from time to time, you can create two files, `vars/Debian.yml` and `vars/RedHat.yml`, with the contents:

```
---
# Inside vars/Debian.yml
__package_config_path: /etc/package/package.conf
```

```
---
# Inside vars/RedHat.yml
__package_config_path: /etc/package/configfile
```

Then, in the playbook using the variable, include the platform-specific vars file and define the final `package_config_path` variable at runtime:

```
---
# Include variables and define needed variables.
- name: Include OS-specific variables.
  include_vars: "{{ ansible_os_family }}.yml"

- name: Define package_config_path.
  set_fact:
    package_config_path: "{{ __package_config_path }}"
  when: package_config_path is not defined
```

This way, any playbook using role can override the platform-specific defaults by defining `package_config_path` in its own variables.

# YAML Conventions and Best Practices

YAML is a human-readable, machine-parseable syntax that allows for almost any list, map, or array structure to be described using a few basic conventions, so it's a great fit for configuration management. Consider the following method of defining a list (or 'collection') of widgets:

```
widget:
  - foo
  - bar
  - fizz
```

This would translate into Python (using the PyYAML library employed by Ansible) as the following:

```
translated_yaml = {'widget': ['foo', 'bar', 'fizz']}
```

And what about a structured list/map in YAML?

```
widget:
  foo: 12
  bar: 13
```

The resulting Python:

```
translated_yaml = {'widget': {'foo': 12, 'bar': 13}}
```

A few things to note with both of the above examples:

- YAML will try to determine the type of an item automatically. So foo in the first example would be translated as a string, true or false would be a boolean, and 123 would be an integer. Read the official documentation for further insight, but for our purposes, declaring strings with quotes (' ' or "") will minimize surprises.
- Whitespace matters! YAML uses spaces (literal space characters—*not* tabs) to define structure (mappings, array lists, etc.), so set your editor to use spaces for tabs. You can use either a tab or a space to delimit parameters (like apt: name=foo state=present—either a tab or a space between parameters), but it's preferred to use spaces everywhere, to minimize errors and display irregularities across editors and platforms.
- YAML syntax is robust and well-documented. Read through the official YAML Specification[168] and/or the PyYAMLDocumentation[169] to dig deeper.

## YAML for Ansible tasks

Consider the following task:

```
- name: Install foo.
  apt: name=foo state=present
```

All well and good, right? Well, as you get deeper into Ansible and start defining more complex configuration, you might start seeing tasks like the following:

---

[168]http://www.yaml.org/spec/1.2/spec.html
[169]http://pyyaml.org/wiki/PyYAMLDocumentation

```
- name: Copy Phergie shell script into place.
  template: src=templates/phergie.sh.j2 dest=/opt/phergie.sh \
  owner={{ phergie_user }} group={{ phergie_user }} mode=755
```

The one-line syntax (which uses Ansible-specific `key=value` shorthand for defining parameters) has some positive attributes:

- Simpler tasks (like installations and copies) are compact and readable. `apt: name=apache2 state=present` and `apt-get install -y apache2` are similarly concise; in this way, an Ansible playbook feels very much like a shell script.
- Playbooks are more compact, and more configuration is be displayed on one screen.
- Ansible's official documentation follows this format, as do many existing roles and playbooks.

However, as highlighted in the above example, there are a few issues with this `key=value` syntax:

- Smaller monitors, terminal windows, and source control applications will either wrap or hide part of the task line.
- Diff viewers and source control systems generally don't highlight intra-line differences as well as full line changes.
- Variables and parameters are converted to strings, which may or may not be desired.

Ansible's shorthand syntax is troublesome for complicated playbooks and roles, but luckily there are other ways to write tasks which are better for narrower displays, version control software and diffing.

## Three ways to format Ansible tasks

The following methods are most often used to define Ansible tasks in playbooks:

### Shorthand/one-line (`key=value`)

Ansible's shorthand syntax uses `key=value` parameters after the name of a module as a key:

```
- name: Install Nginx.
  yum: name=nginx state=present
```

For any situation where an equivalent shell command would roughly match what I'm writing in the YAML, I prefer this method, since it's immediately obvious what's happening, and it's highly unlikely any of the parameters (like `state=present`) will change frequently during development.

Ansible's official documentation generally uses this syntax, so it maps nicely to examples you'll find from Ansible, Inc. and many other sources.

## Structured map/multi-line (`key:value`)

Define a structured map of parameters (using `key: value`, with each parameter on its own line) for a task:

```
- name: Copy Phergie shell script into place.
  template:
    src: "templates/phergie.sh.j2"
    dest: "/home/{{ phergie_user }}/phergie.sh"
    owner: "{{ phergie_user }}"
    group: "{{ phergie_user }}"
    mode: 0755
```

A few notes on this syntax:

- The structure is all valid YAML, and functions similarly to Ansible's shorthand syntax.
- Strings, booleans, integers, octals, etc. are all preserved (instead of being converted to strings).
- Each parameter *must* be on its own line; multiple variables can't be chained together (e.g. `mode: 0755, owner: root, user: root`) to save space.
- YAML syntax highlighting works slightly better for this format than `key=value`, since each key will be highlighted, and values will be displayed as constants, strings, etc.

## Folded scalars/multi-line (›)

Use the › character to break up Ansible's shorthand `key=value` syntax over multiple lines.

```
- name: Copy Phergie shell script into place.
  template: >
    src=templates/phergie.sh.j2
    dest=/home/{{ phergie_user }}/phergie.sh
    owner={{ phergie_user }} group={{ phergie_user }} mode=755
```

In YAML, the › character denotes a *folded scalar*, where every line that follows (as long as it's indented further than the line with the ›) will be joined with the line above by a space. So the above YAML and the earlier `template` example will function exactly the same.

This syntax allows arbitrary splitting of lines on parameters, but it does not preserve value types (0775 would be converted to a string, for example).

While this syntax is often seen in the wild, I don't recommend it except for certain situations, like tasks using the `command` and `shell` modules with extra options:

```
- name: Install Drupal.
  command: >
    drush si -y
    --site-name="{{ drupal_site_name }}"
    --account-name=admin
    --account-pass={{ drupal_admin_pass }}
    --db-url=mysql://root@localhost/{{ domain }}
    chdir={{ drupal_core_path }}
    creates={{ drupal_core_path }}/sites/default/settings.php
```

Sometimes the above is as good as you can do to keep unwieldy tasks formatted in a legible manner.

## Using | to format multiline variables

In addition to using > to join multiple lines using spaces, YAML allows the use of |
(pipe) to define literal scalars, to define strings with newlines preserved.

For example:

```
1  extra_lines: |
2    first line
3    second line
4    third line
```

Would be translated to a block of text with newlines intact:

```
1  first line
2  second line
3  third line
```

Using a folded scalar (>) would concatenate the lines, which might not be desirable.
For example:

```
1  extra_lines: >
2    first line
3    second line
4    third line
```

Would be translated to a single string with no newlines:

```
1  first line second line third line
```

## Using ansible-playbook

Generally, running playbooks from your own computer or a central playbook runner
is preferable to running Ansible playbooks locally (using --connection=local), since
Ansible and all its dependencies don't need to be installed on the system you're
provisioning. Because of Ansible's optimized use of SSH for remote communication,
there is usually minimal difference in performance running Ansible locally or from
a remote workstation (barring network flakiness or a high-latency connection).

# Use Ansible Tower

If you are able to use Ansible Tower to run your playbooks, this is even better, as you'll have a central server running Ansible playbooks, logging output, compiling statistics, and even allowing a team to work together to build servers and deploy applications in one place.

# Specify `--forks` for playbooks running on > 5 servers

If you are running a playbook on a large number of servers, consider increasing the number of `forks` Ansible uses to run tasks simultaneously. The default, 5, means Ansible will only run a given task on 5 servers at a time. Consider increasing this to 10, 15, or however many connections your local workstation and ISP can handle—this will dramatically reduce the amount of time it takes a playbook to run.

Set `forks=[number]` in Ansible's configuration file to set the default `forks` value for all playbook runs.

# Use Ansible's Configuration file

Ansible's main configuration file, in `/etc/ansible/ansible.cfg`, allows a wealth of optimizations and customizations for running playbooks and ad-hoc tasks.

Read through the official documentation's Ansible Configuration File[170] page for customizable options in `ansible.cfg`.

# Summary

One of Ansible's strengths is its flexibility; there are often multiple 'right' ways of accomplishing your goals. I have chosen to use the methods I outlined above as they

---

[170]http://docs.ansible.com/intro_configuration.html

have proven to help me write and maintain a variety of playbooks and roles with minimal headaches.

It's perfectly acceptable to try a different approach; as with most programming and technical things, being *consistent* is more important than following a particular set of rules, especially if the ruleset isn't universally agreed upon. Consistency is especially important when you're not working solo—if every team member used Ansible in a different way, it would become difficult to share work very quickly!

57950624R00222

Made in the USA
Lexington, KY
01 December 2016